SMALL TOWN IN MASS SOCIETY

Class, Power, and Religion in a Rural Community

BY ARTHUR VIDICH AND JOSEPH BENSMAN

A case study of a rural community in upper New York State showing how it reflects the major issues and problems of society. "A creative contribution—particularly in the depth of analysis of the major community institutions."—*Floyd Hunter*. "So good that it may safely be recommended to even the layman normally distrustful of the systematic study of society. It is as captivating as a novel."—*Times Literary Supplement*.

344 PAGES.   1958. $6.00

CONQUEST OF VIOLENCE

The Gandhian Philosophy of Conflict

BY JOAN V. BONDURANT

The distinguishing characteristics of the Gandhian technique, its far-reaching implications, and the importance of continuing experiments in its development, are here explored in terms familiar to the West. "I hope that Dr. Bondurant's book will lead many people to think of this new dynamic force that Gandhi brought into the political and social field. . . . The truth or reality in the idea that he represented will no doubt survive and, I'm sure, influence men's minds more and more."—*Jawaharlal Nehru*.

288 PAGES.   1958. $5.00

AUTHORITY AND POWER
IN THE
FREE CHURCH TRADITION

Authority and Power in the Free Church Tradition

A Social Case Study of the
American Baptist Convention

BY PAUL M. HARRISON

PRINCETON, NEW JERSEY
PRINCETON UNIVERSITY PRESS

1959

Publication of this book
has been aided by the Ford Foundation program
to support publication, through university presses,
of work in the humanities
and social sciences

Printed in the United States of America
by Princeton University Press, Princeton, New Jersey

TO NANCY

CYNTHIA AND JOHN

PREFACE

BAPTISTS are proud of their history and devoted to the principles of their faith. They justifiably boast of great fighters for freedom in America, England, and Holland. They have advocated the principle of separation of church and state and have been in the forefront of the struggle for independency in the secular as well as the religious world. Many of the assertions of the early Baptists were treated as blasphemous and presumptuous and some of the leaders of the movement were unmercifully persecuted as religious fanatics dedicated to the destruction of the true faith.

Their emphasis upon the competence of the individual to discern the mind of Christ within a community of worship and discipline has produced some of the greatest preachers in the history of Protestantism. The Baptists were in the vanguard of the modern missionary enterprise and they contributed important leadership to the Social Gospel movement. They have labored to meet the needs of disinherited people everywhere in the world and have fostered the idea of the gathered church where all who have faith in the gospel shall unite for mutual inspiration and service to the kingdom of God.

This study is written by one who is dedicated to the purpose of the Baptist witness, by one who is profoundly indebted to those leaders of the past and present who have suffered for the principles of their faith. For it is only within a religious environment where free and mutual criticism is respected as a fundamental element of church polity that an effort such as this can be accepted in the spirit in which it was written.

The problem which this study seeks to analyze arises from a discrepancy between the Baptist doctrine of the church and the polity of the American Baptist denomination. For more than a century the Baptists have emphasized the freedom of the individual in all matters of faith and practice. In addition, they have insisted upon the autonomy of the local church and the freedom of the congregation to govern its own affairs apart from the direction of church councils or associations of churches. Thus in its modern expression the Baptist doctrine of the church maintains that there is no authority in church councils and that denominational officials can legally possess no power.

At the same time the Baptists have formed an impressive denominational organization (reflected in the chart on page ix) which in important ways bears a striking resemblance to the large social structures found in the spheres of government and business. The officers of the denominational agencies have obtained a significant degree of influence over the affairs of the local churches. In the face of these circumstances the churches have lost much of their previous prestige and individuals have difficulty finding an effective outlet within the denomination for the expression of their opinions.

Since this study engages in problems of social organization, as well as problems of theology, methods of research were used which are not common to the consideration of a religious group. In order to describe the general nature of the problem a body of known sociological theories was used to provide an analytical framework from which to initiate the investigation. The general theoretical background for the nature of social systems was provided by Talcott Parsons, Robert K. Merton, and Marion J. Levy, Jr.[1] Each of these men follows the logic of functional analysis in which it is determined what requirements are necessary for a social system to survive and at the same time achieve its goals. It is assumed that in the case of a social system like the American Baptist Convention the functional requisites are not appreciably different from those of any other group. Parsons observes that there are certain functional prerequisites common to every social system. They must operate if the group is to engage in integrated activity. For example, every social system must "have a sufficient propor-

---

[1] Talcott Parsons, *The Social System* (Glencoe, Illinois: The Free Press, 1951), and *Essays in Sociological Theory Pure and Applied* (Glencoe, Illinois: The Free Press, 1949); Robert K. Merton, *Social Theory and Social Structure* (Glencoe, Illinois: The Free Press, 1949); Marion J. Levy, Jr., *The Structure of Society* (Princeton University Press, 1952).

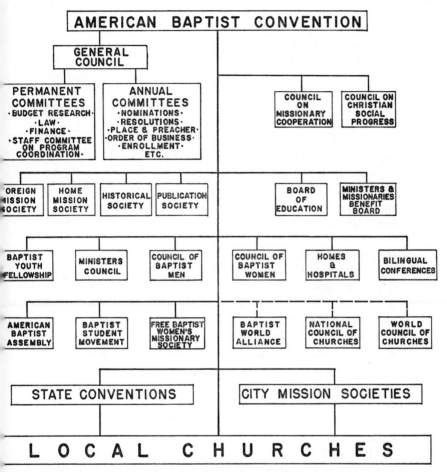

This simplified chart is designed to portray only the primary relationships of the units of the Convention. The simplicity may be deceiving. The comparative power of the agencies, their intricate relationships, and the complexity of any single agency are not represented by the chart. There is no formal hierarchy in the Convention, and to indicate this the official charts place the local churches above the American Baptist Convention.

tion of its component actors adequately motivated to act in accordance with the requirements of its role system, positively in the fulfillment of expectations and negatively in abstention from too much disruptive, i.e., deviant, behavior."[2] This prerequisite applies to a religious group as well as to any other and while it may appear very obvious—nothing more than an imposing vocabulary for common ideas—it is helpful, when one enters the maze of a social system so complex as the American Baptist Convention, to possess theoretical reference points from which to initiate an empirical analysis. It is an advantage to the investigator if these reference points are universal rather than specific. One reason is to be found in Merton's discussion of functional alternatives. He observes that a fundamental social or psychological need can be fulfilled by various types of functions. For example, leadership is a functional requirement of any society; but the nature of the leadership, in terms of training, basis of authority, norms of action, etc., may vary in significant ways. But in any case, if leadership is necessary for any social system and if the Baptists have agreed to unite in a formal effort to achieve common goals, it behooves the investigator to observe with caution Baptist efforts to minimize the power and authority of their leaders.

The problem of church-order within the Convention focuses upon the nature of ecclesiastical authority and power. The theoretical framework for the examination of these issues was provided primarily by Max Weber.[3] However, Lasswell and Kaplan[4] supplied important insights into the nature of power and its relationship to authority not found in Weber's ideal-typical analysis.

Modern social organization, especially in its Western manifestations, has taken the form of the bureaucratic structure. This is true of the church as well as the state and the business organization; it is as true of the denominations with a demo-

2 Parsons, *Social System*, *op.cit.*, p. 27.

3 Max Weber, *The Theory of Social and Economic Organization*, trans. A. M. Henderson and Talcott Parsons (New York: Oxford University Press, 1947), pp. 324-406.

4 Harold D. Lasswell and Abraham Kaplan, *Power and Society* (New Haven: Yale University Press, 1950).

cratic church-order as it is of the ecclesiastical hierarchy. In many important respects the American Baptist Convention is a bureaucratic organization. It is an organization which strives for technical efficiency, places a premium on precision of operation, control by professional experts, speed, continuity of policy, and an optimal return from the money and labor expended. Weber notes that "bureaucratic administration means fundamentally the exercise of control on the basis of knowledge. This is the feature which makes it specifically rational."[5]

The term "bureaucracy" is technically derived and carries no invidious connotation. There are advantages and disadvantages to bureaucratic organization. "But if we recognize that all administrative officials are bureaucrats, the bishop no less than the tax collector, then we may be able to understand the general nature of the problem. . . ."[6] Before engaging in empirical research the writer became familiar with the major studies in bureaucratic theory. These were used as analytical tools to assist in the understanding of the American Baptist Convention. In some cases hypotheses were modified by the empirical research and social theories were revised in order to be specifically relevant for problems of religious organization.

The empirical research included several kinds of source material. In the early chapters historical data were utilized. This included histories of the Baptist movement and early confessions of faith. For the period immediately preceding the formation of the Convention a history of this era was used in order to augment material derived from articles in Baptist journals and papers. Within the modern period a variety of written sources proved helpful. These included annual reports of the proceedings of the Convention, minutes of meetings, journal and newspaper articles, private correspondence from denominational leaders who could not be personally interviewed, committee reports, studies of the organizational problems of the denomination conducted by the Baptists themselves, and directives on organizational procedure circulated among the professional personnel of the Convention.

[5] Weber, *Theory, op.cit.*, p. 339.
[6] Philip Selznick, *TVA and the Grass Roots* (Berkeley: University of California Press, 1953), p. 9.

The writer was able to attend a limited number of meetings of the denominational organizations, including two annual meetings of the Convention and a business and policy session of one of the missionary agencies. One of the most productive sources of information was provided through interviews with Convention leaders. A partial list of these people is given in the appendix. In order to preserve the anonymity which was promised to the interviewees it is not possible to list all the personnel who were interviewed nor is it feasible to cite these persons directly in footnotes. However, a general reference is made in each case to indicate the official position of the various informants. The technique that was used in these personal meetings followed the procedures developed by Merton, et al., for the focused interview.[7]

The hypotheses which had been developed concerning the organizational problems of the Convention provided the basis for the interview schedules. The major areas of inquiry were covered in the case of every individual who was interviewed and special areas of interest for the interviewee were discussed as the writer proceeded through the interview schedule. Rather than asking specific questions about the power structure and patterns of authority within the Convention the schedule focused on the personal experiences of the participant in an effort to ascertain his subjective definitions of the situations in which he was involved. In this way new hypotheses about the problems of the denomination were developed, and in some cases the same persons were interviewed more than once in order to determine the validity of these hypotheses. In general, non-directive procedures were used throughout the interviews: the questions which were asked, especially in the initial stages of the interview, were unstructured and open-ended. When the interviewee proceeded to specific situations the questions usually became more structured and direct.

A dynamic relationship between theory and empirical fact provides the basic methodological principle by which this

[7] Robert K. Merton, Marjorie Fiske, and Patricia L. Kendall, *The Focused Interview* (Glencoe, Illinois: The Free Press, 1956); cf. also Walter V. D. Bingham and V. Moore Bruce, *How to Interview* (New York: Harper & Brothers, 1941).

project was guided. Facts were not considered to be essentially independent of an existing body of sociological theory. If this had been the case the sum total of the facts would result in new and independent generalizations about the nature of the American Baptist Convention. Any similarity between the Convention and other social systems would have been accidental. But the purpose of this study was not to seek for a new sociological theory which would be relevant only for the Baptists; rather, the effort was made to use known theories in order to interpret the particular problems of the American Baptist Convention.

This does not mean that empirical data were adjusted to fit the theories. It indicates that "any *important* change in our knowledge of fact . . . must of itself change the statement of at least one of the propositions of the theoretical system. . . ."[8] "Important" in this context does not connote "interesting" but signifies any fact which is directly relevant for the system of theory which is utilized.

For example, it was noted above that Weber's theory of authority does not fully comprehend the Baptist situation. This does not negate the utility of his theory but does point to a need for readjustment of his analysis. An additional category of authority had to be developed but there was nothing radically new about it and a careful reading of Weber indicates that the idea was already implicit in his theory.

The relationship between fact and theory can best be described in terms of the process of verification. In a study of the Baptists this consisted in the deliberate investigation of the Convention "with the expectations derived from the theory . . . and seeing whether or not the facts actually found agree with these expectations."[9] However, the methodological process is always reciprocal. The important facts which are discovered are related to the hypotheses in such a way that alterations in the theoretical system should be one of the results of the book. But more important is the comprehension of the

[8] Talcott Parsons, *The Structure of Social Action* (Glencoe, Illinois: The Free Press, 1937), p. 7.
[9] *Ibid.*, p. 8.

current Baptist situation with the help of an existing body of social theory.

ACKNOWLEDGMENTS

The research for this study was made unexpectedly pleasurable by the encouragement and suggestions of Professors James M. Gustafson and H. Richard Niebuhr of Yale Divinity School. The idea for this book first emerged in conversation with them. Professor Winthrop S. Hudson of Colgate Rochester Divinity School contributed valuable advice for the historical sections, and he permitted me to cite several of his projects which were still in the process of publication. Professors Horton Davies and R. Paul Ramsey of Princeton University read a preliminary draft and made important suggestions which have been included without citation. I am particularly indebted to Marion J. Levy, Jr., also of Princeton University, who made important critical comments on those portions of the study which deal with sociological theory. I wish to express my gratitude to the leaders of the American Baptist Convention who made this project possible. Not only did they contribute their time but they spoke to many questions which must have appeared naïve or impertinent in view of their intimate knowledge and experience in Baptist affairs. My failure to utilize the good advice of many people completely limits the responsibility of my intellectual mentors for any inadequacies in the present work. I alone am liable for all errors of fact or interpretation which may appear on the following pages. It is a pleasure to recall the help of Mrs. Doris Nystrom in typing and correcting an early draft of this work, and the assistance of Miss R. Miriam Brokaw and Herbert S. Bailey, Jr., whose patient work on the final stages of the manuscript were so important. I am grateful to my father for his continued interest and for assistance in proofreading. I am indebted above all to my wife for assistance with the statistical work and for many helpful suggestions throughout the text, an acknowledgment which falls far short of my larger indebtedness to her.

PREFACE

The author is grateful for permission granted by the following publishers to draw extensively from books or articles published by them: Oxford University Press, for quotations from Max Weber, *The Theory of Social and Economic Organization*, 1947; The Free Press, for quotations from Robert Michels, *Political Parties*, 1949; *Church History*, XXIII, 4 (December 1954), for quotations from Sidney Mead, "Denominationalism: The Shape of Protestantism in America"; *Foundations*, I, 1 (January 1958), for quotations from Winthrop S. Hudson, "The Associational Principle Among Baptists"; The American Baptist Convention, for quotations from *Yearbooks of the American Baptist Convention*, 1907-1957; The Board of Education and Publication of the American Baptist Convention, for quotations from their *Forty-Fourth Annual Report*, 1955, and for quotations from "Basic Papers Prepared for the American Baptist Theological Conference, 1954"; *The Watchman-Examiner*, for quotations from various articles and editorials written between 1922 and 1950. A major portion of this book was a dissertation presented for the degree of Doctor of Philosophy in Yale University.

PAUL M. HARRISON

Princeton, New Jersey
June 1959

CONTENTS

TABLES AND CHARTS

TABLES

CONTENTS

CHARTS

AUTHORITY AND POWER
IN THE
FREE CHURCH TRADITION

CHAPTER I

INTRODUCTION

The Problem of Church-Order

THE Baptists originated in the early seventeenth century within English Congregationalism. Their primary emphasis was upon the voluntary nature of membership in the local church. Only those who personally experienced salvation through Jesus Christ were accepted into the religious fellowship. Churches were independent from external control as exercised by any ecclesiastical official. During the eighteenth century the Baptists and other Independent groups formed local associations, state conventions, and national conventions in order to strengthen their missionary and educational endeavors and gain a greater unity for their evangelical witness. They continued, however, to maintain their loyalty to a congregational polity.

At the present time, the American Baptist Convention[1] with headquarters in New York City is one of twenty-seven Baptist denominations in America. Among these the Southern Baptist Convention is the largest, with 8,000,000 members and 30,-000 churches; while the Independent Baptist Church of America has only fifty members in two churches. The American Baptist Convention with 1,500,000 members and 6,400 churches is the fourth largest of the Baptist groups in the United States. Its membership is limited to thirty-four state conventions north of the Mason and Dixon line and west to California.

In terms of their polity the Baptists are closely related to the Congregationalists, the Disciples of Christ, the Unitarians, and numerous smaller denominations. Theologically, they are more closely allied to the Calvinist Reformed tradition, which

[1] Formerly called the Northern Baptist Convention, it changed its name in 1950. Both titles will be used in this study according to which is more appropriate in the context.

3

includes, among others, the Presbyterians and the Congregationalists. Therefore, the problems which the Baptists face in the modern world are not confined to their own religious movement but are experienced in common by many millions of Protestants in Europe and America.

Before we proceed to a general discussion of the Baptist situation, some basic terms ought to be tentatively defined. First, "power" as it will be used here signifies the ability of a person or group of persons to determine the action of others without regard for their needs or desires. "Authority," on the other hand, indicates a right to exercise power. The people of a community accept the leader as one who ought to lead them and who avoids his responsibility when he does not. The sources of authority are various. A leader may gain authority on the basis of the traditions of a community. This will be called "traditional authority." Or, the leader may possess authority as a legal right which is based on the official and rational laws of the community. This is called "rational-legal authority." The last source of authority is the personality of the leader himself. He may be so endowed that he attracts the loyalty of persons in the community who are willing to follow him even if this requires a disregard for the established traditions and laws; we shall call this "charismatic authority."

This study in the sociology of religion deals with the problem of church-order in the American Baptist Convention. Both "polity" and "doctrine of the church" are included in the term "church-order." The two phrases "theology of the church" and "doctrine of the church" will be used interchangeably to signify the beliefs Christians hold about the nature of the church, its relation to God, and its purpose in the world. Polity, on the other hand, refers to the administration and government of the church, including the relation between individuals and groups within a denomination. A project exclusively devoted to polity would be centered primarily upon the problems of policy-making and power in the church. Such an endeavor would not necessarily include an evaluation of the doctrines about the church.

The American Baptists have often been troubled by inter-group conflicts and inefficiencies of organization. Twice they have cooperated in a study of their polity without seriously analyzing the Baptist theology of the church. Apparently, doctrine of the church was considered permanently valid and essentially isolated from problems of polity. In 1925 an extensive study of the Convention was made and it was noted that the size of the task "required a concentration of attention more on the means of accomplishment than on the ends— more on machinery than on the goal. The Committee could not assess the spiritual values . . . or give adequate recognition in this report to these imponderable objectives."[2]

A more recent survey of the problems of the Convention did offer passing attention to Baptist beliefs, values, and goals. But the professional organization which conducted the study inferred that no matter what the nature of Baptist beliefs and purposes they had no necessary bearing upon denominational polity.[3] The American Institute of Management, which conducted the survey, was generally critical of religious groups in this country because "viewed against the background of modern business corporations, the management practices of religious organizations are appallingly archaic."[4]

A study in the sociology of religion must appraise the dialectic which occurs between doctrine and polity, faith and practice. Polity is the sociological manifestation of doctrinal belief; it is the political expression of the content of the gospel as interpreted by the members of the religious group. How-

[2] "Report on a Survey of Fifty-eight Organizations of the Northern Baptist Convention" (printed for private distribution, 1925), p. iii. (Catalogued by the American Baptist Historical Society, Rochester, N.Y.) In spite of its limitations, this is an excellent empirical analysis of the Convention and will be used in several places below.

[3] *Management Audit of the American Baptist Convention* (New York: American Institute of Management, 1955), p. 1.

[4] *Ibid.*, p. 1. The Roman Catholic Church constitutes an important exception to the generalization. A subsequent study by the American Institute of Management was reported as follows: "The Roman Catholic Church got an 'A' yesterday for administrative efficiency. Its numerical grade was 88, but since 75 is considered excellent and the Standard Oil Company of New Jersey was at the top of the class with 90 plus, the Church's mark was well up in the cum laude category. . . . Last year, the Institute made a study of the American Baptist Convention but did not release any rating to the general public." (*The New York Times*, January 23, 1956, p. 27.)

ever, polity, because it has other functions, is never the perfect expression of religious belief. Even a system of doctrine is never consistent in all respects. One of the most effective ways of discovering internal contradictions within a doctrinal system is to study the dilemmas experienced by the church when its people attempt to express their beliefs through their polity.

One who studies the church-order of a Christian denomination always faces the temptation of castigating the church because its polity does not truly express its theology. The theology of a religious group is often accepted as the fixed norm, the absolute reference by which the actions of the group are to be judged. Deviations from the doctrines of the church are interpreted in terms of human weakness and sin, and in terms of the inevitable tendency on the part of Christian people to adjust their doctrines to the conditions of the secular environment. There can be no doubt that this is often the case. But, as Troeltsch observed, "the great central points of religious development are an independent expression of the religious life."[5] The churches have often made an adjustment to society when they should have been heeding critical prophetic judgments. Sometimes they have refused to adjust because of a profound devotion to their central beliefs. This has been true of the Baptists, who have been loyal to the principle of congregational autonomy even though it militated against an effective denominational organization and detracted from their missionary work. Undoubtedly, their devotion has been motivated by many non-theological factors such as in-group pride and denominational politics, but the Baptists have also been stirred by the conviction that their doctrine and polity is based on the practices of the apostolic church.

It will be shown below that many Baptist leaders are asking critical questions about the Baptist theology of the church. Also, an effort will be made to indicate that there are times when a failure to adjust to new environmental situations is no less damaging to the mission of the church than the tend-

[5] Ernst Troeltsch, *The Social Teaching of the Christian Churches*, II (New York: Macmillan, 1931), p. 1,002.

ency to succumb to secular pressures that are in contradiction
to the spirit of the gospel.

Oftentimes the doctrine of the church remains static while
the polity undergoes a radical adjustment to new situations.
This may occur internally within the church if there is a radical shift in the balance of power. For example, in addition to
its function as the institutional expression of theological statements about the church, another function of polity is to provide a check upon the pretensions of powerful members of the
denomination. In the Baptist situation the desire to curtail
the influence of ecclesiastical personnel was so emphasized
that other needs of the church organization were sacrificed.
This occurred, in one instance, when the Baptists formed the
Convention. They insisted that the autonomy of the local
church be violated in no way, i.e., that the Convention gain
no authority to direct any of the affairs of the churches. But
the effort was futile. In fact, the Convention officials gained
greater power over the activities of the churches than has
ever been recognized as legitimate by the official apologists
for the Baptist movement.

In recent years some Baptists have called for recognition
and acceptance of the power of the denominational leaders.
But it is extremely difficult to make a formal change in the
polity system without altering the doctrine of the church.
Therefore, it is not likely that a significant change will occur
with respect to patterns of authority unless it is preceded by
a reinterpretation of doctrinal formulas. A denominational
official may gain informal power without being recognized by
the members of the church as possessing official authority.

Since power is the ability to determine the activity of others
without their consent, authority may be defined as formal
power. Authority is the legitimate right of the leader to exercise his power. It is a right that is conferred by the people
and supported by their beliefs and traditions. Therefore,
changes in the system of authority must be accompanied by
some changes in the modes of belief.

But the practices of power are quite another thing. When
power comes "into conflict with authority, it is the latter

which gives way . . . by a transformation of its content."[6] In this quotation the impression is given that the beliefs of a social group are unstable and readily modified. Actually, a system of polity is more amenable to change than a doctrine of the church.

One of the fundamental functions of every belief system is to facilitate communication of stable symbols and meanings. Cooperative activity in a social group is impossible apart from general agreement concerning goals and values.[7] From the sociological point of view, theology functions as a relatively stable normative system to which the members of a religious group may appeal for guidance.

In part, theology fulfills this function by interpreting the meaning of history and by determining the place and purpose of the religious group in its social environment. Reference is made to the goals toward which the members of the group are collectively oriented, the relation of these goals to the present and future course of events, and the relation of the whole community to the action of God in history.[8]

On the basis of the previous discussion it is possible to draw a distinction between formal and informal beliefs. These can rarely be systematically defined or codified. But the distinction is useful since both systems have an important and definable role in the life of the religious community. The formal belief system has at least three important functions. The first is the function of identification. The official beliefs describe the nature of the group and sustain it as a useful unit in the society of which it is a part. In the second, the teleological function, the official beliefs serve as formal instruments to define the purpose of the group. The goals, methods, and taboos are prescribed by the belief system. Third is the coordinational function in which the official beliefs formally define the proper mode of relations which are to exist between the various sub-groups within the social sys-

---

6 Lasswell and Kaplan, *op.cit.*, p. 137.

7 Parsons, *Social System*, *op.cit.*, pp. 327-328.

8 *Ibid.*, p. 349. The last sentence is a paraphrase of one of Parsons' remarks concerning the function of an ideology.

tem. The purpose of each sub-group is broadly outlined and the authority of leadership is specified.

The informal belief system functions in quite a different manner. In the first place, it is not a system of written and codified beliefs. The existence of informal beliefs can be discovered only by observing what people actually do as distinguished from what they say they are doing, or should be doing. Rylaarsdam observed the existence of this phenomenon in the Christian church: "The actual functions and expressions of churches change in relation to the actual theological meaning that is given to the Church as the work of God in the world. Not the inherited standards or confessions about the nature of the Church but the current and largely unsystematic belief about it will determine the role of denominations and congregations. A study of the churches as social structures can be an excellent way of discovering what they mean by being churches."[9]

Although Rylaarsdam does not develop analytic categories which distinguish between "formal" and "functional" beliefs, no statement could better describe the intention of this book. For this is a study of the American Baptist Convention as a social structure in order to discover what the Baptists mean when they insist upon allegiance to a doctrine of the church which they do not follow in their actual polity. For example, they constantly reaffirm the autonomy of the local church as a meaningful concept while at the same time reducing the essentials of local autonomy through many of their organizational activities. Another example is their insistence that ecclesiastical officials shall obtain only a limited authority-status; but within the actual situation the officials tend to increase their power with each passing year.

Selznick has observed that formal beliefs often present a serious obstacle to the understanding of a social group. By the very nature of their function, formal beliefs are designed to sustain the common values of the group and establish formal definitions of inter-group relations. He notes that of-

---

[9] J. Coert Rylaarsdam, "The Doctrine of the Church and the Problem of Culture," *Christianity and Society*, XVIII (autumn, 1953), p. 10.

ficial beliefs are presented for public consumption (autonomy of the churches, democracy, limitation of authority, decentralization, and the like) and "it is naturally considered desirable for the attention of observers to be directed toward these avowed ideas, so they may receive a view of the enterprise consistent with the conception of its leadership."[10]

Selznick further observes that it is often the "sincere conviction [of the leaders] that precisely this view is in accord with the realities of the situation and best conveys the meaning and significance of the project under inspection."[11]

In order for severe strains to occur within a social system it is not always necessary that practice come into conflict with formal beliefs. Inconsistencies can arise within the official belief system itself. Marion Levy observes that one of the most common dysfunctional aspects of the beliefs of a social group arises when there is "the presence of goals that are to some extent mutually incompatible. 'Individualism' and 'maximization of the general welfare,' for example, may result in quite sharp conflicts under some circumstances."[12] Levy's illustration is convenient since it is particularly applicable to the Baptists, who wish to maximize the freedom of the individual and at the same time to increase the effectiveness of the Convention. One possible solution to this dilemma is to state that the welfare and purpose of the Convention is not theoretically incompatible with the freedom and needs of the individual. But the ambiguities and tensions which arise in actual social existence cannot be explained so conveniently. Social life is seldom as logical as a system of doctrine. This is especially true if the system has been developed by a theologian who can measure the internal inconsistencies with care and formulate the necessary qualifications. Baptist doctrine, however, was not constructed within the mind of a single theologian; it was developed by many members of a historical community in response to particular situations. It will be seen that the situations were varied in character and the

[10] Selznick, *op.cit.*, p. 8.   [11] *Ibid.*, p. 8.
[12] Levy, *op.cit.*, pp. 178-179.

theological response of the community was seldom structured along systematic lines.

The Baptist Situation

Most modern historians reject the notion that the Baptist movement can be directly traced to the Anabaptist phenomenon in Switzerland and Germany. The ancestry of the modern Baptist churches is to be found in the seventeenth century left-wing Calvinist activity in England and Holland. The Baptists feared and protested against the hierarchical, authoritarian, and centralizing tendencies of the Protestant ecclesiastical movements. As a result they established strong congregations, and by the end of the eighteenth century they were emphasizing the autonomy of the local church and insisting on the competency of the individual in all matters of faith and practice. "For this reason Baptists acknowledge no human founder, recognize no human authority, and subscribe to no human creed."[13]

Mayer points out that despite the diversity of their origin and the unusual degree of tension which has often divided them on issues of critical importance, no Protestant religious group has demonstrated greater tenacity, consistency, and loyalty to its basic emphasis upon individual freedom.[14]

In the next chapter the development of Baptist beliefs within the cultural milieu of the seventeenth century will be considered. Historical and theological data will be utilized within a framework provided by sociological categories. The Baptists successfully discerned the decisive theological issue of the period but not succinctly enough to formulate it in explicit terms. They were therefore unable to prevent serious deviations from their original intention. Freedom was the issue which initially animated the Baptists but it will be argued that the founding fathers of the movement were primarily concerned with the freedom of God, not the freedom of man or the autonomy of the local church. These were second-

[13] F. E. Mayer, *The Religious Bodies of America* (St. Louis: Concordia Publishing House, 1956), p. 259.
[14] *Ibid.*, pp. 259f.

ary concerns; they were instruments to achieve the ultimate goal, the free movement of the Holy Spirit within the churches. Although they often expressed these ideals in unmistakable terms, they never explicitly distinguished between the ultimate goal (the freedom of God) and the means (congregational autonomy and individual freedom).

As a consequence of this ambiguity, the emphasis on polity tended progressively to obscure the original purpose of the founders. A theological individualism displaced the concern for God's sovereignty, and by the turn of the nineteenth century the Baptists placed almost exclusive emphasis upon the sovereignty of man and the freedom of the local congregations from any form of ecclesiastical control.

Even today, the majority of Baptists emphasize a cluster of related ideas which minimizes ecclesiastical authority. But during the nineteenth century they discovered a new interest in missions and evangelism which significantly complicated their problem of church-order. The vast missionary and evangelistic organizations which proved necessary for the advancement of their work eventually culminated in the formation of the Northern Baptist Convention in 1907. According to Baptist doctrines of the church, the officers and professional executives who operated these organizations in the name of the denomination could not be recognized as possessing any legitimate ecclesiastical authority.

Chapter Three analyzes the factors which favored the creation of the Convention. Of no less importance are the elements and conditions which were in opposition to the new organization, for it was the latter which had an equally strong effect upon the present nature of the Baptist problem. Briefly, most Baptists realized that the leaders of the organization would gain a significant degree of power but every effort was made to minimize their influence by limiting their functions and by attempting to eliminate the possibility of conferring any legitimate authority upon these leaders.

Primary concern was centered on the potential power of the full-time professional executives who facilitated the operation of the missionary agencies. In addition to reaffirming their belief in the autonomy of the local church, the founders of the Convention attempted to limit executive power in three ways. First, they stated that executives could make no policies for the missionary organizations. The boards of managers which were directed by the constituency of the denomination would maintain control of the policy process. Second, the delegates to the annual meetings of the Convention would be sent directly from the local churches. Thus "Baptist democracy" would not be compromised by a method of indirect representation and the churches could instruct the missionary agencies concerning their work for the ensuing year. Finally, it was stated that no ecclesiastical organization, whether it be a national convention or an association of local churches, could promulgate legislation which would be binding upon the local churches. In the face of these stipulations it is difficult to determine how the executives were to operate their own organizations effectively or have any important influence upon the activity and thought of the denomination. Nonetheless, the Convention leaders did gain significant degrees of power—in some cases considerably more than was necessary for the performance of their tasks.

The fourth chapter contains a discussion of the problem of power and authority in relation to the contemporary situation in the American Baptist Convention. It is argued that the Baptist doctrine of the church contains fundamental ambiguities and that the locus of ecclesiastical authority has not been sharply defined. The redeemed individual is declared to be a "king in his own right," but at the same time the local church is believed to be the seat of ultimate authority and the denominational agencies are recognized as possessing some kind of power. Although the officials of the Convention theoretically possess no ecclesiastical authority, their actual power is great enough to exert tremendous pressure upon the traditional beliefs of the Baptists.

Few people in the denomination are so credulous that they ignore the existence of the power of the Convention's leaders.

Within the limitations provided by the doctrine of the church, ways have been sought to validate the power of these men. They have been accepted as legitimate authorities, for example, on the basis of their charismatic qualities.[15] But charisma is not the only basis of authority. No less important is the need of the denominational organization to sustain the missionary endeavor. Thus the leaders of the Convention have obtained an "expediential authority," not fully legal, not based on ecclesiastical tradition, but an authority which arises out of the immediate needs of the denominational organizations.

In order to interpret the complex situation of power and authority within the denomination, it is helpful to utilize Max Weber's typology of authority. This heuristic device provides a point of departure for a theoretical discussion of the nature of authority in the Baptist situation even though all the particulars of the Baptist phenomenon are not comprehended by Weber's types.

Within this theoretical framework of authority and power, the next three chapters engage in an empirical analysis of the influence of the professional executives of the Convention, the relations between the various groups in the denomination, and the ideas about the nature of the church which are undergoing change as a result of adjustment to new situations. Chapter Five draws a distinction between the formal and limited authority of the executives and the informal system of power which is necessary to support a leadership that possesses a limited authority. In Chapter Six it is found that the executives, even though their official position is tenuous, exercise a tremendous control over the policies of the denomination and the activities of the local churches. Chapter Seven analyzes the character of the leader's activities and their in-

---

[15] In its original use "charisma" signified a spiritual gift. The personal qualities of the individual were derived from a divine power, and the leader was *possessed* and directed by super-natural forces. However, in recent times, the term has been appropriated by sociologists and others, and often indicates any individual who *possesses* a dynamic personality and who is capable of leading people who believe he is impelled by extra-mundane forces. In this book, the term will be used in its broader, sociological sense. No effort will be made, in other words, to distinguish between charismatic and quasi-charismatic leaders.

clination to place the needs of their agencies before the original goals for which they were created. The tendency for organizational imperatives to undermine the purpose of the organization is widely discussed in sociological literature, but it is found that the Baptist system of church-order accentuates the problem. Since no explicit ecclesiastical authority is tendered the officials of the Convention, the resultant insecurity of the leaders impels them to conserve the gains they have made rather than risk the dangers of a prophetic and imaginative leadership.

In Chapters Eight and Nine Baptist democracy is critically analyzed. It is argued that the effort to preserve a system of "pure democracy" in an organization so large as the American Baptist Convention has involved the denomination in departures from the democratic order which should not have been necessary. The Baptists have insisted that their organization exemplifies democracy at its best, but the protest tends to veil the weaknesses of the system. The Baptists claim that the policies for a succeeding year are formulated by the delegates of the annual meetings. But it is found that the delegates have little influence over the affairs of the Convention except in an indirect manner. The desires of the churches and their delegates can be only crudely assessed by the leadership and it is argued that it is false to claim that the churches are the ultimate power in the denomination.

In Chapter Ten some generalizations are made about the local churches, the state conventions, and their relations with the national organizations. It is found that the original function of the Convention (to serve the churches and help them achieve their missionary and evangelist goals) has subtly changed. The preservation of the Convention as an organization has now become an ultimate goal, a goal to which even the local leadership is often willing to subscribe. Chapter Eleven considers the development of categories of authority which will assist in the analysis of non-authoritarian social systems.

The concluding chapter attempts to focus the critical generalizations of the book upon the central problem of church-order in the American Baptist Convention. An effort will be made to delineate the primary points of contradiction and tension within the Baptist system of doctrine and polity in order to shed light upon the problem of the Protestant non-episcopal tradition in the modern world.

THE FREEDOM OF MAN UNDER
THE FREEDOM OF GOD

In 1907 delegates from Baptist churches in the northern states gave cautious approval to the formation of the Northern Baptist Convention. Every effort was made to limit the power of the Convention and the authority of its officers and professional executives. The new organization was to be a limited instrument for the achievement of goals which the churches could not attain alone, but there were many participants who saw even in this minimal effort a "first step on the road to Rome." By 1957, the year of the Golden Anniversary, a radical alteration of the general attitude had occurred. At the annual meeting of the denomination an extensive debate developed concerning the location of Convention headquarters. Leaders on both sides of the debate—those who wanted the headquarters moved to Chicago and those who wished it to remain in the east—freely admitted that the area which housed the central offices gained great prestige and other advantages with regard to denominational affairs. The professional executives of the American Baptist Convention, once the objects of fear, distrust, and acrimony, were now a coveted people.

These two events illustrate the confusion which has marked the history of the denomination since the founding of the first missionary society in the early nineteenth century. Crucial issues having a profound effect upon the total life of the denomination have never been decided on the basis of a consistent framework of theological principle or, as in many cases, on the basis of any theological ideas.[1]

[1] In the debate on headquarters in 1957 the issue revolved around the idea of "togetherness." In a mimeographed statement the General Council, highest policy-making body of the Convention, recommended that togetherness "is the most important consideration."

Winthrop Hudson observes that the accepted opinion that the existing denominational organization is derived from Biblical precepts or from historic Baptist principles simply is not true. Baptists, he says, were forced to develop a denominational structure in order to solve problems which transcend the local community. The result was an "improvised church order . . . developed somewhat unwittingly and unconsciously, being dictated more by considerations of expediency and necessity rather than by considerations stemming from a re-examination of the nature of the church and its vocation in the world."[2] In another place, Hudson points out that "our denominational structure has not been the product of biblical, theological, or even rational considerations. It was developed on an *ad hoc* basis as an efficient money-raising technique and to serve certain sectional and partisan concerns."[3]

It will be argued that the organizational and theological confusion which plagues the American Baptist denomination is grounded in a disconcerting amalgam of religious beliefs and political theories. The peculiar shifts in the Baptist attitude toward the authority and legitimacy of its leadership, as well as toward the principles of association and autonomy of the local congregation, were born in the conflicts which arose between the early Congregational Independents and Separatists, between right-wing and left-wing Puritanism.[4]

The Freedom of God

It would exceed the limitation established for this study to venture upon an effort to unravel and analyze the history of Baptist origins. But there are indications that the existing "Baptist distinctives" distort the essential intent of the founding fathers of the movement. A reading of the early confessions of faith of the Baptists, both in England and America, does not reveal a primary emphasis upon "the dignity, sanc-

2 Winthrop S. Hudson, "Are Baptists so Peculiar?" *Christian Century*, LXX, 2 (November 18, 1953), p. 1,324.
3 Winthrop S. Hudson, "Stumbling into Disorder," *Foundations*, I, 2 (April 1958), p. 45.
4 James H. Nichols, *Democracy and the Churches* (Philadelphia: Westminster Press, 1951), pp. 32-38.

tity, and competency of the individual." There was a profound concern for religious liberty and freedom of conscience, but it was clearly secondary to the doctrine of the sovereignty of God and never disassociated from it.[5]

Daniel Jenkins also observes that the charge is made too often that Independency encouraged religious individualism. Representative early Independents, he says, made a sharp distinction between themselves and the left-wing sects which emphasized the importance of the Inner Light. Independency's concern "for the rights of the local congregation was not to safeguard an abstract individual liberty but to take seriously the fact of the Church as a community in its most concrete and immediate form."[6]

The earliest Baptist confessions were not primarily concerned with the freedom of the individual and the autonomy of the local church. These were derivative ideas, expressions of the political temper of the time as well as a further development of the left-wing Protestant principles of church-order. The ultimate concern of the first Baptists was for the free movement of the Holy Spirit or the freedom of God; and the Baptists believed that the greatest threat to God's freedom which existed in the seventeenth century was an ecclesiastical order supported by magisterial power.[7]

The effort of the most representative early Baptists to establish individual freedom as a basic tenet of faith was impelled by a religious and political situation which they believed placed restrictions upon the will of God within the religious communions. In the preface to the second edition of the Confession of 1646 it is asserted that the freedom of God holds primacy over every effort to assert individual religious freedom: "And had it [persecution] been against our persons only, we would have held our peace, and committed our cause to

[5] The Confession of 1688, articles I, II, III; Philip Schaff, *Creeds of Christendom*, III (New York: Harper & Brothers, 1877), pp. 643f. Originally based upon the Westminster Confession of 1647, this confession was incorporated with few changes (none in the passages cited) into the Philadelphia Confession of 1688.

[6] Daniel T. Jenkins, *Church Meeting and Democracy* (London: Independent Press Ltd., 1944), p. 10.

[7] Hudson, "Are Baptists so Peculiar?" *op.cit.*, p. 1,324.

God; we may not, nor dare not be neuters in matters of so high a nature, but come in and speak *to the help of the Lord against the mighty*. Therefore, to free ourselves and the truth we profess from such unjust aspersions, that *it may be at liberty, though we be in bonds*, we have published a brief confession of our faith. . . ."[8] The ecclesiastical actualization of this theological idea was motivated by the fear of the possibility that the "new presbyter" might become the "old priest writ large." The early Baptists strived to guard against this by creating a church-order "in the same way that in political construction they were to erect a barrier to tyranny by the reservation of powers to local government and by a carefully devised system of checks and balances."[9]

Among the earliest of the General Baptists were Thomas Helwys and John Murton. Nothing that Helwys and Murton wrote bespeaks exclusive emphasis upon human freedom. Their words on the institution of apostolic succession underline the truth that the Spirit of God must be at liberty to work through all sorts and conditions of men: "How dare any man or men challenge unto themselves a preeminence herein, as though the Spirit of God was only in their hearts, and the word of God only to be fetched at their mouths, and the ordinance of God only to be had from their hands, except they were apostles? . . . This is contrary to the liberty of the gospel, which is free for all men at all times and in all places."[10]

John Smyth, the early associate of Helwys, desiring to assure the free movement of the Spirit, carried the notion of spontaneity to lengths which were repudiated by his own Baptist contemporaries and which would be questioned by even the most radical of modern Baptist individualists. To read from the Holy Bible during church worship was denial

---

[8] Edward B. Underhill, ed., *Confessions of Faith and Other Documents of the Baptist Churches of England in the 17th Century* (London: The Hanserd Knollys Society, 1854), p. 22. Italics added.

[9] Hudson, "Are Baptists so Peculiar?" *op.cit.*, p. 1,324.

[10] Helwys and Murton in a letter to the Mennonites, quoted in A. H. Newman, *A History of Baptist Churches in the United States* (New York: The Christian Literature Co., 1894), p. 43.

of the free expression of the Word of God: "Wee hould that the worship of the new testament properly so called is spirituall proceeding originally from the hart: & that reading out of a booke (though a lawfull eclesiastical action) is no part of spirituall worship, but rather the invention of the man of synne it beeing substituted for a part of spirituall worship. Wee hould that seeing prophesiing is a parte of spirituall worship; therefore in time of prophesiing it is vnlawfull to have the booke as a helpe before the eye. . . ."[11]

In general the tenets of the Free Church tradition were the same for Puritan, Independent, Separatist, and early Presbyterian alike. They are summed up in a statement by Richard Fitz, minister of the "Privye Churche," progenitor of Presbyterian worship. He declared that the "trew markes of Christs churche" consist in "fyrste and formoste, the Glorious worde and Evangell preached, not in bondage and subjection, but freely, and purely. Secondly to have the Sacraments mynistred purely, onely and all together accordinge to the institution and good worde of the Lord Jesus, without any tradicion or invention of man. And last of all, to have, not the fylthye Cannon lawe, but dissiplyne onelye, and all together agreable to the same heavenlye and almighty worde of oure good Lorde, Jesus Chryste."[12]

Soul Competency and the Freedom of Man

The early heritage of the Baptists contains ambiguities which through the passage of time have been transformed into historical contradictions. Even though the central concern of the Free Church fathers was for the freedom of God, it was immediately recognized that the freedom of man in matters of worship and church government was a necessary social corollary of the theological doctrine. Pressed by the secular spirit of individualism current in the eighteenth and nineteenth centuries, and proud of their religious contribution to the movement, later Baptists slipped off their theological

---

[11] John Smyth, *The Differences of the Churches of the Separation*, ed. (London, 1608), quoted in Horton Davies, *The Worship of the English Puritans* (London: Dacre Press, 1948), p. 90.
[12] Horton Davies, *Worship*, *op.cit.*, p. 96.

base and cooperated in the support of an ideology grounded in the spirit of individual voluntarism. In every decade since the beginning of the nineteenth century one can find in Baptist literature reaffirmations of the freedom and competency of the totally independent individual. A statement which epitomizes this emphasis is contained in a book used in polity courses in many Baptist seminaries in the north: "The womb which gives birth to Baptist polity and at the same time endows it with its directive life principle is doctrinal. . . . We refer to the creative idea that the individual is competent in all matters of religion; has within himself by divine gift and right those capacities that make him competent to meet all the demands with which genuine religion confronts him. . . . He has no inescapable need of church to bring him salvation or mediate to him divine grace. . . . It is the doctrine of soul competency that produced the Baptist doctrine of church."[13]

It is not surprising, therefore, that F. E. Mayer, in his brief description of the Baptists, concludes that "the competency of the soul of man in matters religious is the basic principle on which all Baptists are united and out of which all Baptist beliefs grow."[14] A few modern Baptists deplore this emphasis and insist that it is a deviation from the intent of the left-wing Reformers. But these critics are in a precarious position. Living in a time when individual freedoms are threatened by many forces, they find it difficult to attack a crass individualism in the churches and at the same time support a tradition which teaches that the individual must be free in order to assure the freedom of the Holy Spirit. They know that the Free churchmen taught that the Word of God spoken in the churches must become a lively Word, and that this can be achieved only within a tradition which emphasizes man's freedom. But the great strength of the Free churches is also the source of their most serious weakness. The Baptist emphasis upon "soul competency" crystallizes attention upon the possibilities of men rather than upon the power of God.

---

[13] William R. McNutt, *Polity and Practice in Baptist Churches* (Philadelphia: The Judson Press, 1935), pp. 21-22.
[14] Mayer, *op.cit.*, p. 260.

The London Confession of 1646 reflects the original reliance of the Baptists upon the Calvinist tradition which emphasized man's total dependence upon the sovereignty of God. The primacy of the liberty of God is implicit throughout the Confessions: "Faith is the gift of God, wrought in the hearts of the elect by the Spirit of God; by which faith they come to know and believe the truth of the scriptures, and the excellency of them above all other writings and all things in the world, as they hold forth the glory of God in his attributes, the excellency of Christ in his nature and offices, and of the power and fulness of the Spirit in its workings and operations, and so enabled to cast their souls upon this truth thus believed."[15]

The power of man is limited, and by implication his freedom is secondary to the liberty of the gospel. Man does not generate faith out of an empty vacuum of personal freedom and separation from communion with other men. The church as an organized social institution is extremely important, for it is by the agency of the church that the gospel is proclaimed: "Faith is ordinarily begotten by the preaching of the gospel, or word of Christ, without respect to any power or agency in the creature; but it being wholly passive, and dead in trespasses and sins, doth believe and is converted by no less power than that which raised Christ from the dead."[16]

Even though the early Baptists emphasized the freedom and sovereignty of God, they made no absolute distinction between the action of the Holy Spirit in the life of the individual believer and the activity of the Spirit in the church. Nor were they able to make an explicit and well-defined distinction between the freedom of God and the freedom of man. While no sharp distinction is proper or even possible, it probably would have been salutory for subsequent Baptist history if the fathers had placed more explicit emphasis upon God's freedom. It is not difficult to see how the Baptists so readily made the critical shift from concern for the freedom of God to primary attendance upon the competency of the individual

---

[15] London Confession of 1646, art. XXII, *Underhill, op.cit.*, pp. 35f.
[16] Art. XXIV, *ibid.*, p. 36.

believer. The two ideas are so closely and necessarily associated that it was inevitable that the penultimate would displace the ultimate, and that the Baptist form of idolatry would be expressed through the glorification of the human individual and the apotheosizing of the intimate fellowship to which he belonged. The Confession of 1646 expressed the necessary unity between the freedom of the Gospel and the freedom of the individual: "The preaching of the gospel to the conversion of sinners is absolutely free; no way requiring as absolutely necessary, any qualifications, preparations, or terrors of the law, or preceding ministry of the law; but only and alone the naked soul, a sinner and ungodly, to receive Christ crucified. . . ."[17]

The evangelical revivals of the eighteenth century carried the Baptists the remaining distance to a spirit of radical individualism. Calvinistic theology was largely taken for granted, but the great need was to reach those who had felt no religious experience. Evangelical preaching was adapted to the understanding of the common man. Important theological distinctions were ignored in favor of "a religion of the heart rather than of the mind"; and the voluntary status of the churches in America and the fact that ninety percent of the population was outside the churches further contributed to the emphasis upon personal religious experience and freedom for the individual. Thus the resulting theological depression and tensions of church order are not particularly surprising in light of Baptist origins and history. The socioreligious situation was chaotic as well as creative during the era of the birth of liberal democracy and left-wing Protestantism. New relations of religion and culture, manifestly expressed in the changing relations of church and state, were emerging as a result of the flowering of humanistic principles in the political and theological arenas. Free Church theology, and Baptist theology in particular, was almost immediately mixed with the ideals and practices of political democracy.[18]

[17] Art. xxv, *ibid.*, p. 37.
[18] This section is partly informed by a mimeographed paper by Winthrop Hudson, to be used by the Presbyterian Board of Education.

Referring to modern times, someone has said that the Baptists crossed the bridge from religious non-conformity to liberal democracy, and they never returned to the bridge. The situation is made more difficult for the Baptists because of the impossibility of completely unraveling the complex web of ideas which contributed to Free Church development. The ideas of the Independents of Cromwell's army, the writings of John Locke, the theological thought of the Puritan Separatists, and the courageous writings on religious liberty of Thomas Helwys—all contributed to the present Baptist theological milieu,[19] and greater efforts are necessary to clarify the existing confusion.

The Baptist situation since the advent of the Convention in 1907 has been characterized by a constant effort to reorganize the Convention along lines established by current needs. Ideas like efficiency, harmony, unity, and togetherness gain precedence in usage over the central theological ideas of the Christian Church. Baptists tend to give an honorific nod to orthodox Christian doctrines and quickly return to their emphasis and apologetic for the "Baptist distinctives": "Let it be understood now and always that the basic doctrine of Baptists is the dignity, sanctity, and competency of the individual believer. I do not mean to say that we put this doctrine ahead of our belief in the sovereignty of God . . . or of justification by faith . . . or of the necessity of religious experience . . . but it is this belief in the dignity, sanctity, and competency of the individual which Baptists through the years have felt compelled to emphasize."[20]

The author of this statement fails to note that circulation and use of theological doctrines is no less important than the nature of the doctrines which are cherished. There is no more effective way to destroy an idea than to exalt, sanctify, and fail to apply it. The same principle operates in economic theory. In the determination of the health of an economy the velocity of money in circulation is no less important than the

[19] A. C. Underwood, *A History of the English Baptists* (London: Kingsgate Press, 1947), p. 48.
[20] Edward H. Pruden, *Interpreters Needed* (Philadelphia: The Judson Press, 1951), p. 54.

quantity of money in circulation. Like the miser, the Baptists may covet orthodox doctrines, but they have little religious utility if they remain buried under sectarian distinctives. In the present situation these ideas do not exert the same attractive force, nor do they possess the same relevance and power for all Baptists that they had during the period of burgeoning liberalism. There are some Baptists today who are critically analyzing the meaning of such concepts as the autonomy of the local church and the soul competency of the individual. The following quotation is indicative of the critical effort of those who believe these ideas are little more than sacred shibboleths for the support of the existing order:

"It remained for the American churches to absolutize this autonomy of the local congregation. This was done in the name of 'freedom' and even the New Testament. Needless to say . . . the New Testament knows nothing of either the isolated Christian or the isolated Baptist congregation. A local congregation *is* an organic part of every other organization. It can deny this by being independent, but in doing so it shuts off its own source of life and nourishment. It is a branch separated from the vine."[21]

". . . our churches are full of such rugged individualists for whom the church is a casual convenience, or else an arena where the ego can strut like a Daniel Boone or more likely today like a Davey Crockett. It is enough to point out that such a person, and such a doctrine of soul-competency, reflects John Locke more than the New Testament."[22]

The Gathered and the Autonomous Church

Primary emphasis upon the freedom of man also tends to contradict the concept of the autonomous or gathered church.[23]

[21] Harry H. Kreuner, "A Baptist Theology of Church Order" ("Basic Resource Papers for the East Central Regional Theological Conference"). Mimeographed, 1956. Available in Colgate Rochester Divinity School Library, Rochester, New York, p. 25.

[22] *Ibid.*, pp. 14f.

[23] Of course the freedom of God, the freedom of man, and the autonomy of the local congregation are not necessarily exclusive terms. This occurs only when one of the three is treated as an absolute. Without becoming engaged in Hartshorne's problem of omnipotence or in Barth's problem

This second ambiguity in the Baptist heritage is equally important for an understanding of the present organizational dilemmas. When Baptists gather for a discussion of polity or a revision of denominational structure, an impasse is often reached when each of the participants assumes an absolute stand on a different "Baptist distinctive." The ambiguity of the situation can be seen in a recent description of the denominational situation: "There is no Baptist church. There are only Baptist churches. The local church legally is sovereign and may alter its conditions of membership or ordain any candidate for the ministry by majority vote. . . . In the north something like organizational chaos prevailed until the formation of the Northern Baptist Convention in 1907, which affirms the independence of the local church but practices a very considerable control. There are no binding general Baptist creeds or confessions of faith."[24]

In their effort to defend the freedom of the individual against the encroachments of the authority of church or state, Baptists often forgot the primacy of God's freedom and sovereignty over all human creations—including the regenerate individual as well as the church and state. But the Baptist fathers were among the earliest of the neo-Calvinists who believed that the freedom of man is freedom under the grace of God, and that the true depths of human freedom can be searched only in accord with and dependence upon the will of God. These Baptists were true to the Reformation theme that organized religion is in divine terms a human and therefore limited possibility, and that ecclesiasticism, in any form, is a limitation of the freedom of God. On the other hand,

---

of God's absolute freedom, it is only necessary to state that "autonomy" and "freedom" are treated as relational concepts. Autonomy has been defined as "the degree to which a group [or person] functions independently of other groups [or persons] and occupies an independent position in society. It is reflected by the degree to which a group determines its own activities, by its absence of allegiances, deference and/or dependence relative to other groups." Cf. John K. Hemphill and Charles M. Westie, "The Measurement of Group Dimensions," *The Language of Social Research*, ed. Paul S. Lazarsfeld and Morris Rosenberg (Glencoe, Illinois: The Free Press, 1955), p. 323.

[24] Conrad H. Moehlman, "Baptists," *The Encyclopedia of Religion*, ed., Vergilius Ferm (New York: The Philosophical Library, 1945), p. 55.

Baptists generally failed to recognize that "ecclesiasticism" is an inescapable ingredient of human worshipful existence. The displacement of the first idea (God's freedom) by the second (individual or church freedom) is the inevitable result of the failure to recognize that religious expression must assume cultic and limited forms. An effort to establish the pure community or the perfectly free and righteous individual is very likely to result in the unmodified blessing of man bestowed upon his own creation.

This was recognized by the early Baptists, who taught that religious freedom was a necessary corollary to the expression of God's truth, but never an end in its own right. The Confession of 1644 indicates that Baptists established separate communities of faith, not, in the first instance, on the basis of a religious principle, but because it was a matter "for conveniency" within the current religious situation. Nothing is said about the necessity of the absolute autonomy of the local church: "And although we [the seven churches which participated in the Confession] be distinct in our meetings, for conveniency; yet are we one in faith, fellowship, and communion, holding Jesus Christ for our head and lawgiver, under whose rule and government we desire to walk. . . ."[25]

Actually, they were motivated by more than "conveniency" in the establishment of a congregational polity. They believed that the *koinonia* or "gathered church"—apart from the religious establishment of the state—could constitute a church with Christ only as its sovereign. The Confession of 1611 stated that Christ "hath in his Testament set downe an absolute, and perfect rule of direction, for all persons, at all times, to bee observed. . . ." The church is described as "a compainy of faithful people separated frō the world. . . ." It is emphasized that "no church ought to challeng anie prerogative over anie other," since it is Christ only who is head of the church and not the congregations themselves.[26]

It seems clear that the early tradition was not concerned

25 Underhill, *op.cit.*, p. 23.
26 Confession of 1611, Articles 8-12. Cited in W. J. McGlothlin, *Baptist Confessions of Faith* (Philadelphia: The American Baptist Publication Society, 1911), pp. 88-89.

in the first instance with the freedom of the individual or the autonomy of the local church. In fact, the dangers of heresy and corruption in the local communion were explicitly recognized by early efforts to establish inter-congregational discipline. These efforts were designed to assure the gospel preached, "not in bondage and subjection, but freely and purely." Later dilemmas occurred because the tradition was marked by an effort to strive for an impossible ideal, the removal of all manmade impediments, of "any tradition or invention of man," and to institute that discipline which would be "all together agreeable to the same heavenly and almighty word of our good Lord, Jesus Christ."[27]

The impossible ideal of the founders of the Independent and Baptist movement required institutional expression. God was sovereign, but his sovereignty had to be expressed through historical entities. In their effort to disperse the power of presbyter and priest, the relationship and authority of the individual Christian to the local congregation, and the authority and power of the church councils, remained undefined and ambiguous. At the same time it is this lack of definition which should prevent the claims of the modern Baptist extremists. There is no adequate foundation for the claim that the "root belief and life principle" of the Baptists "has been and remains individualism and voluntarism in religious experience, relation and responsibility."[28]

Associational Government

With respect to the history of the Baptist churches and their relationship with associational groups, the record indicates that the connections were not so tenuous as some contemporary polemic would lead us to believe.

The Confession of the Seven Churches in London (1644) affirms that absolute independency is not the prime object of Baptist polity. The distinctive and autonomous nature of

---

[27] Richard Fitz, *The Trewe Markes of Christes Churches, &c*, quoted by Horton Davies, *Worship, op.cit.*, p. 232.

[28] W. O. Carver, "Baptist Churches," *The Nature of the Church*, ed. by R. Newton Flew (New York: Harper & Brothers, 1952), p. 297.

the churches must not mislead the membership into ignoring the true character of the church as one Body in Christ. "Although the particular Congregations be distinct and severall Bodies, every one as a compact and knit Citie in itself; yet are they all to walk by one and the same Rule. . . ."[29] Independency is thus affirmed, but immediately modified, because in addition to walking by the same rule, the churches are "by all meanes convenient to have the counsell and help one of another in all needfull affairs of the Church, as members of one body in the common faith under Christ their onely head."[30]

It can be argued that the intent of this article is to accomplish nothing more than to assure fellowship between the churches and an interchange of advice. The Confession of 1688 is more explicit in defining inter-church relations. It is recognized that there are matters of mutual interest which may affect the life of all the churches and that all are under obligation to accept mutual advice since even the individual church may fall into error. However, it is asserted that the decisions of a council of churches can have no binding influence because a council of churches has no right of ecclesiastical authority:

"The purest churches under heaven are subject to mixture and error; and some have so degenerated as to become no churches of Christ, but synagogues of Satan; nevertheless, Christ always hath had and ever shall have a kingdom in this world to the end thereof, of such as believe in him, and make professions of his name.

"In cases of difficulties or differences, either in point of doctrine or administration, wherein either the churches in general are concerned or any one church, in their peace, union, and edification; or any member or members of any church are injured, in or by any proceedings in censures not agreeable to truth and order: it is according to the mind of Christ that many churches, holding communion together, do by their messengers meet to consider and give their advice in or about

---

[29] Confession of 1644, Article XLVII. McGlothlin, *op.cit.*, pp. 186f.
[30] *Ibid.*

that matter in difference, to be reported to all the churches concerned; howbeit these messengers assembled are not intrusted with any church power properly so called, or with any jurisdiction over the churches themselves, to exercise any censures either over any churches or persons, to impose their determination on the churches or officers."[31]

The "Orthodox Confession" (1678) contrasts markedly with these views on the relations between the churches and associations. It is indicative of the variety of opinion among Baptists who were attempting to establish a polity which would escape "the errors and heresies of Rome," as well as to assure the free movement of the Spirit within the Body of Christ. Messengers to the council meetings were recognized as representatives of the churches, and the councils themselves were "legal" conventions of churches, to be considered as "one church of higher authority than the local church."[32] This confession, however, emerged from the General Baptist movement and Taylor points out that its strong presbyterial character is due to an effort "to approximate as closely to the Calvinist system as they could, without giving up their distinguishing tenets."[33] Their Arminian modifications of Calvinistic theology, especially their greater optimism concerning the nature of man, permitted the General Baptists to be more permissive in their concern for congre-

[31] Article XXVI, Philip Schaff, op.cit., III, pp. 738, 740-741.

[32] William Henry Allison, Baptist Councils in America (Chicago: Press of George K. Hazlitt & Co., A Dissertation Submitted to the Faculty of the Graduate Divinity School in Candidacy for the Degree of Doctor of Philosophy, 1906), p. 18.

Article XXXIX of the confession reads: "General councils or assemblies, consisting of Bishops, Elders, and Brethren of the several churches of Christ . . . make but one church, and have lawful right . . . to act in the name of Christ; it being of divine authority, and is the best means under heaven to preserve unity, to prevent heresy, and superintendency among, or in any congregation whatsoever within its own limits, or jurisdiction. And to such a meeting or assembly, appeals ought to be made, in case any injustice be done, or heresy, and schism countenanced, in any particular congregation of Christ, and the decisive voice in such general assemblies is the major part, and such general assemblies have lawful power to hear, and determine, as also to excommunicate." (McGlothlin, op.cit., p. 154.)

[33] Adam Taylor, The History of the English General Baptists, Vol. I (London, 1818), p. 360. Quoted by Allison, op.cit., p. 19.

gational polity with its restraints upon the power of the ministry.

American Baptists were not significantly influenced by the General Baptists and were opposed to their views on polity as well as to their doctrine of salvation. The first definite sign of formal relations among Baptist churches in America came with the organization of the Philadelphia Association in 1707. Allison shows, through a discussion of the records of the Pennepack Church, which covered the period leading up to the creation of the Philadelphia Association, that church autonomy was not the ultimate principle of Baptist polity. In matters of discipline it was originally agreed that church councils and associations should act as an appellate court. "Such an agreement," Allison says, "shows either a high sense of mutual obligations of churches to each other, or else an indifference to the principles of independency in the presence of practical benefits to be derived from greater centralization."[34] However, the Philadelphia Confession itself was much milder in tone with respect to the authority of associations and councils, and associations in America did not develop into strong synodical bodies in the manner of the Presbyterians. The general fear that the associational organization would dominate the life of the church if it acquired legislative and administrative authority led to the development of local councils of churches which dealt only with matters of ministerial ordination and discipline among the members of the churches.[35] An important distinction must be drawn between the official authority of the associations and their actual power. In cases of extreme necessity the associations and councils exercised a mode of informal excommunication by ostracizing and withdrawing fellowship from deviant churches.[36]

The patchwork history of Baptist councils and associational bodies has been so colored by theological disputes and practical concerns that it is difficult to discover amid the heat of ubiquitous tensions a guiding principle which undergirds the arguments of the protagonists. The viewpoints evinced by

[34] *Ibid.*, p. 26.   [35] *Ibid.*, p. 41.   [36] *Ibid.*, p. 48.

the proponents and opponents have been extreme in their diversity, so that Baptists who study the historical record search in vain for firm support or final refutation of a strong associational polity. Within the boundaries established by the post-Calvinist Free Church movements the Baptists have considered every mode of church-order. In comparatively recent times efforts have been made to establish an associational government which resembles the presbyterial system,[37] while, on the other hand, some Baptists have sought to prove that the church council has no right to exist, even as an advisory body.[38]

In any event, it is clear that Baptist history is freighted with ambiguity, and those who strive to establish the singularity of the tradition are on a weak foundation. The current emphasis upon the absolute autonomy of the local church is undergoing increasing criticism on the basis of the historical record and it appears that the pressures of a new social environment combined with these critical studies may cause the Baptists in the northern states to move in new directions in their effort to discover a realistic mean between anarchy and hierarchical authority.

In a recent article Winthrop Hudson seeks to prove that the associational principle among Baptists in America was not a later accretion which violates the established principle of the theology of the church. Actually, organized denominationalism developed very early, considering the scattered nature of the churches and their limited numbers. The Philadelphia Association and all the early associations "were not Associations of individuals, but Associations of churches. They were composed of delegates or representatives who were designated and authorized . . . to act on behalf of the churches."[39] Hudson says that the early associations were organized to fulfill several functions. They were designed to supply "mutual edification" and "observance of the Lord's Supper"; to supply a suitable and well-trained ministerial

---

[37] *Ibid.*, pp. 96ff.   [38] *Ibid.*, p. 56.
[39] Winthrop S. Hudson, "The Associational Principle among Baptists," *Foundations* (January 1958), p. 15.

leadership for the churches, and to exercise control over this leadership by "the establishment of strict regulations"; to engage in the supply of standard printed materials including confessional statements and treatises on discipline; and to organize the churches for missionary activities to "the western tribes of Indians."[40]

Hudson concludes that the "Association could and did act for the churches" in matters of concern both internal and external to the life of the churches, and it was expected that the churches would "fully acquiesce in determinations of the Association." "While an Association may only 'determine' and 'declare' and not 'impose,' a church is not free to reject the 'advice' and 'counsel' of an Association and still remain a member in communion with the other churches of the Association."[41]

Conclusion

The foregoing review of the diverse elements of Baptist history indicates the existence of several strands within the tradition. These are not always distinguishable and are often paradoxically related, as when it is held at the same moment that the church is absolutely autonomous and the individual is totally free.

The first strand is represented by those who support the doctrine of God's freedom and who believe the initial requirement of church-order is to assure the free movement of the Spirit in all the works of the church. Second are those who start with the freedom of the individual, believing that God can act only through people who are totally unrestrained by social organizations. Third are the Baptists who insist upon the complete autonomy of the local church and feel that this can be the only locus of authority in religious affairs. Fourth are those who see God acting primarily through disciplined groups of churches and who advocate a polity based on tighter associational connections. Finally, in recent times a few Baptists argue for the primacy of God's freedom and advocate a balance of power between the other penultimate

[40] *Ibid.*, pp. 15-18.   [41] *Ibid.*, pp. 18, 20.

"authorities." They call for a form of church government which will not be rigidly established as viable for all times and places but will allow each of the parts of the Body of Christ a special and valid function. The individual may be a prophet and should always be permitted to speak; the local congregation has a real primacy in the life of the church; the association, the council, and the missionary society also have a valid function which congregations and individuals cannot fulfill. Each unit of the church's life, therefore, must be permitted a power and authority which is commensurate with its purpose and character and befits the existing environmental conditions. But all units stand under the sovereign grace of God.

There appears to be no Baptist in the early history of the movement who intended to say anything which resembles the last construction. On the other hand, it is not difficult to discover an early Baptist thinker who could be used to support one of the other ideas: the freedom of God, the autonomy of the local church, the freedom of the individual, or the principle of connectionalism. These ideas did not stand in isolation in the minds of any of the early founders, but neither were they adequately related to one another. The problem seems to be that the early Baptists did not develop an explicit conception of the relations which must exist between the various parts of the church as a social institution. They seldom ceased to think in terms of authority and power, but they did not think in terms of twentieth-century social institutions. The local church could remain independent in the seventeenth century in a way that it cannot today. And because there was no large-scale missionary program to consider, it was not necessary to engage in detailed considerations of the problems of power and authority which have arisen since the advent of these organizations.

Therefore, in a sense the present confusion of theology and church-order in the Baptist denomination is rooted in its earliest history. Recognizing the chaotic conditions within the present situation, some Baptists are calling for a reconsideration of "the normative phase of their history." "Although

Baptists in general have not been accustomed to think in terms of a 'classic' or normative phase in their history, certainly the period in which a group finds it necessary to be set apart for a distinct witness—the period in which a denomination begins its separate existence and explains itself to the Church at large—must in some sense be a norm for testing future developments. If as time passes the needs for which a separate group has been called out no longer prevail, or if the group so forfeits its valid witness as no longer to fill the need for which God created it, then certainly a question mark may be held over the continued existence of the group as a separate entity."[42]

Baptists need to study their heritage. Until recent times Baptists have not been concerned with their history except as a descriptive or polemical exercise. It does not seem likely that the historian will find an unambiguous and normative dogmatic principle upon which to base a modern doctrine of the church. However, a real contribution has already been made in the effort to indicate that the early Baptists were not motivated by a desire to assure individual freedom and the autonomy of the congregation as absolute principles of faith. Since the beginning of the missionary movement in the early nineteenth century, Baptists have been plagued with problems involving their intramural relations. The evangelistic effort of that period led to the development of national missionary organizations which came to exert great influence upon the affairs of the denomination. Even in the last century these national societies came to resemble the highly rationalized bureaucratic organizations more commonly associated with business and government. The emergence of this organizational type constitutes an especially critical problem for the Free churches which are founded on principles of intimate community relations and avoidance of associational-type social patterns. "Both bureaucracy's inefficiency and its menace of efficiency and order are nowhere more apparent than in

[42] Charles R. Andrews, "A Baptist Looks Backward and Forward," *Theology Today*, XIII, 4 (January 1957), p. 507n.

the cultural association of the non-authoritarian church."[43] Nonetheless, "the strong drift of our time is toward large-scale organization with its attendant evils of mechanization and bureaucracy, and the Churches have not been exempt from these."[44]

The problems treated in this study are set in a framework of a theory of authority and power. This is one of the possible ways of analyzing the present denominational situation. Of course there are others. The situation could be studied simply in terms of theological doctrines, and this should be done; but the issues are more complex than a pure study of doctrine would be likely to indicate. The conflicting theological principles which are part of the ideational property of the modern Baptists have provided the focus for many of the tensions which characterize the present situation. In great part, these ideas have been contested by those who have vested interests. The connotation is not Machiavellian. But to ignore the ingredients of power and authority in Baptist denominational life can result only in a truncated view of the total situation with respect to church-order.

[43] Charles H. Page, "Bureaucracy and the Liberal Church," *Review of Religion*, XIV (July 1951), p. 142.

[44] Lesslie Newbigin, *The Household of God* (New York: Friendship Press, 1954), p. 188.

THE FORMATION OF THE CONVENTION

IMMEDIATELY prior to the founding of the Northern Baptist Convention in 1907 the organizational situation among Baptists was chaotic and in continuous flux. The missionary and evangelistic effort was shared by eight national societies which had come into being from 1814 to 1891.[1] Each was completely independent of the others, conducted its own financial campaigns, appointed its own agents and missionaries, and had its own board of directors and membership roles. As a result there was a considerable duplication of activity and inter-organizational competition, but it was widely believed that this method of operation best preserved the principle of congregational autonomy since the societies engaged in specialized tasks and exercised "no power or jurisdiction" over the work of the churches.[2]

A serious movement to create a denominational organization which would coordinate the work of the societies was initiated in the closing decade of the century. In 1896 the three largest societies formed a joint commission to relieve financial problems common to all the national agencies.[3] When it was discovered that the commission could not affect the needed revisions a new commission was formed in 1901 to consider basic constitutional changes. Other "committees came and went, and still no lasting improvement was made in the existing structure and administration of the societies."[4]

In 1906 a general petition was signed by 150 Baptist leaders requesting the professional executives of the three

---

[1] The largest and most influential were the Home Mission Society, the Foreign Mission Society, and the Publication Society. In addition, there was the Educational Society, the Woman's Home Mission Societies (east and west), the Foreign Bible Society, and the Young People's Union.

[2] Robert McClernon, "The Formation of the Northern Baptist Convention" (unpublished B.D. dissertation, Federated Theological Faculty, University of Chicago, 1956), pp. 83-84.

[3] *Ibid.*, p. 96.   [4] *Ibid.*, p. 100.

largest societies to allocate time during the ensuing annual meetings for discussion of the problems and formation of a convention.[5] In May of 1907 the societies held their annual meetings in Washington, D.C., and agreement was reached to form the Northern Baptist Convention. The constitution was formally adopted by the delegates in Oklahoma City in 1908. The legally corporate and autonomous status of the societies was preserved. They were called "corporate agencies of the convention, with specific mutual obligations."[6] The relations between the Convention and the societies were primarily financial in character. The societies were to regulate their budgets in consultation with the Finance Committee of the Convention; financial drives were to receive approval of the Finance Committee; and the societies could incur no indebtedness without approval of the Convention. In return, the Convention promised the societies the support of the constituent churches.[7]

Forces Opposing the Convention

Efforts to unite the denominational work at the national level met considerable opposition. A member of the faculty at Newton Theological Seminary, Dr. J. B. Thomas, believed that "the proposed measure is radically revolutionary." He said that Baptists alone had resisted the "tendency to presbyterianize and to take the authority from the mass of the people and give it to an official body." He was content with the existing method of organization since members of the societies were "permitted to share in the direction of their gifts . . . because they are interested, not because they have been officially appointed as delegates." Commenting on the localization of control over the societies he indulged in an aristocratic *non sequitur*: "The people in the vicinity of Boston are naturally most interested in foreign missions, those nearer New York in home missions, those near Philadelphia in the Publi-

[5] Edward H. Pruden, "The Government of the Church" ("Basic Papers Prepared for the American Baptist Theological Conference, 1954." Hereafter referred to as *Basic Papers*). Mimeographed. Available in Colgate Rochester Divinity School Library, Rochester, New York, p. 4.

[6] McClernon, *op.cit.*, p. 103.　　　[7] *Ibid.*, p. 103.

cation Society, and in each case those nearest and so most interested are best qualified to direct the affairs of the given society."[8]

It is apparent that significant opposition arose from the societies themselves. They required the support of the churches and were ultimately forced to relinquish some of their own autonomy but not until strong dissent had been voiced by a few of their members. One editorial writer expressed the dominant opinion of this group when he made a reasonable and sophisticated assessment of the situation from the point of view of the society executives: "It is true that in the eastern states each of the three greatest societies has a certain constituency. . . . These men very naturally see nothing to change in the relations of the societies. These are men of means and influence; they are on the executive committees of the societies, know how carefully and economically financial affairs are administered, are naturally and generously jealous for the good name and the prosperity of the organization to which most of their attention is given, and make up the conservative element which at once insures competent administration within prescribed lines and resists radical changes of policy."[9]

The situation was confused. There was lack of clarity with respect to the issues involved compounded by a continued failure to define the nature and purpose of the church when it was represented by the activity of councils, associations, national societies, or conventions. In point of fact "represented" is an incorrect term since it implies a power which many Baptists believed could not be claimed by the associational bodies. Even up to the present time no phrase has been developed which adequately defines the relationship between local church and association or convention. One point was clear: "Nobody wants a central committee or cabinet to *govern* the denomination, or to direct of its own free will the entire system of missionary operations. . . . Cooperation does not mean . . . any plan that would interfere with the independ-

---

[8] *The Standard*, 49 (June 1, 1901), p. 1,226.
[9] *Ibid.* (October 26, 1901), pp. 180-181.

ence of the churches, nor does it mean as yet any definite scheme of consolidation of societies or agencies."[10]

At the turn of the century there was a widespread fear that "centralization" would compromise the essential freedom of the churches. This is not surprising since the fear still exists among conservative Baptists, who believe that formal organization is contrary to Christian ideals: "The development of 'system' is inimical to the ideals here presented. System, whether it be hierarchy or organization, has a constant human tendency to impose itself as an obligatory channel of mutual service. Such impositions are dangerous. . . . Now for groups of Baptist churches to organize themselves into a 'system' and to forget the principles upon which our vast world-wide fellowship stands is to destroy that very witness which is peculiarly ours."[11]

A Baptist magazine describes the emotions of the delegates to the first convention in 1907: "Many Baptists started for Washington in fear and trembling. Did this proposed organization mean subversion of all that was dear to the faith? Was it not the plan of a few and not of the many?"[12] Within this general atmosphere the Northern Baptist Convention was born. Every effort was made to limit the power and authority of the national officers of the Convention. The delegates from the churches were not given authority to legislate or speak for their own people. It was believed that such authority would in turn enable the Convention to govern the churches. The result was that relations between the Convention, the societies, the associational groups, and the local churches was purposely couched in extremely vague terms. Some leaders argued for indirect delegational representation, the delegates to be sent from the local associations rather than from the churches. These ideas were discarded on the ground

[10] *Ibid.* (November 16, 1901), pp. 278f.
[11] *Watchman Examiner* (May 4, 1950), pp. 434f.
[12] The American Baptist Magazine (July 1907), quoted by W. B. Lipphard, "We Consider Our Premises" ("Background Material for Special Meeting of the General Council, 1952." Hereafter referred to as *Background Material*). Mimeographed. Available in Colgate Rochester Divinity School Library, Rochester, New York, p. 4.

that the churches must be "directly represented" in order to assure their autonomy.

As finally described in the bylaws of the constitution, the new organization was primarily designed to augment the promotional and budgetary affairs of the societies. Those by-laws which did not deal with financial matters were directed toward the continued assurance of "the autonomy of the churches in all matters of faith and practice." A typical quotation from an early committee report can be cited. It was suggested that an "organic relation" between the societies and the Convention was necessary ". . . to the end that the denomination through its Convention may be able to determine a suitable related policy for all its general activities, by establishing a single coordinated budget for the same, and may provide adequate funds required for this budget; and to the further end that it may be possible to put the various agencies out of debt and thereafter keep them out of debt."[13]

Pressures Favoring Unification

Naturally, the factors which contributed to the formation of the Convention were more influential. Among these were relatively minor events such as the lack of growth of the Baptist movement in the northern states when compared to Methodist expansion, and the increasing membership of the Roman Catholic Church due to the religious sympathy of many European immigrants. Not all the factors which led to the development of the Convention are of equal relevance and no effort will be made to engage in an exhaustive causal analysis. It is only important to recognize the predominant conditions and events which contributed to the emergence of the Convention and the development of its present character.

The threefold purpose of the Convention and the ostensible reasons for its formation are given in the preamble to the constitution: "The object of this Convention shall be to give

[13] *Annual of the Northern Baptist Convention, 1907* (Philadelphia: The American Baptist Publication Society, 1907-1940. Hereafter referred to as *Annual* with appropriate date). Page 3.

expression to the sentiment of its constituency upon matters of denominational importance and of general religious and moral interest; to develop denominational unity; and to give increased efficiency to efforts for the evangelization of America and the world."[14]

Despite an allegiance to the ideals of freedom, autonomy, and democracy, Baptists experienced an equally compelling imperative from other important goals. Chief among these were the missionary, evangelistic, and publication efforts. Those who founded the Convention accepted as a central gospel imperative the command to "make disciples of all nations, baptising them in the name of the Father and of the Son and of the Holy Spirit."[15] In 1907 W. C. Bitting wrote that the Convention must be single in its purpose. "It exists only to unify the denomination and the work of the societies. The convention has no significance except to put the work of the societies upon a basis upon which it has never rested before."[16] A year later he reaffirmed that the Convention "is the expression of the feeling of the unity of Baptists in sustaining the American Baptist Foreign Mission Society, the American Baptist Home Mission Society, and the American Baptist Publication Society."[17] The meaning of the Scriptures was obvious for these men. They must unify the efforts of the churches and create an organization that would possess enough power and authority to coordinate the missionary and evangelistic activities, even though the new organization might conflict with the ideal of congregational autonomy. They believed there was no reason why the essential autonomy of the churches could not be maintained. Without any serious effort to define the meaning and limits of autonomy and freedom they formed the Convention and left the task of definition to succeeding generations of Northern Baptists.

Related to the missionary enterprise was the new problem of urbanization which was making a critical impact upon the life of the Protestant churches. As a result of nineteenth-

---

14 *Annual*, 1907, p. 3.   15 Matt. 28:19.
16 Quoted by W. B. Lipphard, *Background Material, op.cit.*, p. 3.
17 *Ibid.*, p. 3.

century immigration, concentrations of foreign-born people were exhausting the resources and the imagination of the established Baptist churches. Men like Walter Rauschenbusch and Shailer Mathews took an active part in Convention affairs because of their awareness of the problems of the deep city parish and the need for a nationally cooperative religious body dedicated to relief of the problems created by an industrial society.[18] Hundreds of committee reports, speeches, and articles were written about the weakness of Baptists in urban work and the threat of this failure to the life of the denomination.[19] The Baptists were also concerned with the fact that laboring people were rapidly becoming a significant social force. The general failure of the churches in this field led the Social Gospel leaders to point again to the advantages of unified efforts.[20]

The final impetus for the formation of the Convention was provided by the new *Zeitgeist* which started to emerge during the last part of the nineteenth century. Although it was less apparent as a causal factor than missions, evangelism, and social concern, the new spirit supplied an important ideational environment in which to discuss reorganizational projects. World-wide commercialism, the breakdown of communication barriers, the hope for a brave new world which would be free of international conflict and racial animosities, the appearance of giant business corporations, and the new complexity and centralization of organizations in many other social spheres—all contributed to a reconsideration of existing methods of achieving goals which formerly were attained by simpler methods of organization.[21]

These factors played an important role in the changing outlook of the religious leaders at the turn of the century. The small and intimate community church was no longer able to provide the essential resources for the Christian mis-

[18] *Annual*, 1910, p. 179.
[19] *Annual*, 1908, pp. 26ff.; *Annual*, 1910, pp. 21ff., 141-145; *Proceedings, the Baptist Congress for the Discussion of Current Questions* (Chicago: University of Chicago Press, 1895), pp. 58-59.
[20] McClernon, *op.cit.*, pp. 21ff. Cf. also *Annual*, 1908, pp. 26f.
[21] Cf. Nichols, *op.cit.*, pp. 110ff.

sionary programs.[22] Many Baptist leaders considered it imperative to reconstruct existing denominational organizations in order to carry the message of redemption and reform to a changing world. The statements often revealed a significant departure from the traditional emphasis upon individual religious experience and the preservation of congregational autonomy. Four years before he became president of the Convention, Shailer Mathews affirmed: "The Christian spirit must be institutionalized if it is to prevail in the age of institutions. . . ."[23]

The most important way in which the prevailing *Zeitgeist* was expressed in the Baptist movement was by means of a new drive for efficient reconstruction of all existing denominational organizations. The symbol of "efficiency" became the dominant motif in the early life of the Convention, and it remained so until the advent of the "fundamentalist controversy."

The Gospel was preached as the "supreme means of solution of humanity's problems."[24] A call was issued for "an efficiency campaign for the standardization of the local

[22] The Federal Council of Churches was formed during this period, as well as the Baptist World Alliance and the amalgamation of a significant number of allied agencies within various Protestant denominations.

[23] Shailer Mathews, *The Scientific Management of the Churches* (Chicago: University of Chicago Press, 1912), pp. v-vi. Baptist leaders still find it necessary to emphasize the theme of unity and organized cooperation since there are so many who continue to value the freedom of the local church to the exclusion of other values. Hudson writes: "Since the effective social community has become vastly larger than the old congregational neighborhood, a wider church order than provided by an insistence upon the independence of the local congregation would seem to be necessary if Christians are not to be disqualified from their responsibility to the larger community in which they now live." Winthrop S. Hudson, "The Church and the World," *Basic Papers*, p. 2.

In the same set of papers another committee reports on the issue: "The independence of the local congregation was an adequate structure in a time when the effective unit of living was to a very large extent the local community. But the problems and concerns which trouble the Christian conscience today are no longer restricted to the common life of 'the isolated settlements and small towns of agrarian America. . . .' Thus 'a structure designed to discipline only the immediate neighborhood to Christian living' can serve only 'to disqualify Christians from their responsibility to the larger communities of industry, commerce, state, and culture.' " John E. Skoglund, "The Nature of the Church," *Basic Papers*, p. 27.

[24] *Annual*, 1913, p. 195.

church."[25] The congregation as a community of like-minded people gathered together by the presence of the Holy Spirit, but joined in fellowship without regard for the life of other churches, was no longer considered a full and legitimate activity by many Baptist leaders. There was a need for unification of the denominational effort, signifying that the churches must reorganize along "standard" lines in order to make an effective witness in the world. An early resolution of the Convention stated: "We therefore recommend that the Executive Committee be asked to consider ways and means for pressing the efficiency campaign among the churches, and for tabulating results."[26] In an earlier year it had been observed that "the increase of efficiency in the local church is the most important task to which the Northern Baptist Convention can address itself."[27] Baptists had become increasingly concerned with the quantitative indicators of success, believing that this was positive evidence of rich quality in the life of local congregations.[28] A dominant motif of the modern American social environment had become an essential part of the life of the churches.[29]

The Baptists were susceptible to emphases upon efficient action, achievement, and success. They were an emergent denomination anxious to grow and exercise their influence upon "moral and religious matters." Many of their leaders were at the forefront in the Social Gospel movement, which in itself had a strong achievement impulse. The names of Rauschenbusch and Mathews are found throughout the Con-

[25] *Ibid.*   [26] *Ibid.*
[27] *Annual*, 1911, p. 49.   [28] *Ibid.*, p. 50.
[29] Parsons, *Social System*, *op.cit.*, pp. 182ff. *passim*; Robin M. Williams, *American Society: A Sociological Interpretation* (New York: Alfred M. Knopf, 1952), pp. 390-394. One of the themes in these sociological studies concentrates on the idea that the goals of personal achievement and success have been internalized by a tremendous number of people in our society. The result is a depersonalizing of the individual. He is not valued as a whole person but as a being who is "good" and deserves love and respect only if he achieves certain accepted and quantitatively assessed goals. "Good" is assimilated with "success" and the desirable neighbor is one who shows signs of climbing the achievement scale. It often happens that little attention is given the methods he uses in the ascent so long as they are efficient. It will be shown in a later section that there are interesting parallels to this mode of evaluation in the "rating" of ministers in the Baptist denomination.

vention yearbooks. The latter wrote a revealing statement concerning ministerial training: "I believe that the fundamental conception of a theological education looks to church efficiency, i.e., the preparation of men trained to lead the churches to the performance of their peculiar function in a given community, rather than the training of men to remember and defend a general message. My idea of a pastor is . . . a man who institutionalizes a belief and an attitude toward life rather than a man who simply proclaims a truth. I am convinced, therefore, that the fundamental conception of a minister's education must be changed from that of a man with a message to that of a leader of a social group with a definitely religious and moral function."[30]

This emphasis upon the non-theological category of efficiency results in part because of theological developments in the Free Church movement. Left-wing Puritanism drew a clear distinction between the spheres of revelation and the natural processes of history.[31] Baptists, with the exception of a minority of "deviants" like Mathews, never lost sight of their "basal position . . . the response of the human soul to the revelation of God in Christ. . . . Our emphasis is upon the regenerate life, which finds its formal expression in believer's baptism."[32] Therefore, on the one hand, there was an essential rationality in the experience of regeneration of the human soul, but, on the other hand, a substantive irrationality in the formation and existence of large social groups. There was a readiness among Baptists to recognize the possibilities of sin in systematized social organization, but seldom did they admit the possibilities of redemption in such activity.[33]

[30] Mathews, *op.cit.*, pp. 44-45.

[31] Nichols, *op.cit.*, p. 125.

[32] George E. Horr, *The Baptist Heritage* (Philadelphia: The Judson Press, 1923), p. 33.

[33] This interpretation of human organization is contrary to Max Weber's understanding of social action. He too, interprets history in terms of a dichotomy between rational and irrational activity; but irrational behavior is that mode of social action which is not systematically organized to achieve effectively the explicit goals of the group. (Cf., Weber, *Theory*, *op.cit.*, p. 92.)

Weber used "the process of rationalization" as a conceptual category which indicates that a social group, when confronted with a choice between

However, the Baptists did create the Northern Baptist Convention, thereby engaging in what Weber calls "the process of rationalization." When this occurs, Weber notes, the means of organization tends to displace the original goals of the social group. The Baptists became so interested in the organizational means that even before the Convention was formed a "doctrine of efficiency" started to develop: "The test which the apostolic church . . . applied to its various oper-

---

an empirically adequate or less adequate belief or mode of action, will eventually choose the former. When this occurs the inadequate beliefs will be discarded. Thus, it is sometimes called the "process of de-mystification." In action terms the concept indicates that there is a tendency toward (1) rationalizing the goals, i.e., striving for goals which are empirically attainable; and (2) utilizing means which are most suited to the achievement of the given goal. (Weber, *Theory*, *op.cit.*, pp. 122f. Cf. also Parsons, *Structure*, *op.cit.*, p. 751.)

"Efficiency" was never defined by the Baptists, but it is clear that the term referred to organizational techniques of action in relation to their imperative goals. Shailer Mathews described efficiency by means of seven basic principles of institutional organization. It can be noted that a few of his principles are roughly parallel to categories developed by Weber to describe rationalized bureaucratic organization. (Weber, *Theory*, *op.cit.*, pp. 330-332; Mathews, *op.cit.*, *passim.*)

Mathews' Principles	*Weber's Categories*
Efficiency centers upon operation, the discovery of the purpose of the church within the given situation, and the attainment of goals by the best procedural techniques available.	A continuous organization of official functions bound by rules.
Standardization of operation in terms of functions rather than in terms of "speeding up" existing programs.	Specified spheres of competence.
Division of labor between management and the workers.	Hierarchical organization of offices.
Education in specialized tasks.	Technical rules or norms for the regulation of official activities.
Cooperation instead of intergroup competition.	The incumbent of an office does not appropriate the office for his own ends.
Proper equipment for efficient operation; preservation of written records of all activities.	Acts and decisions are formulated in writing.
Appeal to motives that shall insure the performance of tasks.	Administrative staff separated from ownership of the means of production.

ations, whether in its own organization or discipline, or in the extension of its administrative power, was its efficiency in accomplishing the mission for which the church itself was called into being. It is this idea which has been historically the fundamental principle of Baptist polity."[34]

Another important factor which contributed to the formation of the Convention was the failure of the national societies to achieve the goals for which they were established. This circumstance was not due to the failure of any particular agency so much as to the competitive and inefficient nature of their combined activities. Each national society "had increased in scope and efficiency" at the turn of the century, "so that difficulties of inter-relationship were accentuated by 'overlapping functions and territorial influence.' "[35]

In addition, there was inadequate cooperation between the local churches and the national societies. The denomination was divided into territorial units in such a manner that local associations and state conventions could dominate the activities and policies of the churches in their respective areas. The local churches insistently affirmed their belief in autonomy, but in reality were often prevented from supporting the work of the national organizations if such cooperation did not accord with the executive secretary of the state organization.[36]

Probably more than any other single factor, the financial condition of the national societies induced the denominational leaders to consider seriously the creation of a centralized organization. In 1897 the debt of the Foreign Mission Board was $292,721, and the other societies were in similarly awkward straits.[37] Many leaders were convinced that the situation could be remedied only by creation of a more centralized organization. Complaints from the constituency indicated that interest in missionary projects was slackening because decision-making was confined to an elite group. Even official board members of the societies sometimes complained that

[34] William A. Allison, "The Basis of Baptist Polity," *The Standard* (March 30, 1907), p. 923.
[35] Pruden, *Basic Papers, op.cit.*, p. 28.
[36] *Annual*, 1907, pp. 7-9.
[37] McClernon, *op.cit.*, pp. 96f.

they had little control over the policies which were formulated within the exclusive executive committee sessions. Approval by the wider membership was of "the rubber stamp variety. . . . All things considered, it appears that the societies were not great examples of Baptist democracy in action."[38]

Within this situation the churches responded in an expected manner. When the local constituency discovered they would not be heard, they withheld their contributions. This was their only weapon since increased participation of the churches could be achieved only through alteration of the constitutions of the societies. Despite opposition from influential board members and contributors to the societies, these agencies were no longer able to resist the movement toward unification under the banner of a national organization.[39]

More serious, however, was the failure of the societies to engage in full cooperation with respect to their missionary endeavor.[40] It was in support of this work that the national agencies were most competitive. The promotional campaigns, whether viewed from the educational or fund-raising perspective, were becoming partially self-defeating efforts as each society propagandized the churches in its own behalf.

In this situation leaders appeared who affirmed that changes in organization were "necessary, imperative, and feasible." W. C. Bitting wrote that there was too much emphasis upon individualism which damaged fraternity and cooperation. "Our churches are insular, washed by the separating seas of an over-emphasis on independence." He criticized those who opposed all formal cooperation because, he believed, the Baptists compromised their independency in a more extreme but subtle way—"the whole missionary operation is not controlled by the churches, but by societies of individuals."[41]

Fifteen years earlier Henry Morehouse, secretary of the Home Mission Society, had called for a radical revision of inter-organizational relations because of the "undemocratic"

38 *Ibid.*, p. 87.   39 *Ibid.*, p. 88.
40 Lipphard, *Background Material, op.cit.*, p. 3.
41 W. C. Bitting, "What Changes, If Any, Are Desirable and Feasible in our Missionary Organizations and Methods?" *The Standard* (December 28, 1901), pp. 480-482.

and inefficient mode of operation of the existing agencies: "The unwieldiness, and unmanageableness, and practical worthlessness of our annual meetings are generally recognized. But how can we help it? What is the remedy? This is our answer: State representation on the basis of Baptist membership."[42] Even today the majority of Baptists would consider this a radical suggestion, but Morehouse's recommendations often had a prophetic temper. He could have been speaking to the present generation of Baptists when he said, "Our anniversaries are not 'mass meetings' to fire the hearts of the people . . . but meetings to do the Lord's business with earnest and thoughtful hearts."[43]

The Nature of the Convention

Even Bitting and Morehouse agreed that the Convention should not be a powerful policy-making or legislative body and that its existence should be contingent upon the will of the churches. It was to be legitimated in a fashion radically different from that of the church-type organization. It was an organization born out of a response to pragmatic and immediate needs, an instrumental entity possessing no direct authority from God to exist in its own right. It was a social instrument to fulfill the desires of the local congregations and meet the needs of the societies. The Baptist attitude toward all associational structures is preserved in the original "Declaration" of the Convention. This statement affirms "belief in the independence of the local church, and in the purely advisory nature of all denominational organizations composed of representatives of the churches."[44] In the view of many present-day Baptists there is no reason why the character of the Convention and its relationship to the churches needs to be reconsidered. In 1952 it was declared: "Our denomina-

[42] Lantham A. Crandall, *Henry Lyman Morehouse* (Philadelphia: The American Baptist Publication Society, 1919), p. 106.

[43] *Ibid.*, p. 106.

[44] *Annual*, 1908, p. 7. No change has been made in this original charter; cf. *Yearbook of the American Baptist Convention*, 1957 (Philadelphia: The American Baptist Publication Society, 1941-1957), p. 11. Hereafter referred to as *Yearbook* with appropriate date.

tional machinery is the means by which our churches carry on a year-round ministry beyond the reach of their own parishes. It also serves as a means of carrying on our work in a business-like way, helping our churches to do their own tasks at home, and making our impact upon public affairs."[45]

In brief, the Convention was created to establish instruments to realize normative goals within a rapidly changing society. The need was translated into organizational structures but these in turn were molded within a framework supplied by the Baptist interpretation of "the New Testament organization of the church." The Convention provided the means for achieving the missionary and evangelistic goals, but the demand to maintain the autonomy of the local church was no less imperative. The tension between these imperative goals has been at the root of the Baptist problem. Important anomalies have been born out of this tension. The Convention was created by "delegates" from the local churches, but a significant number of Baptists continued to insist that the churches had no right to delegate authority to any individual or group. Therefore the Convention, although it has increased tremendously in power and prestige, still operates without benefit of legitimated ecclesiastical authority. The succeeding chapters will constitute an analysis of the Baptist effort to solve the problem of the presence of power and the absence of authority.

[45] Carl W. Tiller, "We Consider Our Boards, Agencies, Conventions, and Schools," *Background Material, op.cit.*, p. 1.

CHAPTER IV

AUTHORITY AND POWER IN THE
BAPTIST TRADITION

EMERGING as they did from the neo-Calvinist Free church movement of the seventeenth century, the Baptists have always regarded the problem of authority and power as a fundamental concern. The attitude of the left-wing Protestant churches was expressed by John Cotton when he cautioned all the world to "learn to give mortal man no greater power than they are content they shall use, for use it they will. . . . It is necessary . . . that all power that is on earth be limited, church-power or other. . . ."[1]

While it is true that the radical ideals of the Puritan left-wing were stimulated within an environment of religious persecution, they were "derived in the first instance from the two theological doctrines of the sovereignty of God and of human bondage to sin."[2] Because concentrations of power lead to rebellion against God, the churches must be independent of government, voluntary in membership, and limited in authority. No official could be trusted to wield the administrative instruments of both church and civil government. Thus the Baptists insisted upon the separation of church and state, and for the same reason they were of the opinion that church officials should not exercise authority over more than a single congregation.[3] No church leader could legitimately claim special access to the divine power, and since God is the only absolute sovereign it follows that all religious authority must

[1] Cf. Winthrop S. Hudson, *The Great Tradition of the American Churches* (New York: Harper & Brothers, 1953), p. 53.

[2] *Ibid.*, p. 49.

[3] Some modern Baptists insist that the minister has no special authority even in his own congregation. "The pastor of a Baptist church is simply the preaching member of that church. In a congregational meeting he has one vote . . . and the vote of the most insignificant member of the church counts for just as much as the vote of the pastor." (Pruden, *Interpreters Needed, op.cit.*, p. 56.)

53

be penultimate and limited. The church "executive must always be subject to correction by the will of Christ, for which a partial criterion was at hand in the Scriptures."[4]

But difficulties arose when these doctrinal ideas were expressed through the polity of the churches. The Baptists believed it was sufficient to point to the Scriptures, the personal experience of the Holy Spirit, or to the gathered congregation of believers as the principal mediators of divine authority. But emphasis upon the autonomy of the local churches ignored the sinful potentialities within these religious groups. The divine presence among the people was sometimes interpreted to signify the possession of God by the community, so that the will of the congregation was equated with the will of God. When God is possessed by the local church, external direction from ecclesiastical officials is obviously superfluous.[5]

One of the primary problems in every religious community is the discovery of a method for historical expression of the divine sovereignty. In any case, the sovereignty of God must be historically mediated, whether it be through "spontaneous inspiration" of special individuals or by means of an official priestly class which preserves and transmits the oral or written tradition. However, every form of polity contains possibilities of corruption. The genius of the Free Church polity lies in the conception of the limitation and balance of power; but this form of church government tends to break down when an effort is made to eliminate the effective authority of those leaders who have been given ecclesiastical responsibilities.

---

[4] Nichols, *op.cit.*, p. 268.

[5] This phenomenon is neither new nor is it confined to the left-wing Protestant tradition. Martin Buber shows that primitive religious societies undermined the authority of the chief priests "by establishing, within the tribe but external to the official tribal life, a secret society in which the actual, the true, the 'holy' communal life is lived, free from the bonds of the 'law' . . . but in holy action." The problem always arises, that if the authority of the priests "is disputed and extended to all, then the actual dominion is taken away from God; for without law, that is, without any clear-cut and transmissible line of demarcation between that which is pleasing to God and that which is displeasing to Him, there can be no historical continuity of divine rule upon earth." (Martin Buber, *Moses*, London: The East and West Library, 1946, pp. 186f.)

The Authority of the American
Baptist Convention

The crux of the problem of authority was recognized by many of the leaders who participated in the formation of the Convention. Some believed the Convention itself would provide the answer:

"So far as organization is concerned, these problems center in the task of getting efficiency without dependence upon external authority.

"We are our own spiritual masters. Of course there is difficulty in having so many masters, and the process of getting cooperative efficiency with us has been one of long development. We have taken step after step, and at last we have evolved the Convention."[6]

The need for some form of social mediation of God's sovereignty led the Baptists to locate ultimate historical authority in the Holy Scriptures. But even the authority of the Bible must gain social expression in the religious community. The Bible may be the normative referent to which the various personal authorities turn, but in every case its meaning must be interpreted and the problem remains: who are the interpreters and what is their authority? The Baptist answer is ambiguous.[7]

On the one hand, the authority of Scripture "was to be exercised under the guidance of the Spirit of Christ operative in the Christian community."[8] Therefore, under the gospel, the local church was the ultimate authority. But the Baptist effort to scatter authority throughout the land does not cease with the positing of authority in the local communion. On the foundation of the doctrine of the priesthood of all believers, the same people who affirm the authority of the community

6 Shailer Mathews, "President's Address to the Convention," *Annual*, 1916, p. 22.

7 The Baptists are not alone. With the possible exception of the fundamentalists, the entire Protestant view of authority is ambiguous. (Cf. Rupert E. Davies, *The Problem of Authority in the Continental Reformers*, London: The Epworth Press, 1946, pp. 10, 154, *passim*.)

8 Walter J. Harrelson, "The Biblical Basis of the Gospel," *Basic Papers*, *op.cit.*, pp. 3-4.

hold that "once saved, any person has free and direct access to the Father through the one and only High Priest, Jesus."[9] In Baptist thought there often seems to be more involved than an effort to sustain a tradition of prophetic criticism of the community by means of an inspired individual. McNutt affirms that the true church "will be a fellowship of the religiously competent, with every man a priest, a spiritual democracy, with every man in God a king."[10] With such royal opportunities offered every individual in the Baptist denomination it is not difficult to discover one of the primary sources of a constantly threatening disorder.

However, there are many spokesmen who deplore the individualism inherent within the Baptist doctrine of the church. "Individualistic voluntarism has no place in the New Testament," says one Baptist who was writing a report for a committee of the Convention. "The fellowship," he continues, "is the mother which gives birth to each new child."[11] In the contemporary situation some of the basic issues have been discerned. For example, the contradiction of positing two ultimate authorities—the individual and the community to which he belongs—has been recognized. Nonetheless, the tension still exists between the kings—"each man on his throne" holding "absolute sway over his own realm"[12]—and those who believe that "private interpretation of the Bible must always be subjected to the testing of the Spirit, and this testing takes place in the regenerate Christian community. . . ."[13]

It is clear that the Baptists are faced with a more critical problem than the autonomy of the local church.[14] The intramural tensions inherent in this principle may be superseded by

---

[9] Pruden, *Basic Papers, op.cit.*, p. 2.
[10] McNutt, *op.cit.*, p. ix.
[11] Skoglund, *Basic Papers, op.cit.*, p. 18.
[12] McNutt, *op.cit.*, p. 24.
[13] Harrelson, *Basic Papers, op.cit.*, p. 19.
[14] Lesslie Newbigin simplifies the problem of congregationally-ordered churches when he asserts that there is no "intelligible reason why we should be asked to acknowledge the spiritual authority of the local fellowship over the individual but to deny the spiritual authority of the regional or ecumenical fellowship over the local." It is evident that many Baptists do not acknowledge the spiritual authority of the local churches over the individual except in a very limited way. (Newbigin, *op.cit.*, p. 120.)

the anarchic potentialities of a radical individualism. The problem of authority of the regional or associational group in relation to the local church would be considerably simplified if the locus of authority at the congregational level were a settled issue.

But Baptists have a genius for obscuring the problem of authority by means of a labyrinth of theological doctrines. There is no effective way of predicting what a given document will pronounce on this vital issue. According to one source there may be no possibility of a mediated authority beyond the New Testament: "Christ is the only Head over, and Law-giver to, His churches. Consequently, the churches cannot make laws, but only execute those which He has given. Nor can any man, or body of men, legislate for the churches. The New Testament alone is their statute book, by which, without change, the body of Christ is to govern itself."[15]

Or, the local church may be the primary locus of authority: "We Baptists are the recognized democrats of the Protestant world. The local church is our depository of ecclesiastical authority. The Association has no authority over the local church; the State Convention has no authority over the Association; and the Northern Baptist Convention has no authority over the State Convention. All these are voluntary cooperative associations created for the sake of greater effectiveness in the business of the kingdom."[16]

A third possibility, as pointed out above,[17] is that the individual under God may be the supreme authority. A fourth variation, of more recent origin, may be expressed in many ways. This final perspective represents a more realistic effort to account for the existing power of the associational groups and to discover a biblical rationale for the support of this power.

In 1954 a committee of the American Baptist Theological Conference observed that authority extends beyond the limits

---

[15] Edward T. Hiscox, *The Standard Manual for Baptist Churches* (Philadelphia: The American Baptist Publication Society, 1890), p. 14.
[16] Mrs. W. A. Montgomery, "President's Address," *Annual*, 1922, p. 38.
[17] McNutt, *op.cit.*, pp. ix, 24.

of congregational membership. If missionary work is an "integral part of the responsibility and authority given to the church by its Lord," then Baptists must agree that in working through a national society or its board, the local church "has virtually delegated parts of its authority to that board."[18] But this unanticipated shift of power and confirming of authority is not to be treated lightly by the national leadership. They receive a warning from the same committee which indicates that final ecclesiastical authority remains with the local church. The authority given to the national executives is provisional and the position they enjoy is precarious, depending, as it does, upon proper rendition of the Baptist tune composed by the local churches: "At the same time it must be clear that such delegation of authority can remain justified only in so far as the board retains the confidence of the church and can be regarded as a fit repository for the authority involved. Unless the church has the right to terminate the delegation of authority when the necessary confidence has been shattered, then it could have had no right to delegate the authority in the first place. Under the Baptist system the Boards and their officials are necessarily the servants of the churches, not their masters. To give up authority once for all would be, not a justifiable limitation, but a violation of the autonomy of the church."[19]

This quotation seems to indicate that God may work through the national boards only if the local churches permit Him to do so. Since He had nothing to do with the creation of these boards, except in an indirect way, He can guide them only through the medium of the local churches. If for some reason communication between the local churches and the national boards is seriously impaired, then, according to the Baptist theology of the church, these boards inevitably would become secularized because God's only means of communication with them had been destroyed. On the other hand, if the local churches become corrupted the national boards possess no legitimate authority to criticize or correct them. According to Baptist polity, in such a situation the national boards

[18] Pruden, *Basic Papers, op.cit.*, p. 19.
[19] *Ibid.*, p. 20.

would be servants of God but only by means of the diseased churches.

It is beyond argument that the boards should serve the local churches and in some sense should be responsible to them. In a strict historical sense they were brought into being by the churches, but from a theological perspective a distinction must be made between the desires of the churches— which may be corrupted—and the needs of the churches. Since it is possible that God conceived the national boards as a corrective for the sins of the churches, it is dangerous on principle to preclude the possibility of conferring official authority upon the ecclesiastical officers of the boards. This authority need not be unlimited, and according to Baptist principles it should not be. But it seems no less a violation of the freedom of God and of the original intention of the Baptist fathers to deposit ultimate authority under God with any historical individual, whether it be the local church, the state association, the national boards, the General Secretary of the Convention, or a prophetic layman in the local congregation. "The recognized democrats of the Protestant world" seem to have forgotten the first principles of democracy as developed by the Independents: the separation of powers and the freedom of God to speak through the most unlikely of historical individuals.

This is not surprising since with regard to the authority of leadership Baptists have been preoccupied with control and restriction rather than with the element of freedom which is no less necessary for leaders than for the constituency. Baptists attended to the limitation of the leader's authority and power, but they have largely ignored the problem of the fulfillment of his duties. From the Baptist point of view the chief responsibility of a leader is to avoid seeking enough power to meet his responsibilities. But without authority and freedom the ecclesiastical leader cannot be held accountable for failing to achieve goals to which he has been assigned. Baptist voluntarism has resulted in an effort to pulverize ecclesiastical authority and power. Realizing that concentrations of power contain great demonic potentialities, the Baptists have placed a higher value on the minimization of power than on establishing effective means to attain other goals. If the Baptists had enjoyed substantial success in achieving the primary goal of their polity there would be considerably less ground for criticism. But it will be argued in the succeeding chapters that the Baptist denomination has been no more successful in establishing a "democratic polity" than many other Protestant denominations which do not place primary emphasis upon this goal.

According to Pruden's committee on church government, "our system is based upon the assumption that churches of regenerate believers will be sensitive to the promptings of the Spirit and will do their proper share voluntarily."[20] This places an unbearable pressure upon the motivations of the regenerate soul and reveals a faith in the power and goodness of the individual which is unsupported by traditional Christian doctrine. "Moral and spiritual suasion," the committee reports, "are the means at our disposal. If they fail us it is because we have failed."[21]

The Problem of Authority in the Present Situation

Notwithstanding the ambiguities and restrictions on their authority, the executive officials of the American Baptist Convention have managed to gain enough power to meet their responsibilities with reasonable effectiveness. Since they have no official ecclesiastical authority they seek to secure their position by other means, and they have been remarkably successful in their efforts. It has often been observed that the American Baptist Convention "has no authority, but has very great influence."[22] In order to analyze the character of this influence as well as the problems which surround the executives of the Convention, it is best to draw a clear distinction between power and authority. Power signifies the ability to carry out one's own will despite the inertia or resistance of

[20] *Ibid.*, p. 20. [21] *Ibid.*, p. 21.
[22] "Baptists," *Encyclopedia Britannica*, Vol. III, 1953 ed.

others;[23] it is the ability to influence or control the actions of others even though there is no institutional sanction for this control. However, "power may be, and generally is, used to acquire legitimized status and symbols of recognition."[24] Therefore, power is a more comprehensive term than authority; in fact, authority is a specialized function of power.[25]

Authority is defined as formalized or institutionally recognized power. "Authority is thus the expected and legitimate possession of power."[26] Since authority is the more specialized concept it will be used whenever the intent is to indicate that kind of power which is officially legitimated and voluntarily accepted by the group. This does not signify that those who wield authority always satisfy every member of the constituency, but that despite particular dissatisfactions the constituency recognizes the right of the leader to lead. However, when a leader exercises power, which, within this analytical framework could be called "illegitimate authority," he is controlling the actions of others despite their wishes, or he is controlling them without their knowledge. The latter often occurs in the Baptist situation because the Baptists are unwilling to confer authority upon their leaders and are equally unwilling to recognize that they have attained power apart from authority. Thus they do not possess adequate analytical instruments to discern the existence of "illegitimate authority."

Those Baptists who do recognize the existence of power either ignore the situation because they enjoy its fruits and recognize it as a functional necessity of every social system,

23 Weber, *Theory*, *op.cit.*, p. 152.

24 Parsons, *Essays*, *op.cit.*, p. 172.

25 Marion Levy defines power as "the ability to exercise authority and control over the actions of others." More accurately, it should be "authority and/or control." Power can exist apart from institutional sanction. (Levy, *op.cit.*, p. 333.)

26 Lasswell and Kaplan, *op.cit.*, p. 133. This definition is in agreement with Parsons, who describes authority as the "institutionally recognized right to influence the actions of others, regardless of their immediate personal attitudes to the direction of influence." (*Essays*, *op.cit.*, p. 171.) It is also in agreement with Weber's definition of authority or imperative control which "is the probability that certain specific commands (or all commands) from a given source will be obeyed by a given group of persons." (*Theory*, *op.cit.*, p. 324.)

or they deplore it because they enjoy no benefits and engage in an effort to eliminate it as an "un-Baptist" phenomenon. But power is required for achievement in any field whatsoever.[27] Even though it contains the seeds of corruption,[28] power in itself is not an evil thing. It is necessary for life, which is capable of both good and evil.

Those leaders in a social group who are given responsibilities and goals to achieve will strive for legitimate authority from their constituency in order to gain the necessary support for the achievement of the group's goals. Those who hold power will seek to legitimate it; that is, they will seek authority.[29] If, as in the case of the Baptists, the ideology of the group does not permit the granting of legitimate authority to the leaders, any struggle for power will probably be increasingly complicated. Each group will strive to establish itself as the legitimate authority.

The Baptist denominational executives are given responsibility and limited power, but no legitimate authority. In order to overcome the lack of official status, they seek more power and when they are successful in this enterprise they seek authority. Relatively speaking, it has not been difficult for them to acquire the power necessary for the achievement of their assigned tasks. This has been accomplished by means of an unanticipated formation of an informal system of interpersonal and inter-group relations which bypasses the formal rules of order. The distinction between the formal and informal systems of action is a category of interpretation which enables the observer to answer crucial questions concerning the Convention. Why do the national leaders possess considerable power when the Convention itself does not have any "legislative power" or legal authority? What is the actual—

[27] Eduard Heiman, *Freedom and Order* (New York: Charles Scribner's Sons, 1947), p. 119.
[28] Never "absolute corruption." Acton's dictum is in error because absolute corruption presupposes absolute power, which is a historical impossibility. Power and authority are both relational concepts. Even in the limiting case of slavery the leaders must exercise caution because of the constant threat of a revolutionary uprising. (Weber, *Theory*, op.cit., pp. 62f., 276ff.)
[29] Lasswell and Kaplan, op.cit., p. 137.

as distinguished from the official—locus of authority in the Convention? Is the informal power of the executives gradually becoming legitimated on a formal basis? Or, to reformulate the last question: are there any signs that the Baptist interpretation of the nature of the church is changing in order to adjust to changes in the environment?

According to sociological theory, authority is generally associated with the formal system of action, i.e., the officially sanctioned relations of the group. Power is associated with the informal system.[30] Even before the Convention came into being the national executives of the missionary societies discovered that their duties extended far beyond the specific functions of the organizations. Whether they wanted it or not[31] their positions enabled them to exercise tremendous influence in the life of the denomination. They made decisions about the content of the denomination's educational and pamphleteering enterprises, the fund-raising activities, the development of seminaries and colleges, in addition to determining the policies of the missionary boards.[32]

Hudson notes that fifty years before the Convention was formed a large number of important posts were held by a small group of influential men. Francis Wayland, President of Brown University, was active in the affairs of the Triennial Convention from its inception until the middle of the century. During those years he held the following posts: recording secretary of the Triennial Convention, secretary of the Baptist Convention of Massachusetts, secretary of the Boston Baptist Foreign Missionary Society, member of the Board of Trustees

[30] Recall that Lasswell and Kaplan defined authority as formal power. Conversely, power could be called informal authority. (*Power and Society*, *op.cit.*, p. 133.)

[31] Indications are that most executives desired all the power they could acquire. Hudson notes that a power struggle was in progress among the denominational leaders shortly after the creation of the Triennial Convention (predecessor of the Foreign Mission Society) in 1814. At one of the annual meetings a movement to create a General Convention was set aside. "Apparently, Luther Rice had feared that some maneuver to seize control of the Convention was afoot because he pointed out that the . . . arrangement could easily be abused by an 'active and intriguing man.'" ("Stumbling into Disorder," *op.cit.*, pp. 5f.)

[32] *Ibid.*, pp. 14ff.

of Newton Seminary, board member of the Baptist Missionary Society of Massachusetts, board member of the Baptist Education Society of Massachusetts, board member of the Evangelical Tract Society, member of the Boston Standing Committee for the Triennial Convention, and editor of the *American Baptist Magazine*. "Wayland was not a unique figure in this respect. Actually, all the offices of the various societies and boards in Massachusetts were held by a dozen men. In New York and elsewhere the situation was the same."[33]

The by-laws and resolutions of the Convention prevent a single individual from holding so many posts today,[34] but the situation has changed only in degree. This circumstance, however, should not necessarily be interpreted as an undesirable appropriation of power by men of evil intent, but rather as an inevitable emergence of leadership which occurs in any social system.

The Authority of the Professional Executives

It was argued above that rational-legal authority—as the term was used by Max Weber—has not been conferred upon the officials of the American Baptist Convention. Actually, the professional executives do exercise a form of rational authority which is not explicitly defined by Weber. It is not *rational-legal* but *rational-pragmatic authority*. These terms will be further defined below.

Authority exists, Weber says, when there is "the probability that certain specific commands (or all commands) from a given source will be obeyed by a given group of persons."[35] The commands are obeyed because the group believes the leader has the legitimate right to issue them. If the submissiveness of the group is motivated on the basis of other reasons, the relationship is not to be described in terms of authority: "Loyalty may be hypocritically simulated by individuals or by whole groups on purely opportunistic grounds, or carried out in practice for reasons of material self-interest. Or

33 *Ibid.*, p. 20.
34 *Yearbook*, 1957, pp. 22, 27.
35 Weber, *Theory, op.cit.*, p. 324.

people may submit from individual weakness and helplessness because there is no acceptable alternative."[36]

TRADITIONAL AUTHORITY

An authority relation exists only when the claim to legitimacy is treated as valid. According to Weber there are at least three sources for the validation of an authority relation: law, tradition, and charisma. In the second instance, authority may be legitimated on the basis of long-standing traditions which extend beyond the memory of any of the members of the group.[37] Traditional authority has never played a crucial role in the history of the Baptists. Revolt against a normative ecclesiastical tradition was one of the motivating forces of the earliest Baptist leaders. Although there are signs that the negative attitude toward tradition is significantly changing, this movement has not gained enough force to warrant serious consideration as a basis for the legitimate authority of the denomination's leaders.

However, there is a variant of traditional authority which has played an important role in the history of the Baptist movement. Weber notes that traditional authority is accepted by the group on the basis of the sanctity of the order, i.e., the group and its powers of control have always existed.[38] Many Baptists argue that congregational polity is the only valid pattern for the Christian church. Since the Baptists idealize this form of government it is assumed that their churches are the most hallowed of all Christian communities. But even this expression of traditional authority is based on the more sacred tradition of Holy Scripture: "The New Testament is accepted by Baptists as a sufficient and trustworthy rule of faith and practice, and it has been our boast that we needed no other authority, since the gospel may be understood

[36] *Ibid.*, p. 326.
[37] *Ibid.*, p. 341.
[38] A minority of Baptists whose concern for establishing the sacred origin and uninterrupted succession of the movement is greater than their passion for objective scholarship has attempted to establish a lineage originating with John the Baptist. For the majority of Baptists this merely provides occasion for humorous remarks.

and experienced by any normal individual who sincerely seeks to walk in the truth of it."[39]

As it is with the sovereignty of God, so it is with the authority of Scripture: it must be mediated through persons who are the "bearers" and interpreters of the authority. Contemporary Baptists are becoming increasingly aware of this fact: "Neither a church nor an Association legislates in matters of faith and practice. Christ is the legislator. The role of a church and an Association is to judge or interpret or 'determine' the mind of Christ as it is made known to them in the Scriptures by the inward illumination of the Holy Spirit. Thus, when a matter is 'determined' and 'declared' by an Association, the ultimate ground is the authority of Christ and not the authority of the Association."[40]

There is little dispute among Baptists that the ultimate ground of the Christian church is the authority of Christ. Conflicts arise when the "authority under Christ"—the mediated authority—is established. It has been observed that the Baptists suggest several possibilities for the locus of this authority, none of them resembling the answer of the ecclesiastical-type religious organization. Baptist polity is based on sacred precedents and implicit biblical imperatives which indicate that no human organization, not even the church itself, may supersede the authority of Scripture. The emphasis is in agreement with the Reformation tradition, although within that tradition the nature and type of mediated authority has been variously defined. With respect to the locus of mediated authority, Baptists seem to be gradually moving away from a radical individualism and a corresponding emphasis upon the autonomy of the local church, toward a modified ecclesiastical method of validating authority.[41] Within a framework

[39] *The Baptist* (August 11, 1925), pp. 709f.

[40] Hudson, "The Associational Principle among Baptists," *op.cit.*, p. 20n.

[41] Baptist individualism passed through its most radical phase near the turn of the present century. At this time, Edward Hiscox wrote that it was the privilege of the individual to "read the Bible for himself, without dictation from, or dependence upon anyone, being responsible to God alone for his use of the sacred truth." He went further: "All men have the right, not only to believe, but also to profess and openly declare, whatever religious opinions they may entertain, *providing they be not contrary to*

established by the authority of biblical imperatives, Baptists are discovering modes of authority supported by methods of legitimation generally associated with ecclesiastical organizations. At a recent annual convention it was stated that "the authority of the Holy Spirit cannot be claimed alone by the local church. It is also an authority which belongs to denominational leaders, to 'guide,' 'judge,' 'rebuke.' "[42]

RATIONAL-LEGAL AUTHORITY

Weber's second mode of legitimate authority, the rational-legal type, is primarily applicable to the hierarchical ecclesiastical institution. Validation of authority within this church-type is based on rational and legal grounds. Among the members of the religious community there is a commonly accepted "belief in the 'legality' of patterns of normative rules and the right of those elevated to authority under those rules to issue commands. . . ."[43] Thus, the official of the church exercises authority because of his legal right, not because of any special attributes of his person. He must obtain impersonal qualifications such as theological education and ability to perform liturgical rites, but his authority flows primarily from the occupation of a legally established office.

According to the theology of the hierarchical-type the church exists because it was directly instituted—legally established—by God. The mediated locus of authority is the church as a whole, although this proliferated authority is rationally channeled through the hierarchy of church officials which represents the real locus of authority.

The American Baptist Convention also gains its legitimacy by means of rational rules. But the nature of the legitimation is clearly different from that of the church-type. As noted previously, the Convention has a right to exist according to

---

common morality, and do no injustice to others." (Edward T. Hiscox, *The New Directory for Baptist Churches*, Philadelphia: The Judson Press, 1894, p. 12. Italics added.)

[42] Walter J. Harrelson, "The Church and Its Baptism" (unpublished paper presented at the American Baptist Convention, Seattle, 1956), p. 3. Mimeographed.

[43] Weber, *Theory, op.cit.*, p. 328.

the "principles of Baptist tradition," but only so long as it does not actually legislate or claim any legal authority over the faith and practice of the local churches. However, depending on the vagaries of the particular local church and the character of a given situation, the Convention does exercise "considerable influence over the affairs of the churches."[44] When the Convention passes a budget resolution or decides on a new policy, the churches conform because the membership of the denomination generally accepts "the legitimate right," but not the legal right, of the delegates and officials to create policies and formulate budgets. In such a situation the churches are accepting the American Baptist Convention as a legitimate and rationally established authority. Therefore it is at least partially true to claim that the churches do not obey the dictums of the Convention solely because they fear economic reprisal, have self-interested motivations, or for any other reasons that could be given for obedience which extend beyond the meaning of rational authority.[45]

However, the acceptance of an associational body as a legal authority offends the sensitivity of a significant number of Baptists, even though the early Baptist associations did have diciplinary powers. For at least two centuries "official Baptist opinion"[46] has held that higher church councils are nothing more than human creations, and that no such council can have jurisdictional authority over a local church. They were created by the churches to serve the churches. Therefore, the American Baptist Convention, an associational body, can gain whatever legitimate authority it possesses only on a basis of authority that will be called *rational-pragmatic* or *rational expedient*. This signifies that the Convention is an expedient;

44 Merton indicates that "influence" may take many forms. He lists, among others, coercion, domination, manipulation, advice, exchange, and defines each. Several of the forms of influence—most notably manipulation, advice, and exchange—are operative in relations between the Convention and the churches. (Merton, *Theory, op.cit.*, pp. 419-421.)

45 Weber, *Theory, op.cit.*, pp. 325f.

46 This can never signify more than "majority opinion," but is no less significant from a sociological point of view because of its informal character. Informal or unofficial systems of belief and practice can often be more potent forces than official systems which have outworn their usefulness and do not gain the support of the constituency.

it is a temporary institutional means pragmatically conceived for the achievement of a higher purpose of the religious group. The Convention itself does not express that purpose through its own being since its existence is justified only when it achieves the goals for which it was established.

Therefore, the Convention and its officers do not possess a form of rational authority which is comparable to the legal authority of a priest or bishop in the ecclesiastical-type. The authority of the professional executives of the Convention is gained primarily through their ability to achieve assigned goals. The "influence" they exercise—generally acknowledged as considerable—is grounded in something other than rational-legal authority. The source of their influence is twofold: the formal system of authority and the informal system of power. The primary basis of their legitimate authority is pragmatic rather than legal.

The "ordinary" laymen, in the eyes of many Baptists, may enjoy more prestige, status, and authority than the "office" of executive secretary. Even though "specified spheres of competence" are delineated in the Convention and there is a "systematic division of labor," the incumbent of an office is not provided "with the necessary authority to carry out these functions," nor are "the necessary means of compulsion clearly defined."

According to Weber, rational authority is grounded in the acceptance of the leader as one who has the legal right to exercise imperative control over the social group. If he is not obeyed he has access to controls and sanctions. The use of these may be strictly defined and carefully limited by the rules of the group, but the official would be failing the community if he refused to use them in times of disorder. The executive professionals of the Convention do not possess any such privileges in their relationship to the churches of the denomination. They may exercise control, and instrumental sanctions are available, but they do not obtain any legal force. For example, executive officers of the national and state conventions occasionally utilize economic sanctions or the power of propaganda to bring ministers, churches, or other secretaries "into line."[47] The individual or group which is obedient to these pressures is not accepting authority but is succumbing to influence or power. It is this system of informal power as contrasted with the system of formal authority which plays a necessarily prominent role in Baptist organizational life.[48]

Weber believes that the "purest type of exercise of legal authority is that which employs a bureaucratic administrative staff."[49] While the Baptists do not have a highly developed system of rational-legal authority they have developed a complex administrative bureaucracy in order effectively to achieve their goals. Therefore, two generalizations may be drawn: (1) that bureaucratic organization appears as a response to

[47] Actually, this process works both ways. Because many local churches bring pressure to bear upon the work of the associational groups, many leaders believe they are justified in using this kind of power. One leader comments on the situation: "We are a denomination which maintains that the local church is the source of everything. Yet much of our literature is designed to promote the interests of autonomous organizations apart from the local churches." (Bryan F. Archibald, "A Study of Promotion," *Background Material, op.cit.*, pp. 21f.) A minister makes a similar observation: "And finally, without any disposition to be unpleasant to anyone near or far, let all who hold positions of trust in high places have a jealous regard for their standing as leaders and workers on the local level. Nothing is more devastating to morale and the good prospect of a better future for the Cause than the failure of people who exercise influence in the decisions of the Convention . . . to be themselves powerful assets in the local church and community." (Ivan M. Rose, "A Critique," *ibid.*, pp. 2f.)

On the other hand, the churches are often engaged in effective activities to influence the denominational leaders. One writer indicates that to a group of conservative Baptist churches "must go the credit or the blame for the growth of separatism among Northern Baptist churches. They have reduced it to a philosophy supported by the use of some Scripture and the avoidance of others. They have propagandized separatism until they make many pastors and laymen feel that to continue cooperation with the missions of the ABC is to be unfaithful to our Lord." (John W. Bradbury, "A Study of Withdrawing Churches," *ibid.*, p. 3.)

[48] This situation is not peculiar to the Baptists, but applies—as do other generalizations in this study—to the experience of most Protestant churches. It has been observed that "outside the Roman Catholic Church institutional authority is generally weak, partly because in their pluralism the institutions too clearly represent something else than God, Christ and Scriptures or the Christian community." Institutional authority may play an important supporting role in ecclesiastical Protestantism, but in the case of evangelical Protestant churches it "can become a matter of wholly minor significance and even the . . . [authority] of Scriptures is often made secondary to personal experience of the power of the gospel." (H. Richard Niebuhr, *The Purpose of the Church and Its Ministry*, New York: Harper & Brothers, 1956, pp. 72, 73.)

[49] Weber, *Theory, op.cit.*, p. 333.

the modern organizational environment independently of the authority which supports it, or (2) that rational-pragmatic authority provides sufficient ground for the creation of a bureaucratic order. Both of these may be true. From the point of view of the Baptists the evangelistic goals had to be achieved and an efficient administrative organization became an imperative for the denomination. Because of that, rational-pragmatic authority was assumed by the leadership of the bureaucracy and served as a support for the further development of the complex administrative structure.

Pragmatic authority, because it is not rationalized to the extent found in the "pure type" of legal authority, is always supported by obedience and loyalty on the part of the constituency. It can be distinguished, however, from obedience to a recognized legal authority. It is much more difficult to determine why the constituency obeys the leaders who have only pragmatic authority. Do they follow the guidance of the executives because they accept them as legitimate authorities, or simply because the executives possess instruments of sanction and control? A definitive answer is not possible, partly because of the ambiguity of Baptist beliefs and practices, but also because any decision of this kind—even within the system of rational-legal authority institutionalized by the Catholic Church—is characterized by mixed motives. The Catholic layman probably obeys his priest because he is devoted to Christian beliefs or is loyal to the authority of the church; but he may also fear the secular power of the church or recognize opportunity for non-religious benefits if he obeys.

The expediential or pragmatic authority of the Baptist executives is substantially undergirded by their opportunities to gain informal power. Some sources of this power can be isolated. First, the executive official can exercise important sanctions in order to control the deviant person on his own administrative staff. Ultimately he has the power of demotion and dismissal, although, according to the official rules, he must work through his board of managers. But the subordinate can "be brought into line" without using these controls. For example, he can be assigned an inordinate amount of unpleasant tasks, such as field trips which carry him far from home. This was reported as used by one executive secretary in past years.[50] On the other hand, of course, is the power of the executives to reward their staff through advancement or assignment to prestige tasks. In any event, control over the administrative staff makes an important contribution to the power and authority of the chief executive of a denominational agency.

A second source of power is control over procurement and allocation of monies. This was discussed briefly above, but because the potential power that can be derived from this source is always considerable it needs to be developed in greater detail. The economic determinist would interpret the Baptists primarily from this perspective, but no source of power is more widely proliferated in the denomination than that which is related to procurement and distribution of money. The financial activities of the Convention have been characterized by adjustment, counteradjustment, compromise, committee studies, new bylaws, etc. One of the principles which underlies all these machinations is the effort to separate policy-making from control of funds. This bears remarkable similarity to one of the classical rules of bureaucratic procedure: ". . . It is a matter of principle that the members of the administrative staff should be completely separated from ownership of the means of production or administration."[51] Obviously, no Baptist executive can "own the means of production," which would constitute ownership of the churches. The executives, however, can exercise remarkable control over finances in several ways. The most direct method involves the work of the missionary churches which are receiving substantial support from national or state agencies. Indebted financially to the agencies, these churches are morally and economically bound to accept the guidance of denominational officials including the choice of pastoral leadership. This appears perfectly normal by most social standards, but is a direct refutation of the principle of local autonomy.

[50] Interview with an executive secretary.
[51] Weber, *Theory*, *op.cit.*, p. 331.

Another way in which executives can exercise influence over the disposition of funds is through their advice to the financial committee of the Convention during the annual process of allocation of funds. This committee, composed primarily of laymen,[52] is quite inured to the conflicting claims of the agency executives. The executives are their first advisors and within the limits established by budget allocation they exercise the greatest degree of control aside from the committee members themselves. In order to offset the influence of the executive secretaries the financial committee is advised by a budget research subcommittee which meets more often than the financial committee and employs full-time assistance.[53]

Financial power is not confined to those who are active at the national level. Affluent laymen often play a crucial role in denominational affairs. For example, the late J. L. Kraft, the cheese merchant, was one of the benefactors who was instrumental in acquiring Green Lake, the Convention's extensive assembly grounds in northern Wisconsin. Also, ministers of large churches and state secretaries acquire power through their ability to direct funds toward the activities of the Convention or by threatening to withdraw support.[54]

A third source of power is the voting strength of one's constituency. An executive who directs a missionary society which can claim the loyalty of a large number of delegates to the Convention is always certain to gain more attention than the national executive of a smaller agency who can claim no such support. The nature of one's constituency, however, is very important. The national executive engaged in rural church work or inner-city parish activities may enjoy the sympathetic support of his people, but since they are not able to attend the annual meetings they represent an attenuated power.[55]

[52] *Yearbook*, 1956, p. 21. [53] *Ibid.*, p. 22.

[54] Constituency support, a prime source of power, cannot be measured in terms of numbers alone. Thus a single minister may be more influential than some state secretaries. The support of one millionaire may be "worth" more than the ability to direct the funds of many small, semi-cooperative churches.

[55] Other important sources of informal power which contribute to the pragmatic authority of the national leaders will be discussed in more detail below.

CHARISMATIC AUTHORITY

According to Weber a third source for the validation of the authority relation is the charismatic power of an individual who "is set apart from ordinary men and treated as endowed with supernatural, superhuman, or at least specifically exceptional powers or qualities."[56] Charismatic authority and rational pragmatic authority represent the chief sources of legitimation for the activities of the executive professionals of the American Baptist Convention. This represents an interesting amalgam because charismatic authority is "outside the realm of everyday routine and the profane sphere. In this respect it is sharply opposed both to rational, and particularly bureaucratic, authority. . . ."[57] Charisma is the antithesis of the routine control of action. A compromise between these two types of authority is not surprising for the Baptists. In a sense they have been able to operate with a relative degree of effectiveness amid contradictions of heteronomous-autonomy that would drive a Roman Catholic bishop to distraction. Some Convention executives have not only overcome the antitheses but have combined charismatic and rational authority, the result being what in popular jargon is known as a "Baptist pope."[58]

A charismatic executive possesses the ability to marshal support from various sectors of the denomination. Not all executives are able to do this, but those who can are in a position to play an important role in the formulation of denominational policies. This is a well-known phenomenon in the denomination and was especially prominent during the years of the "fundamentalist controversy."[59]

[56] Weber, *Theory, op.cit.*, p. 358.
[57] *Ibid.*, p. 361.
[58] Personal interview with a division chairman of a missionary society.
[59] The fundamentalist wing of the church was probably more dependent upon charismatic leadership than were the liberals. This was true because of a failure to develop a rationalized organization, with the result that the leaders could not maintain the support of the constituency without dependence upon charismatic personalities. There is evidence that some of the fundamentalist leaders were more concerned with their personal failure to gain adequate recognition from the Convention than with the work of the denomination itself. These men would be representative of the "pseudo-charismatic type." John Straton, who in the 1920's was called

For example, one executive of the Convention attracted personal support from diverse groups, even gaining the guarded respect of the fundamentalists. His colleagues, on the other hand, receiving nothing but criticism from this powerful faction, were in no position to oppose his policies. In fact, he was often called upon by other executives to gain support for programs which might antagonize the fundamentalists.[60]

Strictly speaking, it is not accurate to pin the charismatic label on every Baptist leader who displays qualities which attract the loyalty of large numbers of people. Charisma is a concept generally reserved for those unique persons in history who have made a profound break from the bonds of routinized activity and who have been a revolutionary force in the history of their society. However, the descriptive utility of the term has been so great that it has been used more loosely to describe the authority and attracting power of persons of otherwise limited endowment and mediocre attainment. Charismatic authority will be used here in the more generalized sense: to denote those qualities of personality which enable a leader to gain a following for his ideals and spontaneous support from the constituency for the achievement of his goals.

In order to analyze the Baptists it is important to note the conditions which favor the development of charismatic movements. Parsons notes that Weber had relatively little to say on this subject. Since Weber's time, evidence has accumulated to support his theories. Parson's description of these conditions tends to be extreme, but, nonetheless, is in general accord with the Baptist predicament: "Any situation where an established institutional order has to a considerable extent become disorganized, where established routines, expectations, and symbols are broken up or are under attack is a favourable situation for such a movement. This creates

---

"the fundamentalist pope," was described as "too ambitious to work closely with any group he could not dominate." (Norman F. Furniss, *The Fundamentalist Controversy, 1919-1931*, New Haven: Yale University Press, 1954, p. 109.)

[60] Summary statement of material derived from personal interviews with an associate secretary and a member of the General Council.

widespread psychological insecurity which in turn is susceptible of reintegration in terms of attachment to a charismatic
movement."[61]

Interviews with Baptist leaders indicate a general agreement on their part with most of Parsons' argument. One member of the General Council deplored what he called the "aristocratic dictatorship"[62] of a former executive secretary of one
of the societies. He stated that "dictatorship" was possible because of the structure of the organization: "It's too loose, there
are no adequate checks and balances. That's what we're trying
to get in the present plan for re-organization. We don't want
absolute control for the General Council. But if they make the
over-all policies it will reduce the possibility of the executive
secretaries gaining absolute control of the Convention's programs. At the present time, there are no checks to curtail
the dynamic personality. I know this is both good and bad.
A rigid structure can stifle a creative person, as often happens
in the Episcopalian set-up, but this is no more dangerous than
having the periodic appearance of some superman who gains
too much power."[63]

Under the present constitutional arrangement the executive
professionals of the denomination have no alternative but to
depend on the strength of their personal ability and the extension of their individual influence in order to compensate
for a lack of rational-legal authority. A state secretary described his method of operation in the following manner: "I
don't have any right to tell the churches what to do with respect
to any issue just because I'm the state secretary. I can't do a
thing if the people don't want me to. I operate in such a way
that my programs are carried out by pastors because they
want to carry them out, and I have to make them want to.
Let me give you an example. If I know that one of my churches

[61] Talcott Parsons, "The Institutionalization of Authority," in Weber,
Theory, op.cit., p. 71.

[62] The leaders who are intimately acquainted with a charismatic associate are usually intimidated rather than attracted by his qualifications, a
reaction which is not surprising considering the competitive organizational
structure of the Convention.

[63] Personal interview with a member of the General Council.

is going to appoint an uneducated minister from one of the Bible schools, I write to the pulpit committee and ask them if they want me to preach. I always want to preach to these people before I talk business with them. . . . When I get to the church I don't talk about the work of the state convention from the pulpit. I preach straight from the gospel and try to give them a real inspiring sermon. Then I've got them!"[64]

Most state executives describe themselves as "a pastor's pastor," seldom as an administrator, an executive, or a policymaker. When the executives do refer to these functions they are merely acting as a "funnel" through which the churches—"the real policy-makers"—can express their desires. One state secretary wrote as follows: "I found during my tenure of office that the relationship is one very closely akin to that of a pastor of a local church. . . . On an associational basis it is also quite evident from my experience that the associational leadership looks very definitely to the office of the state secretary for related interest that flows down from the local church, or rather, up from the local church through the district association and on to the state convention. . . . This has all been done, may I say, without any indication whatsoever of an over-all or seeming hierarchy imposing upon the pastors of the churches certain things, but has come from a common basis of understanding and fellowship that makes for wonderful relationships in our entire work."[65]

Because of the tenuous authority-relation between Convention officials and the churches, the officials are often forced into a type of public relations which will enable them to establish direct contact with the constituency and exercise their personal charismatic power. One secretary wrote: "I have given 200 messages in the past 9 months." And another executive described the situation in familiar terms: "One of the great problems of our democratic setup, as far as the state secretary and the local church is concerned, is that of being unable to exercise any authority when it is quite evident that

[64] Personal interview.
[65] Confidential correspondence to the author.

77

a pastoral change is needed. . . . Oftentimes conditions become most deplorable before any call for help is extended."[66]

The executive officials at every level of the denomination are incessantly struggling against the threat of institutional chaos. The Baptists, within their system of church-order, have unconsciously created contradictions in order to "preserve pure democracy." It is a contradiction to give the executives official responsibility but no official authority. To absolutize in principle the idea of local autonomy and to create, at the same time, associational organizations which compromise the absolute, is a contradiction. It is often observed that the Baptists are preoccupied with checks and balances. This is inaccurate. Actually, they have been primarily interested in checks. The resulting lack of balance has been offset only by gradual development of an informal system of power, the unanticipated appearance of a rational-pragmatic authority, and an effort—conscious or unconscious, on the part of those who appoint executive officials—to recruit men who possess personal charisma.

The fundamental anomaly in the Baptist situation, in fact a circumstance viewed with wry humor by those who are aware of it, is that, despite their noblest effort, the Baptists have not succeeded in their program to check authority or to balance power. This, of course, was inevitable, for had they succeeded the result would have been no effective leadership, complete separation of the local congregations, an absence of common symbols, limited inter-church communication, no denominational unity, and no evangelical program. Their methods of creating and controlling power will be discussed in the next chapters.

[66] Confidential correspondence.

CHAPTER V

THE FORMAL SYSTEM OF AUTHORITY AND
THE INFORMAL SYSTEM OF POWER

The Function of the Formal and Informal Systems

THE PROCESS of institutional rationalization results in a division of labor, a complex order of role assignments and functions, and a formal system of hierarchical authority. Relationships of individuals within the organization are patterned in such a way that they become the means for the achievement of the official goals of the group. In brief, one of the functions of formal organizational patterns is to relate individual actors to a social group which is dedicated to a set of goals which officially transcend the needs and desires of any of its members.[1] Therefore, even when the ideology includes a complete subordination of the individual to the group—as occurs in a totalitarian system—there always exists a tension between the needs of the group and the needs and desires of its members. The elements of strain are significantly increased when the group includes within its ideology a dedication to the rights and beliefs of the individual. This aspect of the problem of rationalization is particularly crucial within the American Baptist Convention since the freedom of the individual is one of the sacred shibboleths of the belief system.

In addition, the formal patterns of organization are bypassed by the personnel of the Convention because of their desire to be treated as ends rather than means. The goals of the American Baptist Convention, no matter how sacred, are seldom valued by the individuals to the extent that they are willing to subordinate themselves utterly to the aims of the organization. This tendency on the part of the individuals is reinforced by a fundamental tension within the belief system:

[1] Selznick, *op.cit.*, p. 251. For another description of the relationship between individual actors and their social system see Parsons, *Social System*, *op.cit.*, pp. 24-26.

group loyalty in conflict with the high value the Baptists place upon the sacred integrity of the individual. The situation is considerably relieved by the fact that many of the individual's needs are fulfilled by the group itself. Organizational membership breeds organizational loyalty, and the individual will seek self-realization and recognition by means of the success of his particular group. Personal identification with the institution of which one is a member becomes part of the social process. Nevertheless, the individual will seek particular self-realization within this order. He will tend to break the "rules" and traditions of the organization in order to gain what he believes to be his personal needs. This will be true of the lowest functionary, who does not follow the "proper channels" for the obtaining of paper clips, as it is for the executive officer who often finds it necessary as well as desirable to formulate policy without requesting the guidance of his elected board of managers.

This process can be distinguished from the practice of by-passing routinized channels in order more effectively to achieve the desired goals, even though in actual circumstances the two processes are sometimes indistinguishable. In the latter instance, the personnel decide that the officially established procedures for achievement of the desired goals are not adequate or efficient. The formal channels will be bypassed, not so much to achieve personal power, as to realize the goals to which the organization is committed.

Both of these patterns of social action tend toward the breakdown of the formal system of organization. The official role assignments are altered and the hierarchy of authority is reshuffled. This may even lead to an alteration of the division of labor. The complexity of the process is obvious, and within any large organization important changes may result from the tensions which occur when alterations are made in personnel, or as conditions in the external environment demand adaptation of patterns of action and methods of policy-making.

The informal system demands the major portion of our attention in this section. The formal structure, however, provides both the special environment within which the informal patterns and relations must operate, and the official reference point for the resolution of conflicts which occur within the informal operation.[2]

The informal structure within the American Baptist Convention, as in secular social systems, reflects "the spontaneous effort of the individuals and subgroups to control the conditions of their existence."[3] The conflicting nature of the Baptist imperative goals places unusual strains upon the formal organizational patterns. These strains result in a need for an efficient and adaptive social structure which will preserve the existence and integrity of the institution. Also, the organization must be able to achieve its imperative goals within the limitations established by the formal beliefs and prescribed patterns of action. With regard to "conflicting goals," specific reference is made to three factors previously investigated: the "soul competency of the individual believer," "the autonomy and authority of the local church," and the necessity for co-operation and inter-group discipline at the organizational level in order to strive for "the evangelization of the world."

The formal system of authority and control does not supply the means for the achievement of the official goals. In fact, the official independence of every organization within the denomination, from the local church to the state association and the national society, serves as a barrier against intergroup control and discipline. It is for this reason that the professional executives have found it necessary to create informal lines of communication and power in order to gain more effective control of the "conditions of their existence."

One of the functions of the informal system within the Convention is to supply an effective leadership which can bypass the limitations set upon the associational organization by the contemporary Baptist ideology and official charters. Although the authority of the executives is formally limited, they have discovered techniques for providing the essential leadership either through broad interpretation of the formalized author-

2 Selznick, *op.cit.*, p. 251.
3 *Loc.cit.*

81

ity, or by exercise of power not expressly extended by the official organizational bylaws.

For example, although each national society is officially autonomous and independent of the needs and desires of the other societies, when an important officer within one of these organizations proves to be incompetent or uncooperative, thus adversely affecting the work of the other organizations, methods are readily available for the restraint or removal of this official. A case of this nature arose in recent years. In the words of one executive: "There wasn't any real difficulty involved in replacing him. And it wasn't a case of intervening in the affairs of another society without provocation or simply for our own interests. His ineffectiveness had already reflected upon the work of several societies. The problem was brought to the attention of certain members of his board of managers. It was pointed out that executives in other societies found it impossible to work effectively with him. A 'prestige church' in -------- was mentioned as a possibility for his future. The necessary contacts were made and an informal decision had been reached before the next official meeting of his board of managers."[4]

At this point the formal lines of authority are utilized. Prior to the board meeting other "key" members of the board are judiciously informed with regard to the business at hand, and the whole board accepts the resignation without objection and with only two or three members of the board knowing that the pressure to remove their executive came from outside the "independent" organization. Even the informed board members might have experienced great disillusion had they known that the initial complaints concerning the executive had come from the lowest levels of his own office staff.

This illustrates the fact that the informal patterns of power often work in unorthodox directions, "upward" as well as "down" and "across," and that in certain instances the power of a clerk may far exceed his official authority.[5] It further in-

[4] Interview with an executive secretary.
[5] Herbert A. Simon, "Decision-Making and Administrative Organization," *Public Administration Review*, IV (1944), p. 21.

dicates the functional significance of both the formal and informal systems of power. It is not possible for all activities and decisions of the Convention and its organizations to be made within the limitations of either the formal or the informal systems of authority. Formal authority is generally reserved for the settlement of disputes, and is usually "related to the appointment, disciplining, and dismissal of personnel."[6] At this point Mr. Simon is not discussing the American Baptist denomination, where often, it is true, the final settlement of disputes is not made by the "official" hierarchy. Because inter-organizational relationships within the Convention are so tenuous, the informal system of power and decision-making must assume a disproportionate share of the operational load. Actually, very few inter-organizational decisions are made along the official "lines of authority."[7] The important policies and decisions are informally developed and formally sanctioned. The unusual importance of the informal system within the life of the Convention is made necessary by the restrictions placed upon the leadership, which is expected to achieve goals exceeding the limitations of their authority. Within the denomination there is a tremendous gulf between the official system of authority and the informal system of power.

When so much weight is placed upon the informal aspects of organizational activity, the social system cannot be designated as a highly rationalized structure. But even an unrationalized system has a functional significance. Failure to rationalize the inter-organizational framework of the Convention has not been totally dysfunctional for the denomination, just as, conversely, formalization is not entirely beneficial. While it may prove necessary to achieve a higher degree of formal authority within the institutional framework of the Convention, it has been no less essential to sustain the work of the various agencies until this goal is reached. But whether or not a greater degree of rationalization is desirable, failure to define the status and authority of the Convention's various

---

[6] *Ibid.*, p. 19.

[7] This generalization is based on ideas derived from several interviews with various personnel. The intention of this and succeeding chapters is to verify the statement.

professional offices has served a useful purpose from the point of view of the officials themselves. In the words of one executive, "If we leave things undefined structurally as well as theologically, we can operate the Convention pretty much as we please."[8] He did not mean that the executives desire and strive for complete freedom from sanctions. He was merely operating on the assumption, for which there may actually be little real foundation, that the "grass roots" of the denomination "is not ready for any significant revision of their concepts of church polity and ecclesiastical authority." Therefore, it is assumed to be easier to achieve denominational goals within the present informal system than to rationalize the system merely to better achieve these same goals.

Another function of the informal system is the ease by which "undesirable" centers of power are rendered ineffective. The fundamentalists were the most obvious recipients of this effect of informal power. During the years of the controversy between the liberals and the fundamentalists, the latter were unable to gain even a minority share of the executive positions at the national level.[9] They were powerful at the state and local level, and were often able to control budget procedures and general policies within these areas.[10] At the national level they were always ineffective although extremely vocal, and according to Furniss they were often unethical and derisive.[11] The fact that the fundamentalist groups, even at the height of their power, could not make their appeal through the machinery of any official hierarchy, enabled those who controlled the informal system to control the ultimate policies of the Convention. If the minority groups pressured the executive officials to do something in their favor, the executives needed only to point to their lack of real authority. Since no one had official power, how could anyone be brought to task for inequities, no matter how obvious they may have been?

The most important function of the informal system of power is to promote the achievement of the denominational goals within the existing anarchical framework of the Amer-

---

8 Interview with a sub-executive.   9 Furniss, *op.cit.*, pp. 112, 117.
10 *Ibid.*, p. 110.   11 *Ibid.*, pp. 106, 108, 113, 115.

ican Baptist Convention. A superficial loyalty to the autonomy of the local church and the absolute freedom of the individual can be maintained, and at the same time the executive officials can exercise enough informal influence to gain the support of the majority of the local churches. So long as the belief is sustained that the executives have no power which exceeds the official limits of their pragmatic authority, and so long as they remain in the background of the official celebrations and annual meetings, leaving the speechmaking and voting to the ministerial and lay-delegates, it is assumed that the principal tenets of the ideology are not violated.[12]

There are many leaders within the denomination who are annoyed with this method of self-deception, and they become fearful when a new charismatic leader appears on the lower levels of the hierarchical ladder.[13] As Baptists these leaders believe that the dispersal of power is an essential of Free Church polity, but at the same time the churches through the machinery of the denomination must be effective enough to register a significant impact on the secular world, and an educative impact upon the members of the local churches themselves.

The existing patterns of action which appear so chaotic actually permit the leadership to formulate policies while acquiring only the indirect approval of the churches; i.e., they do not receive directive guidance from the churches but only act in a way which they believe will be least offensive to the greatest number of local communions. When complaints do arise from the grass roots, the areas of authority and responsibility are so poorly defined that it is almost impossible to discover who made the policy decisions and who is to be held accountable for that activity which is believed to be undesirable.[14]

Therefore, depending on one's perspective, the informal system of power relations is both functional and dysfunctional.

---

[12] Interview with an associate secretary.

[13] Edward B. Willingham, "We Consider Our Tensions," *Background Material, op.cit.,* pp. 8-12.

[14] Tiller, *Background Material, op.cit.,* pp. 3, 5.

The purpose of the system is to accomplish certain defined ends without violating the current Baptist emphasis on the freedom of the individual and autonomy of the local church. But individuals cannot be called free, nor can the churches be called autonomous if the issues which are of vital importance for each of them are beyond their control. In other words there is little functional unity within the Convention. Robert K. Merton has observed that "social usages or sentiments may be functional for some groups and dysfunctional for others in the same society."[15] From the point of view of the Convention's leadership, especially that of the professional leaders, the informal power relations may be considered as beneficial. The "uninformed" and "conservative" constituency is not permitted access to the means of decision- and policy-making because they cannot exercise significant influence through the official channels of authority. From the point of view of the constituency the current emphasis upon freedom and autonomy and the resultant need for an extremely elaborate informal system of power prevent them from effectively operating at any meaningful level of the decision-making process.

The Power of the Professional Executives

In many respects centralization and rational bureaucratic organization are in conflict with the current Baptist theology of the church. The tendencies toward impersonalization, the premium placed on technical knowledge, and the removal of the formulation of important decisions from the aegis of the local churches which accompanies rational and centralized social systems are necessary for the achievement of the common goals of the denomination. But they are all equally opposed to the ideals of the Baptist ideology. The organizational needs were too pressing to deny the drive toward centralization of administrative, financial, and policy-making operations. The need for a coordinating organization with an established leadership resulted in an informally organized Baptist elite,

---

15 Merton, *Social Theory* (1949), *op.cit.*, pp. 29, 51.

a group of leaders whose authority has never been fully legitimated. The influence of certain members of the elite sometimes reaches inordinate proportions because, for the most part, the power of the leadership is veiled and was neither intended nor recognized by the founders of the denominational structure. The creators of the Convention's charter left the boundaries of responsibility and influence poorly defined, and the resulting social relationships are so fluid that the layman or local minister is left in a hopeless quandary when he attempts to understand the mechanism of the Convention or act intelligently within it.[16]

It is difficult to explain the rationale of the Convention because of the ambiguous nature of the power of the professional executives. *Within* his own society an executive's authority is legally legitimated and his duties are delineated with a reasonable degree of clarity. A bylaw of one of the societies is worded as follows: "The Executive Secretary shall be the executive officer of the Board and shall have general charge and oversight of the work of the board; all divisions and departments shall report to him for instruction and advice, and he shall be kept informed constantly by the heads of all divisions and departments of the condition and progress of the work for which each head is responsible. . . ."[17]

On the other hand, the official authority of the executive secretaries is non-existent with regard to inter-organizational

[16] This was discovered through conversation with many ministers and lay people within the Convention, but it was most dramatically illustrated at two of the Annual Conventions in 1956 and 1957. At the first Convention the leaders were proposing a reorganization of the Convention structure; at the second a proposal was brought to the floor of the Convention to move the denominational headquarters to Chicago or some other city in the midwest. In both cases it was clearly indicated by the constituency that they had an inadequate comprehension of the nature of the issues. Many of them had some grasp of the problems involved if the outcome were to have an effect upon their local situations. For example, a discussion with a group of ministers from West Virginia revealed that reorganization would be poorly received in their churches. Therefore, they were opposed to it although they seemed to be in favor of some kind of reordering of the structure of the Convention. But there were many lay people and ministers who had no opinion on the subject and felt morally constrained *not* to vote because of their lack of knowledge.

[17] *The Board of Education and Publication of the American Baptist Convention*, 44th Annual Report, 1955 (Philadelphia: The Judson Press), p. 90.

87

affairs. The autonomous nature of every church, association of churches, and national agency within the denomination precludes the possibility of official inter-organizational authority. Even the General Secretary of the Convention has limited authority in inter-agency affairs. He is called the "principal administrative officer of the Convention and of the General Council," and he "shall act as representative of the Convention in accordance with its Bylaws. . . ."[18] But this does not confer upon the General Secretary any authority in relation to the societies or the local churches or the local or state associations. He is merely the administrative officer of the Convention, "under the direction of the General Council,"[19] and it must be recalled that "The American Baptist Convention declares its belief in the independence of the local church, and in the purely advisory nature of all denominational organizations."[20] This is strictly defined in order to indicate that the Convention cannot exercise any ecclesiastical authority over the affairs of the autonomous agencies of the denomination.

The executive secretary of a society is officially responsible to his board of managers. The constitution of one society reads as follows: "The Board of Managers shall have the management of the corporate affairs; shall have the power to elect its own chairman and recording secretary, and the executive secretary and treasurer of the Board of Education . . . and to define the powers and duties of each. . . ."[21] It should be noted that the boards of managers of all the societies are always elected by the delegates to the American Baptist Convention.[22] Therefore, through the delegates to the annual conventions and boards of managers of the various agencies, the professional executives are indirectly responsible to the constituency of the local churches. Because the executives are responsible to the churches only through their boards of managers, the boards serve as a shield or buffer between the

18 *Yearbook*, 1956, p. 13.
19 *Ibid.*, p. 13.
20 *Ibid.*, p. 11.
21 *The Board of Education and Publication*, *op.cit.*, p. 83.
22 *Ibid.*, pp. 82, 83. Cf. also *Yearbook*, 1956, p. 23.

executives and the "vagaries of the local constituency." Actually, the executives often attempt to maintain the fiction that the real creators of policy are the delegates to the annual conventions. In the words of one executive: "We merely implement the policies which the delegates formulate for us from year to year. This is the only way that our claim to democracy can be upheld."[23] This is the direction that conversations with the executives usually take. However, only a few executives maintain this theme throughout an extensive interview or series of interviews. When they are asked how the delegates make policy, how the local churches direct the delegates, how the delegates know which issues are significant, which needs are greatest throughout the denomination, etc., it develops that "a certain amount of direction from the top is necessary in every modern religious body."[24] The delegates to the annual meetings, an associate secretary said, "cannot be expected to know all the problems involved in far-flung missionary activities," or, he could have added, even in the city mission in the nearby area of urban disintegration, or even in the more familiar area of fund-raising and public relations.

Within our modern technological environment a central, rationalized organization is essential for the achievement of the goals desired by a larger number of local groups. The making and implementing of policy, the problems of financing and budgeting, the various kinds of specialized knowledge necessary for foreign and home mission work, publicity problems and problems of education and research, the administration of a large force of sub-executive and office secretaries— all of these require a higher degree of centralized planning and a greater investment in centralized authority than was anticipated when the Baptists formulated their ideology within the milieu of the eighteenth and nineteenth centuries. Leadership by experts is primarily the result of the technical specialization that is the unique characteristic of rationalized or-

23 Interview with an executive secretary.
24 Interviews with an executive secretary and an associate secretary.

ganization.[25] In the American Baptist Convention the result is that the power of policy initiation and determination no longer rests with the local church, but rather with the technically experienced, full-time leadership.[26] The professional leaders of the agencies are no longer—if they ever were—the passive executors of the will of the churches expressed through the boards of managers of the various agencies. The officials not only initiate the policies, they implement them as well. There are times when they do encounter opposition to the formulation of their plans, but they are still able to control the implementation of policy, a power which enables them ultimately to determine the nature of the policies even if they do not originally formulate them. Robert Michels noticed this phenomenon in relation to democratic political parties: "The technical specialization that inevitably results from extensive organization renders necessary what is called expert leadership. Consequently the power of determination comes to be considered one of the specific attributes of leadership, and is gradually withdrawn from the masses to be concentrated in the hands of the leaders alone. Thus the leaders, who were at first no more than the executive organs of the collective will, soon emancipate themselves from the mass and become independent of its control."[27]

Reasons will be given in a subsequent section to indicate that within the American Baptist Convention this condition is not so clear-cut as described by Michels with regard to secular democratic politics. But it is true that "organization implies the tendency to oligarchy." If Michels is correct, even in a general sense, whatever residue of democratic procedure remains within the Baptist denomination is due to disappear almost entirely, because "the increase in the power of the

[25] Robert Michels, *Political Parties* (Glencoe, Illinois: The Free Press, 1949), p. 31.

[26] For example, Hudson observes that "It must be confessed that most Baptists, as yet, would not be willing to admit that their witness in the contemporary world is being crippled by an undue emphasis on the independence of the local church; nor would they readily acknowledge that they are confronted by the necessity of developing appropriate means for achieving a wider church order." ("Are Baptists so Peculiar?" *op.cit.*, p. 1,324.)

[27] Michels, *op.cit.*, pp. 31-32.

leaders is directly proportional with the extension of organization."[28] There is no reason to suppose that the tendency toward more complex organizational forms which has been present within the Baptist movement since its earliest days in America is going to be curtailed. However, there is no necessary reason why organization *qua* organization must be aristocratic or oligarchic in nature. It seems clear that some kinds of organization, e.g., representational, are more "democratic" than other kinds, such as a monolithic structure. However, a lack of awareness on the part of the leaders concerning the possibilities of different degrees of representation, and a general assumption on the part of leaders that the denomination is democratic because it is Baptist, offers no relief from oligarchic tendencies. Baptist leaders have done little critical thinking along these lines. The general assumption of the leaders is illustrated by the phrase, often repeated, "We are proud of our democracy." One executive said, "We may not be as efficient as the Roman Catholics but one of the men from the American Institute of Management, who was a Catholic, admitted that his church could learn a lot from our democratic procedures."[29]

The general tendency of the leadership of the Convention is to convince themselves as well as the laity that the Baptist denomination knows nothing of "leaders" in the bureaucratic or oligarchic sense. The denomination merely has "executive employees" and managerial boards, which are sensitively responsible to the desires of the grass roots. But this only serves to conceal from everyone, leaders and laity, the danger which threatens the cherished democracy.

Although recognized by many people, it has not been publicly admitted that the executive secretaries and their staffs, who officially are confined to the implementation of policy,

[28] *Ibid.*, p. 33.
[29] The reference was to the "Management Audit" of the American Baptist Convention made by the American Institute of Management in 1954. Of the three men who attended the sessions of the General Council one was a Roman Catholic who was apparently impressed by the fact that the Council members were free to speak as they pleased within the sessions, a freedom which does not necessarily indicate the existence of a democratic procedure throughout the entire Convention.

have also become the initiators of the policy.[30] The establishment of an administrative staff to implement the decisions of the churches leads to a policy-making authority not originally intended by the founders of the Convention organization. But this cannot be classified as an "unanticipated consequence,"[31] since it was this circumstance which was most feared by the fathers of the American Baptist Convention. However, the need for an established and full-time leadership is too great to be overcome merely by anticipating its undesirable effects. If the Convention refuses to legitimate on a formal basis the leadership necessary for the achievement of its concerns, a group of leaders with tremendous informal power will appear. There is no easy way to prevent this. In fact, because the power is unintended and veiled it is oftentimes considerably greater than the official ecclesiastical authority of the Episcopalian or Methodist bishop, or the Presbyterian moderator.

In the first place, there is no way for the constituency to know who has the power. There can be little effective check upon the power of the leadership when most lay people have no knowledge of Convention affairs, never attend a national, state, or even a local associational meeting, do not know the names of their officials nor anything about the policies they are making, and are not represented in any way at these meetings if they fail to attend in person.[32]

In the second place, an executive leader may possess charismatic authority, a phenomenon which is familiar within all types of social organization. But in the American Baptist Convention, where the pragmatic is the only form of rational authority, an unbearable burden is placed upon the limited legitimacy of the Convention officials if they confine their activities to the formal system of authority. Therefore, the charismatic type becomes a requirement for the continuing work of the organization. Many of the leaders deplore the presence of the charismatic type but are resigned to a necessity

---

[30] This point will be discussed in the next chapter.

[31] Merton, *Social Theory* (1949), *op.cit.*, pp. 50-51.

[32] Methods of representation at denominational meetings will be discussed in Chapter VII.

for such leadership since it lends so much support to the functioning of the informal system. But it is much more difficult to control the power of the charismatic personality when the formal rules within the official charter of the Convention are unrealistically conceived with respect to the power needs of the denominational leaders. A calculated balance of power is essential for every democratic order, but an attempted elimination of power merely establishes a condition which is conducive to social chaos and a greater likelihood of the emergence of charismatic personalities. The Convention has been fortunate in the appearance of charismatic leaders who have contributed positive and dynamic guidance to the denomination in times of crisis, but these leaders have been restrained by the internal conflicts which have plagued the Convention for the past three decades.[33] No leader has been able consistently to unite a majority of the forces by attracting the allegiance of the fundamentalists, the liberals, the executives, and others. However, the executive leader who possesses charismatic authority enjoys a unique power within the informal structure of the Convention.

An executive secretary of one of the major societies may gain the support of an extensive agency on the basis of his administrative skill and his official or rational authority, but if charismatic qualities are added to this formal authority the executive will gain the support of the active lay constituency at the local level. His personal appearances through his field contacts, his mediation work with the conflicting forces of the denomination, his sensitivity to the needs of widely opposed groups and his ability to attract their loyalty, will all contribute toward the creation of a grass-roots support which evinces primary dedication to him and his concerns.[34] Once this kind of support is obtained it can never be ignored in the policy-making counsels of the other leaders. Just as there is no possible way for such an individual to obtain

---

[33] Willingham, *Background Material*, *op.cit.*, p. 10.

[34] Three persons who were interviewed, a member of the General Council, an executive, and an associate secretary, each had the same particularly effective leader in mind while discussing this issue.

this kind of power by official means, there is no official road which the other leaders of the Convention can follow to restrain this power. It has been the experience of the Convention that the denominational organization is wedded to the hopes and desires of the charismatic leader until sickness or death do them part. One of the reasons is that while the non-charismatic executives might attempt to coordinate their informal power to restrain or remove the charismatic personality, there is always a critical need within the hierarchy for a man who can exercise the power to mediate between the power blocs of the denomination. One charismatic executive of recent years, who enjoyed the respect but not the general affection of many of the other executives, was periodically on call by these men to mediate conflicts which threatened their organizations, not his own. He was passionately dedicated and had the ability to enthrall the conservatives on one day, the liberals on the next. Such a man is not readily disposed of, even though several leaders reported that their tolerance level reached the breaking point when he exerted this same kind of authority in executive meetings.[35]

Therefore, although informal, the power of the executives may reach startling proportions. Modern Baptist emphasis upon ultimate authority of the individual believer, the authority of the local church, and the corresponding "containment" of the authority of the executive professionals resulted in unanticipated consequences. Being permitted nothing more, at least at the official level, than an instrumental function with no ecclesiastical authority, the executives were forced to substitute informal power for official authority. In individual cases, this can far exceed the power of many executives or ecclesiastical officers of the "authoritarian" religious orders. This has occurred for several reasons, some of them having been mentioned in the preceding paragraphs.

The founders of the Convention did not anticipate the *impossibility* of policy formulation by autonomous churches. They did not anticipate the fact that the system of direct representation could not work within an organization so large

[35] *Ibid.*

and widespread as the American Baptist denomination. We shall come back to this later, but it can be pointed out now that if every church in the denomination sent its official quota of delegates, the annual meeting would contain an absolute minimum of 12,744 voting representatives."[36] (With 430-odd delegates, the House of Representatives of the United States government has been characterized as "unwieldy.")

In the second place the founders of the Convention did not recognize the interdependent or organic nature of the denomination and the fact that a denominational publication or missionary activity controlled by full-time professional workers would affect the dynamics of the most remote local communion. Because the work of every local church is important to the life of the Convention, it is incumbent upon the executives to see that these churches act and believe in a way which the leadership of the denomination feels is healthy for the Convention. Thus it was not anticipated that the executive leadership would feel a constant need to strive for that informal power which they were not officially given. This refers to an organizational rather than an individual need. While it is true that some leaders strive for power because they do not gain enough personal satisfaction from their official status, it has been necessary apart from this personal motivation for the executives to gain a degree of power which is commensurate with the extent of their responsibility.

In the third place, the founders did not anticipate the potential influence of the executives when they utilized nothing more than the limited official authority that was given them. The right to direct the affairs of an agency whose capital value may exceed by two or three times the yearly budget of the entire Convention has obvious implications for the power of the executives of that organization.[37] When such

36 This figure is based on the number of churches cooperating with the Convention in 1956, namely 6,372, and on the basis of the bylaw which states that "voting members shall consist of two delegates and one additional delegate for every one hundred members above the first one hundred, appointed by any cooperating church from its own membership. . . . " (*Annual*, 1956, pp. 13, 41.)

37 For example, The Home Mission Society listed $26,047,706 on the

administrative authority is combined with charismatic authority, as in the case of the executive mentioned above, the power of the individual may attain almost irresistible proportions.

There appears to be an interesting disjunction at this point. On the one hand, the various executives may achieve extreme power over the affairs of the Convention; on the other, there is no one who possesses the kind of authority for coordination which is necessary for the work of the denomination and for the guidance of the leaders. Because their official authority is limited to the administration of their agencies and is not supposed to flow over into the work of any other organization of the Convention, the structural form of the denomination resembles what one executive called "a hydra-headed monster."[38] Like the beasts of mythical literature, the heads are often found in conflict with one another at the expense of the body.

It will be noted in more detail below that no executive obtains unmodified power. In their daily activities they tend to check and balance one another. There has been a change in degree, but there has been no material change since the inception of the Convention in their conflicts for their "rightful" portion of the "unified budget."[39] The constant strife over the budget apportionment is reflected in many of the decisions of the secretaries. Cooperation is a desirable thing between the agencies but only so long as the successful work of one agency does not detract from the program of the others. Because of this competitive tension, it requires an unusually gifted personality to rise above the level of his peers. However, this has happened in the past and several executive leaders believe there is another "personality boy" appearing in the higher reaches of the second echelon.[40]

There are other powerful forces which tend to restrain and limit the activities of the secretaries. The action of the execu-

---

asset side of their balance sheet in 1956. The unified budget for the Convention for 1957 was $8,764,527. (*Annual*, 1956, pp. 310, 63.)

[38] Interview with an assistant secretary.

[39] Interviews with a member of the Budget Research Committee and an executive secretary.

[40] Personal interviews.

tives is kept in bounds by their fear of group pressures. Actually, these pressures can be very great, or even oppressive, from the point of view of the executive leadership. The result is that countervailing pressure groups are formed to balance the original forces, until the denomination consists of a myriad of power blocs of national executives, state secretaries, conservative ministers, liberal ministers, wealthy laymen, rural church workers, city secretaries, social action advocates, political reactionaries, and many others.

Most people who are active within the denomination will belong to more than one of these groups, thus complicating the inter-group relations. But there is a tendency for the groups to form sympathetic constellations as particular issues arise; and, by virtue of this fact, larger power blocs will be formed on a temporary basis. For example, during critical phases of a theological conflict the groups will probably coagulate around the "conservative" and "liberal'" nuclei. On the issue of "Churches for New Frontiers," tension arose between those who wanted funds to be used for areas of slum disintegration and those in favor of middle-class churches. In this case, the blocs would assume a new alignment, perhaps some of the executives uniting with proponents of social action and city mission men, as against those who believed the denomination should be strengthened with new, higher-status churches before it extended its benevolent activities. All of these political relations are informal but essential for the work of the denomination because there exists no official means for supporting the activity of the executives when they are met by an effective opposition bloc. From one point of view denominational politics becomes the basis for reinforcing or opposing the decisions of the leaders, decisions which are made in the national offices during the year and confirmed by the gathering of the delegates at the annual Conventions. It is because this process of approval is necessary for the continued activity of the denomination that the claim is generally made that the Baptists are a democratic group. But if an informed constituency is one of the requisites of a democratic order, the Baptists can make no strong claim at this point. This problem will be discussed more fully in a succeeding section.

The Pragmatic Authority of the
Executive Leadership

According to the official procedures of the American Baptist Convention, the general directive policies for the Convention are initiated within the local churches. While it is not expected that the scattered congregations will formulate or implement specific aspects of a general policy decision, all important decisions formulated at the state or national level are theoretically supposed to be referred back to the local churches for final approval. As in most denominational organizations which attempt to maintain a semblance of democracy, policies are ostensibly formulated by the delegated representatives of the churches, even though it is recognized by the constituency that policy implementation must be carried on by the professional personnel. Any major alterations of policy and ultimate approval for all policies must be presented to the Convention's delegates for consideration. Most Baptists who are active in Convention affairs seem fully aware and are content with the fact that policy decisions cannot always follow this arduous and inefficient route. Therefore, at least when the Convention is not in session, the boards of managers of the various agencies are permitted to make these decisions. Writing on this subject, Mayer says: "Though the local church still retains its autonomy, the Convention is now so organized that duly elected delegates through interlocking boards conduct the various activities formerly conducted by the various societies."[41]

This statement is in error at several points. The local church is not really autonomous; the delegates are seldom "duly elected"; the boards are not interlocking in the classical sense of that term; and the delegates do not actually "conduct the various activities" of the Convention. However, Mayer

[41] Mayer, *op.cit.*, p. 268.

was no better or less informed than the average Baptist; in fact, he derived his information from Baptist sources.[42]

Officially, the activity of the Convention is to be guided by the local churches by means of the delegated representatives. The staff personnel are simply hired to follow the directives which issue from the delegates and to implement the formulated policies. Most leaders who were interviewed explained the workings of the Convention in this way and affirmed their belief in the system. However, all agreed that "it is not a very efficient system." In the opinion of the executives, lack of efficiency seems to arise primarily from faults in the inter-organizational arrangements. "If the societies could just get together and forget their differences, we might be able to work something out with the state secretaries and the General Council."[43]

Among the younger men who were interviewed there is a tendency to believe that the people do not have adequate opportunity to participate in the affairs of the Convention. Oftentimes this was followed by a comment on the merits of a "representational method such as the Presbyterians have." The older and more established executives deplored lack of lay participation, but only one mentioned associational representation as a desirable goal.[44] Whenever this was suggested as a solution the retort would be, "but that's Presbyterian. It is hardly democratic." Most Baptists seem in agreement that the Presbyterians have the "second best method," but that their policy is formed at the top levels and is then carried to the churches, where there is no opportunity for the decisions to be modified. One executive said, "freedom is lost in this way. Guidance comes from the 'professionals' rather than from the 'amateurs' in the local churches who are guided by the Holy Spirit." (He did not explain why the Holy Spirit prefers amateurs.)

---

[42] No citation is given for the quotation Mayer used above. Most of his primary sources represent the conservative wing of the denomination, probably because these are the most readily available publications. (*Ibid.*, pp. 261ff.)

[43] Interview with an associate secretary.

[44] Interview with an executive of a sub-committee of the Convention.

Although the original charter of the Convention mentions "unity" as one of the three goals of the organizational movement, cooperation is seldom mentioned as an end-in-itself in official Baptist literature. The primary reason Baptist churches cooperate with one another through the national agencies is to expedite the missionary and evangelistic work of the denomination. Such phrases as unity, fellowship, and "the great Baptist family" are usually used in association with the implementation of some other goal: "The great mass of Baptist churches have realized the necessity of cooperation, in order that every church, however small, may have a share in missions, in order that overlapping and neglect may be avoided as much as possible, and in order that educational and other projects that demand, in terms of money and personnel, more than any local church can supply, may be properly taken care of."[45]

It is generally admitted by the leadership of the denomination that the local church has lost much of its cherished autonomy, and as a result a significant power as the initiator of policy, a power that it probably has not had in any significant sense since the formation of the Triennial Convention in 1814. The leadership recognizes the travesty of full local autonomy, but there seems to be a general hesitancy to publish this fact to the constituency. The semi-official literature which emerges in mimeographed form from the various organizational and theological conferences often contains realistic appraisals of the situation of the modern local church, i.e., dependent upon the Convention for its meaningful existence. But this kind of literature is never widely distributed throughout the denomination.

Even in the semi-official literature it is not observed that policy-making authority has passed out of the hands of the delegates to the Convention and even from control by the boards of managers of the agencies. There is a division of interpretation at this point. It is hard to discover what role vested interest plays in the statements of the leadership, but

[45] Pruden, *Basic Papers*, *op.cit.*, p. 19.

most non-professional leaders want to believe that the boards still have control over the policy-making functions of the agencies of the Convention. Thus the majority of the leaders, both executive and non-executive, publicly insist that the policy-making authority is only once-removed from the purview of the local churches. Pruden, a past President of the Convention, says, "one must admit that a church, in working through a board, has virtually delegated parts of its authority to that board."[46] He further believes that such delegation of authority is "essential to an effective obedience to the Lord of missions," and constitutes a "necessary limitation of the independence of the local church."[47] But in his view the locus of authority still remains with the churches. The churches delegated the authority in the first place and have the full right to terminate that delegated authority at any time which they see fit: "Under the Baptist system the boards and their officials are necessarily the servants of the churches, not their masters. To give up authority once for all would be, not a justifiable limitation, but a violation of the autonomy of the church."[48]

Thus most denominational leaders, other than a minority of the professional staff, believe that the policy-making authority rests, at least indirectly, with the delegates from the churches. For obvious reasons, the minority is unwilling to make a public statement to the effect that they have the greatest influence within the denomination. The non-professional leadership clearly believes in the limitation of the authority of the professionals, a belief that does not appear in accord with the facts: "The authority thus entrusted to the boards and their officials is limited to the administration of the work in question, and in no wise gives them authority over the churches themselves. . . . If a church does not fulfill what would seem to be its moral obligations over against a mission board, the board has no means of coercion. . . . Our entire system is based upon the assumption that churches of regenerated believers will be sensitive to the promptings of the Spirit and will do their proper share voluntarily."[49]

[46] *Ibid.*   [47] *Ibid.*   [48] *Ibid.*, p. 20.   [49] *Ibid.*

This expresses a belief that seems to be widely held among modern Baptists. The Holy Spirit works only at the level of the local communion; seldom, if ever, does the Spirit move through the efforts of the state or national boards. Thus a dichotomy is established between the associational groups and the local congregations. An essential difference is declared with respect to the nature of the two groups. The result is a tendency toward the total secularization of the associational agencies, but, on the other hand, an idealization of the spiritual potential of the local communions.[50]

If, however, the Baptists are justified in their spiritualization of the local communion, and if only the "churches of regenerate believers can be sensitive to the promptings of the Spirit," they are correct in their insistence that it is absolutely incumbent upon the associational and national leaders to wait upon the direction of the churches for all important ecclesiastical decisions. But two problems remain. A theological question must be asked with regard to the tendency to apotheosize the local church, especially when it results in the secularization or "de-spiritualization" of the associational religious groups. The second problem, which involves the authority of the executive secretaries, is not unrelated to the first. It is impossible for an individual or group to operate responsibly within any social system without some degree of power, especially if one is assigned the role of leader. Within a religious group this power must include theological justification. It is necessary, therefore, for the leaders of the Convention to create some rationale for their authority in order to assure the means for meeting their responsibilities. Many of the leaders solve this problem by frankly—but not publicly—rejecting the current ideology of the Baptists. They believe that if God is really free to act He can work through an executive secretary and his staff no less than through the meeting of the local churches. This means that the right of the national agencies to exist must include ecclesiastical justification and authority in the sight of God, even if this notion

[50] In this connection it is interesting to note that denominational officials are designated by nomenclature drawn from the world of business and politics: executive secretary, president, treasurer, board of managers, etc.

is presently rejected by the majority of Baptists. Therefore, many Convention leaders believe that loyalty to the national agencies or to the other associational groups may often take precedence over loyalty to the variety of opinion expressed by the local communions.

One top executive conveyed this opinion by relating an amusing incident. During the telephone shortage a few years ago he had requested a special extension line, explaining to the telephone company that he was an executive secretary. He received a polite refusal on the basis that an "office secretary" could not request special privileges. "But," he continued, "when I explained that an Executive Secretary is comparable to a Stated Clerk in the Presbyterian Church, or to a Bishop in the Episcopalian Church, I received the phone the following day."[51] This is an interesting status-definition by a Baptist official, who had more to say in the same vein (used in another section of this study).

Not all national executives interpret their office in this manner. In at least one national agency, morning devotions are held prior to the daily work of the agency. This is not done because the executive secretary feels that his staff is lacking in piety, but because "we need to gain personal and individual guidance before we start out on our designated tasks. Oftentimes our work has been criticized because our methods bear resemblance to secular institutions."[52]

A staff member in another agency could give no theological reason for the existence of his functions and his office other than the fact that he was personally dedicated to the work. He did not believe he owed any loyalty to the denominational offices for his ideas and beliefs, and he said that if his beliefs changed he should quit the job or even attempt to dissolve

---

[51] Interview with an executive of the Convention.

[52] A sub-executive in another agency who deplored this perspective and who believed his office was legitimate not only because it had been instituted by the local churches but because it was theologically legitimate, told of a time when he called the abovementioned agency on a matter of immediate urgency. When he was informed that their prayers could not be interrupted and was asked to leave a message, he retorted angrily, "Just tell them God called!" This apparent blasphemy conveys the attitude of many members of the so-called "neo-orthodox younger generation," an attitude oftentimes completely incomprehensible to those leaders who have an antecedent theological orientation.

that aspect of the work of the agency. Admittedly, it is very difficult to draw the line between prophetic self-consciousness and community loyalty, but the tendency of many executives is to maintain devotion to a radical individualism. They believe the legitimacy of their office is derived solely from personal religious experience and in no way from the ecclesiastical authority of their denominational agency or association. Many of the executives act in a responsible way toward the work of the Convention because of dedication derived from personal experience rather than because of loyalty to the experience of the Baptist church as represented by the work of the associational groups.

People who hold this point of view, no less than the ecclesiastically oriented, are constrained by organizational commitments which are instruments of control within any rational social structure. But they are guided by a sense of social loyalty toward their particular groups rather than by a belief in the theological legitimacy of their agencies. If they maintain a personal belief in the work of the agency they are aware that the stability of the group depends largely upon their actions as staff members.

The difference between these two types is subtle indeed. Perhaps it can be illustrated by another quotation from Pruden which indicates the highly individualistic nature of some Baptist thinking: "Inherent within the Baptist understanding of the gospel is a truth which is the essence of the free way of life for all peoples. It lies in the fact that we hold a spiritual rather than a material view of the church. That is, we regard the church as a fellowship of persons who are redeemed by Christ and possessed by the Holy Spirit. The church is therefore not an ecclesiastical organization, although it may express itself at times through organizations. The church is not dependent upon the continuance of forms and ceremonies, the perpetuation of a priesthood, or the maintenance of a specific organization structure in order to fulfill the will of Jesus Christ, its Head."[53]

[53] Pruden, *Basic Papers*, *op.cit.*, p. 19.

104

THE POLICY-MAKING POWER OF EXECUTIVE LEADERSHIP

The Policy-Making Process

A CASE STUDY of a meeting of a board of managers in progress is the best method for determining the validity of much of the foregoing material. The official duties of the executive secretary include the "general charge and oversight of the work of the Board"; to act as chairman of the Headquarters Executive Council, which functions as an advisory body to the executive secretary; to be responsible for the work of the members of the Executive Council.[1]

On the official hierarchical scale, the Executive Committee stands above the Executive Council. It meets bi-monthly and consists of the chairman of the board, the executive secretary, the four divisional chairmen, and "additional members of the board sufficient to make a total number of fifteen."[2] It is significant that a quorum for this committee is five members[3] and that this number corresponds with the number of executive professionals on the committee.

Next above the Executive Committee is the Board of Managers itself, which meets three times a year, unless there are additional special meetings. The board consists of about thirty-nine members, including the officers and executives. The board is revolving in membership, twelve new members being elected by the Convention at each of its yearly meetings. Officially, the board is the supreme authority in the affairs of

[1] *The Board of Education and Publication, op.cit.*, p. 90. This Council, and the corresponding group in other agencies, is the chief policy-making body of the agency. In the smaller agencies it may include members of the boards of managers, but in the larger societies it contains only executive professionals. In this particular agency it includes "the Executive Secretary, the Assistant Executive Secretaries, the Treasurer, and the Executive Directors of the Divisions."

[2] *Ibid.*, p. 87.

[3] *Ibid.*, p. 91.

the society. It manages all "the corporate affairs," has the power to elect its own officers, but more important, the power to elect the executive secretary and other professional workers of the society.[4]

A chart of this organizational arrangement is quite similar to the chart of the American Baptist Convention, with the local churches holding the place of supreme authority.

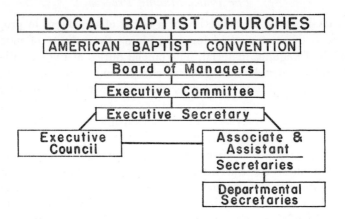

The dynamics of the board meetings indicate that a different process is in operation than is prescribed by the official charter and bylaws of the organization. The general procedure of a board meeting is as follows: First, the entire board meets and the important issues and order of business are presented by the professional staff members. Questions and objections are raised by the board members and are in turn answered by the staff personnel. The meeting is then adjourned.

The board then disperses into committees which correspond to the general divisional or functional organizations of the society. The purpose of the committee meetings is to raise further questions about the problems or programs which have been presented in the general meeting; discuss matters of importance for each of the committees; and supply the board members with general information and background with regard to the work of the society and its divisions in the past

4 *Ibid.*, pp. 83-91.

and the projected work of the future. Officially, these committee meetings are led by a non-professional member of the Board of Managers. Actually, the staff personnel who are present tend to dominate the meeting while ostensibly playing the role of resource leaders.

In the third phase of the board meeting the entire board meets again and the various committees make their reports, including their reactions to the problems presented at the previous general session by the staff personnel. Again, the professional personnel often intervene at this point; especially if there is serious disagreement as to the advisability of the policy decisions under discussion, the executives are usually able to amass enough technical information to control the situation. This process of general sessions and committee meetings is repeated throughout the days devoted to the board's meetings.

The board members of the various societies are acutely aware of and critical of many aspects of this process, although, again, it is not a problem which is widely discussed outside the circle of leadership of the Convention. For example, the Administrative Committee of the Council on Missionary Cooperation (the fund-raising agency) has come under sharp attack by some of the members of the council. As in the case of the executive committees of the societies, the administrative committee of the council is elected annually by the council, consists of ten members, and exercises the functions of the council between sessions. It "approves staff personnel, reviews and recommends a budget, appoints committees, and generally seeks to expedite the work of the CMC according to the bylaws":[5] "Criticism from many different sources indicates that there is considerable opinion to the effect that the Administrative Committee is apt to be dominated by the plans of staff members living in New York who come prepared to unload their ideas. Inasmuch as there is often not time enough adequately to discuss all measures, the other members of the Committee feel that they are simply giving assent to an

[5] Archibald, *Background Material*, *op.cit.*, p. 9.

already cut and dried program. This program is later recommended to the CMC in session, which is so large and unwieldy that it does not discuss and think through things as it ought."[6]

The executives are well aware of the power they obtain in their capacity as full-time workers. One executive of wide experience who had been a board member in two agencies before becoming a professional leader in a third commented on this problem: "The Board of Managers (of our Society) rubber-stamps everything we do. In nine years I do not recall one thing they turned down after we had suggested it. In fact, so long as I worked with this Board we have never run overtime on any meeting. We meet three times a year, and never during Board meetings have I left the office later than five o'clock. Not only have they never turned anything down, so far as I can recall there have only been two or three arguments between the Board and the staff. If we foresee a disagreement we will take our material to the chairman of the Board before the meeting, explain it to him, get him on our side, and everything runs smoothly. I assure you, it is the same thing on all the Boards."[7]

This is undoubtedly an exaggeration of the situation. The relationship between the board members and executive professionals varies in accord with the nature of the policies under discussion as well as with personalities and situations. For example, the decision was finally made at the annual convention in 1958 to move convention headquarters to Valley Forge, Pa. The issue was fraught with controversy. The technical problems were so complex that it was beyond the ability of any man, professional or lay, to fully comprehend the implications of the move. Various power blocs in the denomination were competing for the benefits of relocation. The fundamentalist-liberal tensions were renewed again, but for the first time in more than two decades the liberals were divided in their assessment of an important issue. Even the powerful Roger Williams Fellowship was split in two or three ways. The result was that everyone had a strong opinion, no

[6] *Ibid.*, pp. 9-10.
[7] Interview with an associate secretary.

one could be trusted as an objective informant, and everyone had expert advice to impart. In one instance, an executive secretary presented for the routine approval of his board his own elaborate plan for the location of headquarters. He found only a single supporter on the board and his plan was completely rejected.[8]

This is an exception to the general pattern. As a rule the board members are not so "well informed," nor do they find their executives so subjectively involved in a situation. With regard to the routine policies which in the long run are of far greater significance than the location of headquarters, the board members lack information and have only a limited time for discussion of the matters presented to them.

Of course the board members are generally anxious to revise the procedures in order that they may participate in a more meaningful way in the policy-making process. But they do not know what steps to take other than to make the present organizations "more democratic in procedure" and to send out pre-meeting orientation literature to the members.[9] The first suggestion is too vague to warrant comment, and the second would constitute little gain since the professional executives would be formulating the pre-meeting material.

The possibility of pre-meeting orientation material arose several times at a board meeting of another society. The executives raised five objections to this procedure. The mailing costs would place strains upon an already limited budget; additional office help would be needed for the mailing, or the present staff would have to be diverted from essential duties; it would require enormous labors on the part of the executives to formulate in writing all the data and supporting arguments which are usually given at the meetings; the problem of communication would not be solved because no written report would adequately inform the board; and, finally, it was difficult to obtain the data—especially of a statistical nature—in time for the meeting, and often the result would be that the material would be out of date by the time of the meeting.

8 Interview with a board member.
9 *Ibid.*, p. 10.

The question was closed with a statement by an executive: "However, we will try to make the information we send you more complete."[10]

Board members are inadequately informed prior to the meetings, but, because they are often overworked within their own professions, they probably would not have time to study a massive orientation report. This has had an unanticipated effect upon the dynamics of the meetings. One committee meeting proceeded as follows: The people were seated in a small room in the following order:

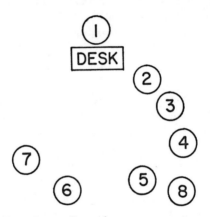

1. Executive staff member
2. Chairman of the committee, a Baptist educator
3. A youth representative
4. An educator
5. A sub-executive of the society
6. A professional representative from the ABC
7. An educator
8. Observer

The discussion was on a new campaign for Christian higher education which had been presented in outline form at the general session immediately preceding the committee meeting. The chairman opened the meeting with some general remarks about the critical need for education among Baptists, indicating his favorable attitude toward the proposal to raise $6 million for this purpose. From this point on he acted pri-

10 Interview with a sub-executive.

marily as time-keeper and moderator, making an excellent effort to understand the financial and statistical aspects of the proceedings and further interpreting the comments of the executive. Almost immediately the meeting became a question-answer session with an occasional expression of opinion by the members of the committee. The meeting lasted sixty-two minutes, the conversation being divided among the participants in the following manner:

1.	Executive staff member	twenty-six minutes
2.	Chairman	eleven minutes
3.	Youth representative	did not speak
4.	Educator	five minutes
5.	Sub-executive	seven minutes
6.	Executive professional	five minutes
7.	Educator	eight minutes

When the committees had returned to give their reports at the second general session of the morning, one of the committees which was composed primarily of college students gave its report. The secretary of the committee read a few of the resolutions which had been passed and then became confused. She said she had not been able to record all the minutes; turning to the executive who had attended their meeting she asked him to give the remainder of the report, adding, "We move whatever Mr. ---- says!" The executive arose with the quip, "This is indeed a unique opportunity and I shall take full advantage of it." The "rubber stamp" character of these board meetings is not usually so humorous. Speaking along these lines, one commentator wrote that he had received a letter on the subject from a city mission secretary: "The Council on Missionary Cooperation is an expensive, luxuriant rubber stamp. It is too large to classify as a Board of Directors; too unrelated to headquarters to be able to discuss policies meaningfully or vote intelligently on issues; too little time allowed for intelligent planning or thinking. We do not think—we listen to speeches and rubber-stamp policies presented by staff."[11]

[11] Archibald, *Background Material, op.cit.,* p. 9.

It is interesting to compare this judgment with the "official" statement of the CMC on the process which they call "cooperative planning": "The Council on Missionary Cooperation, composed as it is of a representative group from all sections of our territory and every phase of our work, is alert to discover new and more effective methods of helping individuals and individual churches to serve our Lord better, locally and unto the ends of the earth. Before any method of missionary promotion is adopted as a national plan, it has been studied by the General Director and his staff and by the State and City Directors and by various committees and by the Council itself. Further, it has been subjected to testing in many churches or areas."[12]

Perhaps one of the most significant powers of the professional staff is their ability to control the funds, to know how much money is available for various enterprises, how much has been spent on past projects and remains for future work. A past president of one of the subsidiary agencies of the Convention reported during an interview that he had once been planning-chairman for an annual meeting of his organization. He asked a sub-executive of the agency for $1,000 to cover the costs of the conference, but was told that it was not available and that he would have to pare down his speaker list. "But after the conference I found that there was $600 surplus, because she [the sub-executive] started pushing for a publication which she had indicated for some time that she had wanted. It was a program material book which emphasized the new organizational set-up of our agency. She wanted to publish it under the guise of 'a follow-up of the conference.' [Her executive superior] negated the project—called it ' sheer junk.' But this is an example how staff can bypass the 'real policy-makers.' "[13]

Another weakness of the board members as policy-makers is the poor communications which exist between the members themselves. They are widely scattered throughout the country

---

[12] "A Manual for the Department of Missionary Cooperation of a State Convention or City Promotional Area" (mimeographed, no date; but issued by the Council on Missionary Cooperation within the last decade), p. 4.
[13] Interview with a minister.

and are seldom acquainted with each other to the extent that they know the limitations and abilities of their fellow members. In addition, they are seldom chosen as board members because of their over-all knowledge of the work of the agency, but because of their specific familiarity with some aspect of the agency's activity and their commitment to the general goals of the agency. This in itself is a weakness as well as another source of influence for the executives. When the executive asks a board member for advice based on *his* area of experience and knowledge, the implication is that the board member is not an expert in the *other* work of the agency. One educator, a member of the Board of Education and Publication, said, "When I raise critical questions about our publication policies and the possibility of getting better books for our Baptist colleges, I cannot follow through because they always talk about lay-aversion to higher quality books and the financial condition of the publication work."

While there are no available funds for the education and inter-communication of board members, the executive secretary of a society may contact anyone he wishes at the expense of the agency. He knows the problems; he knows the personal qualifications of each of the board members and which member should be contacted for every given problem; and he can draw reasonably accurate projections regarding the possible areas of tension and disagreement, and make his plans accordingly.

The greatest power which the executive secretaries exercise over their boards is their ability to control the character of the personnel on the boards. According to Convention by-laws the boards are elected by the delegates to the annual convention, the board members having "been nominated by the Nominating Committee of said Convention. . . ."[14] However, each executive of the various agencies submits to the nominating committee a list of names which is usually accepted by the committee without question. One board member explained the process as follows: "Disagreements sometimes occur, but we have methods for handling them. One year we

[14] *Board of Education and Publication, op.cit.,* p. 83.

submitted a man's name, and we felt it was crucial to have him on the Board. But the nominating committee was controlled by an unfriendly clique and they did not submit his name to the Convention. We wanted the man and we wanted him very much, so we merely elected him as Vice-chairman the first time the board met. This is also the way we get around the rule on three year appointments—that is, when we feel it is necessary."[15]

Thus the executive secretary of a board, in cooperation with a few of the board members, can determine the nature of the personnel of his board, and by this means, the policies which will be made.

The intent of this section is not to indicate that the boards of managers of the various agencies lack all influence or authority. However, their real power does fall far short of their official authority. In times of crisis, as in the case of an incompetent executive, the board can exercise its official right to remove him or refuse to reelect him. This has happened but it is not a common occurrence. The executives recognize that their power is not unlimited and their tendency—as will be examined more fully below—is to be cautious and conservative.

Michels' deterministic interpretation of bureaucratic organization and its effect upon the democratic process is substantially accurate, but one important qualification needs to be made. In a paragraph describing the organization of political parties he portrays a situation which is strikingly similar to the problems faced by the Convention:

"Nominally, and according to the letter of the rules, all the acts of the leaders are subject to the ever vigilant criticism of the rank and file. In theory the leader is merely an employee bound by the instructions he receives. He has to carry out the orders of the mass, of which he is no more than

---

[15] Interview with a board member. E.g., *ibid.*, pp. 85-86. This typical bylaw reads: "The Board at its first regular meeting . . . shall organize for the ensuing year by electing, by ballot, the following officers: a Chairman, a Vice-chairman, an Executive Secretary, a Recording Secretary, and a Treasurer. It may, at its discretion, elect Assistant Executive Secretaries or other officers."

the executive organ. But in actual fact, as the organization increases in size, this control becomes purely fictitious. The members have to give up the idea of themselves conducting or even supervising the whole administration, and are compelled to hand these tasks over to trustworthy persons specially nominated for the purpose, to salaried officials. The rank and file must content themselves with summary reports, and with the appointment of occasional special committees of inquiry. Yet this does not derive from any special change in the rules of the organization. It is by very necessity that a simple employee gradually becomes a 'leader,' acquiring a freedom of action which he ought not to possess. The chief then becomes accustomed to despatch important business on his own responsibility, without any attempt to consult the rank and file."[16]

The last two sentences require qualifying remarks before they can be used to interpret the activity of the Convention. The executive officials of the agencies are extremely sensitive to *what they believe* to be the attitudes, beliefs, and desires of the rank and file. They deliberate with great caution before engaging in a program which will stir discontent among the lower echelons of the denomination. But this cannot be characterized as a reinforcement of the democratic process, for the executives are not acting in response to the freely expressed opinions of a majority of the people in the denomination; rather they are bowing before the inordinately vocalized statements of the minority groups. But the composition of the populace of the Baptist denomination in the northern states has probably undergone a significant alteration during the last twenty to fifty years. No one really can be sure of this since a study has never been made, but if—as is assumed by many observers—the constituency of the denomination is no longer dominated by economically and educationally under-privileged groups, this fact should have important implications for the activities of the leadership.

The denominational leader cannot be characterized as responsive to the grass roots, but on the other hand he is not

16 Michels, *op.cit.*, p. 34.

"accustomed to despatch important business on his own responsibility, without *any* attempt to consult the rank and file." However, due to the nature of the Convention's procedures for assessing the opinions of the constituency, consultation often amounts to nothing more than a poll of the "feelings" of the executive professionals. One executive spoke of new programs developed at the national level: "The idea of Churches for New Frontiers was inaugurated and hailed as 'the great longing of all the churches.' I don't know how we made this discovery. There is not one man in the New York offices who knows what the longing of the churches is. We don't know their needs. In fact, we show our greatest concern for them only when their financial contributions fall off and the societies themselves start to suffer."[17]

In a different context another executive commented on the same subject. Speaking about what he called the "inadequate structure of the Convention," he said, "either someone becomes a dictator and does everything, or plays it safe and does nothing. We believe we have an excuse for doing nothing because Baptist leaders must first discover what the churches want. We'll wait forever!"[18]

Executive ignorance of the opinions of the constituency is not a recently discovered phenomenon. Six years before the Convention came into being one of its founders wrote: "Of what use is it now for an official to declare that his society 'is perfectly willing to bow to denominational sentiment,' when he, and everyone else, well knows that we have no means of discovering it."[19]

It is at this point that one of the most important functions of the boards of managers must be considered. As noted above, they do not exercise as much influence in the policy-making process as indicated by the official description of their duties. In this respect Michels' description of the political process within a democratic order can be fruitfully applied to the Convention. But the board members are not left without an im-

---

[17] Interview with a sub-executive.
[18] Interview with an associate secretary.
[19] Bitting, *op.cit.*, pp. 481-482.

portant role in the life of the denomination. It is interesting to note, however, that the function of the boards has undergone an important transformation since the creation of the Convention. The original intention of the founders was for the board members to act as the principal policy-making representatives of the denomination. The professional executives were employed simply to expedite these policies. In the present situation it is the executives who are the primary policy-makers, the board members acting as a liaison between the constituency of the denomination and the professional policy-makers. The members of the boards play a role that involves a two-way representation. As the limited participants of the policy-making process at the national level they act as the representatives of the churches to the societies; but when they return to their churches they interpret for the constituency the meaning of the actions taken at the national level.[20]

It needs to be observed that each board member does not exercise the same degree of influence as all the others. There are many members who have acquired their position because of the requirements of geographic representation or to mollify tensions between political blocs within the Convention.[21] These members will not be taken into the confidence of the inner circle of the board. In this way informal centers of power appear within other centers of power, and the peripheral member of a board of managers may exercise less influence than a wealthy layman or a "prestige minister" who may never have been on a board of managers. On the other hand, there have been board members who have exercised great power, not in the official capacity as national leaders, but because they occupy an influential place in Baptist work at the level of the state associations.

[20] According to Parsons, every associational organization requires "an internal differentiation of roles with respect to the functions of the collectivity as a unit. . . . Internally this may be called a leadership role. When the special concern is with relations of the collectivity and its members to other persons and collectivities, it may be called a 'representative' role." (*Social System, op.cit.*, p. 100.) Thus the board members are both "leaders" and "representatives," and although they do not enjoy the policy-making power of the professionals, in their dual capacity they do exercise considerable influence.

[21] *Yearbook*, 1957, p. 27.

While as a general rule the professional executives exercise the greatest influence over the affairs of the Convention, and as has been pointed out, the official controls upon the executives operate inadequately, it is very important to point to a converse circumstance. Just as there is a lack of official *check* upon the executives, there is also missing a system of formal *support*. Because they lack official authority when the pressures upon the executives become too great, perhaps in the form of a dissident political group, there are no official sanctions which the executives can bring to bear upon the potential oppressors. Therefore, appeal is made to the political arena of the denomination, the same dynamic field which assists in controlling the activity of the executives. Thus, denominational politics becomes the basis for reinforcing or opposing executive decisions.

The dynamics of the American Baptist Convention can be characterized by a structural arrangement which can be charted in a concentric-circular manner. The situation is extremely complex, due to the movement of some people from one circle to another, and due to the fact that some people possess little power, although they have official authority, and others possess great power where they have no authority. Therefore, a graphic representation must include secondary circles of power superimposed upon the primary concentric arrangement. (Cf. chart, p. 119).

Michels' description of political orders is better adapted to static and rigid hierarchical class systems with an executive elite at the apex exercising almost total control over the decision-making process. But, like most non-totalitarian social systems, the American Baptist Convention is pluralistic and in constant flux. Michels' interpretation is more useful when he criticizes Pareto's class theory because the latter presents a theory which is essentially stable, modified only by an occasional replacement of the elite group by another elite. His remarks can be more directly applied to the Baptists at this point, for within the Convention there "is not a simple replacement of one group of elites by another, but a continuous process of intermixture, the old elements incessantly attract-

118

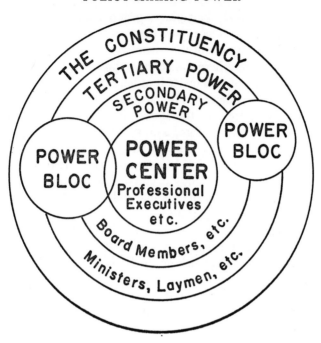

ing, absorbing, and assimilating the new."[22] The executive leaders are constantly seeking new sources of reinforcement as the old power centers disappear or shift their loyalties. New programs and ideas require new supporting groups. The denominational situation is flexible and dynamic—some would say "loose and chaotic"—but the tendency toward the development of a situation characterized by a "managerial demi-urge" is critically modified by a situation of inter-group tensions accentuated by theological instability.

Limitation of Executive Power through Inter-Agency Competition

In order to understand the limitations of the executives as well as their power, it is necessary to discuss in greater detail the relations of the Convention's agencies. Contrary to the reported opinion of the laymen, the executive professionals

[22] Michels, *op.cit.*, p. 378.

seldom form a closely knit power group which cannot be effectively opposed.[23] The report mentioned in footnote 23 indicates that the attitude of the executives is formulated within a competitive atmosphere. Since this report is not easily available it may be helpful to quote it at length:

"The employed officer has become the most important factor in the situation. He sees the Board members and other volunteer workers come and go, and observes that the employed personnel are really the chief continuing force in the organizations. The work for which he is responsible often has been established only after a struggle, and has been maintained with difficulty. He therefore has a natural inclination to overestimate its relative importance.

"The pressure of inadequate financial support is always upon him, and, as a rule, he believes that contributors should generously support the work on the basis of faith, and should have little if anything to say regarding policies or programs. He has come to feel that he has a vested right in his work and status, and doubts that a division of responsibilities among employed officers, Board members, and representatives of his supporting constituency can be planned for without unduly restricting his prerogatives. He fears the personal consequences of attempts to coordinate the work of his own Board with that of others, and frequently opposes efforts to that end. . . .

"Moreover, he is sometimes inclined to encourage the view that the work of the denomination should be conducted with the freedom from management responsibility which is commonly regarded to be consonant with the Baptist idea of freedom in theological matters. This attitude comes about naturally

[23] A committee which studied the Convention in 1925 reported that "church members feel that the program is 'imposed' upon them, that it is 'handed down' to them, and that the accounting for funds contributed is not satisfactory. They criticize the character of information furnished regarding the program, and seriously object to reference to recurring deficits, which they consider a means of exerting pressure to increase contributions. They criticize the Northern Baptist Convention as not representative, and they also feel that it is a mere mass meeting. They express great concern over the growth of what they term a 'bureaucracy' in Boards, Societies, and State Conventions. . . . " ("Report of a Survey of Fifty-eight Organizations," *op. cit.*, p. 41.)

because the denominational organizations are not a unit, and because they are not controlled by a single coordinating head."[24]

The last paragraph applies to the current situation concerning the work and authority of the General Council of the Convention. Until recent years the General Council has been one of the weakest agencies in the denomination. It operated on a microscopic budget, the members often having to finance their own passage to council meetings. It had no executive officer, a fact which constituted a serious limitation of power. Finally, its purpose was poorly defined and its policy-making authority was severely limited. Between sessions of the Convention the General Council is described as possessing "all the powers vested in the American Baptist Convention."[25] But in the minds of many council members this merely constituted a further refinement of an authority which was already poorly defined.[26]

In recent years the opinion of many denominational leaders has been changing. It is now believed that the General Council must assume a more significant role and act as a coordinating group for the various agencies. One of the reasons for this change in attitude is the increasing power of the Convention's promotional organization, the Council on Missionary Cooperation. This agency exercised considerable control over both the promotion and distribution of funds, and many leaders feared its unique position in the policy-making process. An executive of another agency expressed the opinion of many others concerning the power of the Council on Missionary Cooperation:

"They gained tremendous power over the years because the promotional work involved so many people and so many different kinds of activities. Everybody in the denomination has heard of the CMC because they contact every church in order to raise money. To increase the contributions of the churches to the Convention, they have helped hundreds of churches in their over-all work. This was fine, but then they

24 *Ibid.*, p. 42.   25 *Yearbook*, 1956, p. 15.
26 Lipphard, *Background Material*, *op.cit.*, pp. 11ff.

started telling the societies what kind of literature was needed so that nobody would be offended and the budget would continually rise. Nobody ever said it that way, but that's what it amounted to."[27]

The influence of the Council on Missionary Cooperation and its predecessor organizations had been accumulating over the years. After the annual convention of 1946, when the fundamentalist controversy was at least temporarily laid to rest, there was a power vacuum in the denomination which only the CMC was capable of filling. The societies were specialized in purpose and the General Council had no money, no executive, and little authority. Leaders who had long feared a central administrative agency started looking toward the General Council as a possible countervailing power to thwart the interests of the CMC. The weakness of the General Council was deplored: "Seldom has the General Council manifested concern over these larger and crucially important aspects of our denominational life. Time and again during the past 35 years I have sat in meetings of the General Council when its agenda consisted of numerous irrelevancies. . . . Only occasionally has some serious and vital problem relating to the health of the denomination and the unity of the Convention come before the General Council."[28]

The atmosphere was becoming increasingly favorable for reorganization toward a greater degree of centralized authority. Denominational publications such as the *Crusader* discussed the competitive conditions, and the existing inefficiencies and various plans were suggested. Some of these were limited in scope while others called for a total reconstruction of the Convention.[29] Not all of the plans favored the General Council, but that agency enjoyed what one member of the Council called a "psychological advantage." He said, "We are the only group which represents the whole denomination without having any special ax to grind. We don't raise funds;

[27] Interview with an assistant secretary.
[28] Lipphard, *Background Material, op.cit.*, p. 11.
[29] *Crusader*, January 1956, pp. 8-9; April 1956, pp. 6-7; June 1956, pp. 3-5; Summer 1956, pp. 8-9.

we are not missionaries or anything else; but we are interested in all these things."[30]

The "autonomy" of the societies again became an issue in the reorganizational debate. But since their autonomy is more fictional than real, it was used more as a shibboleth to maintain existing balances of power than to sustain an existing and necessary independence. According to the bylaws of the constitution the societies have not had real autonomy since 1907. The delegates to the annual meetings are at the same time the voting delegates of each of the cooperating organizations.[31] This means that the delegates could vote for greater policy-making power to the General Council and reduce the influence of the societies. A member of the Council remarked that "this is one reason why the societies are so afraid of us."[32] Therefore, if it is possible for the Council to convince the constituency that it is the only organization which can act impartially and effectively, the constitutional means exists for the implementation of the Council's authority.

The strains which exist between the agencies of the Convention have often been described by Baptists as "the root of our difficulties." In part, it is these conflicts which act as a restraint against the appearance of an oligarchy. The tendency among Baptists, however, is to regard tension as a factor to be eliminated. Seldom is it regarded as a source of fruitful creativity or as a restraint against concentrated power. But competition among the agencies can become so great that energies which would be better devoted to support of the missionary tasks are shunted off to meet internal threats. The pride of the national societies is commented upon by one of their executive secretaries. One source of tension, he says, is "inherent in the relationship of our Missionary Societies to the overall fellowship. Our Societies are incorporated in their own right and are older in organization than the Convention itself."[33] In the same article it is observed that the structural

---

[30] Interview with a member of the General Council.
[31] *Yearbook*, 1956, p. 23.
[32] Interview with a member of the General Council.
[33] Willingham, *Background Material, op.cit.*, p. 8.

arrangement of the Convention itself is conducive to inter-organizational conflict. Strains arise in "the relation of our state promotional agencies to the national organization. . . ." There is also "the tension which appears from time to time concerning our City Societies and their relation to the state and national organization. . . ." And finally, we must "not omit reference to tensions which have existed within the framework of our Convention organization itself."[34]

If they were viewed from this perspective alone, the executive professionals could be made to appear very weak since so much of their effort is directed toward immediate security within a cauldron of discord. It is evident that one important aspect of their work is the establishment of their individual positions as well as the health of their agencies. Willingham comments on this subject: "The relationship of employed personnel, one to another, has at times been complicated and a source of real tension. The place of such important groups as the Council on Missionary Cooperation, the Finance Committee and the various other councils, commissions and committees should be so clearly set forth that there could be no occasion for misunderstanding, friction or tensions."[35]

It was pointed out during personal interviews that the general health of the American economy has contributed to the minimization of the competition between agencies and personnel. A member of the Budget Research Committee said, "The years I have been on the committee the economy has been rising. The budget income of the Convention has been on the increase almost every year. When they request it, it is much easier to justify a larger share to one of the societies if all the others are getting an increase. I do not know what would happen if we had a series of low years."[36] Another member of the same committee was able to comment on the depression years. "The depression was not bad for us because oddly enough people seemed to cut down on their

[34] *Ibid.*, pp. 8, 9.
[35] *Ibid.*, p. 9.
[36] Interview with a member of Budget Research Committee.

religious contributions much later than on other things. So we were able to make a gradual adjustment."[37]

As mentioned above, the Budget Research and Finance Committees, in cooperation with the executives of the various agencies, determine the percentage of allotment each agency is to receive. This has been the procedure for many years and contributes to a conservative tendency in the policy-making of the Convention. The proponents of new or "controversial" projects have had to struggle with the permanently established societies in order to obtain a portion of the budget. The Council on Christian Social Progress is a case in point. After many years of dedicated effort this agency has reached a point where it is receiving $37,549, which is .0043% of the total budget and only $2,000 more than is allotted to the "Reserved Item" in the budget.[38]

As pointed out above by the Commission of 1925, the executive of every society is convinced that his program represents or should represent the core of the Baptist witness. He may not intend to disparage the importance of other agencies, but he has a natural reluctance toward new ventures which will involve a subtraction from the funds of his own group. Therefore, the needs of a disrupted world—the original impulse of the Baptist missionary movement—now constitute only a part of the criterion for budget allotment. The maintaining of existing organizations and policies has become a primary requisite for those who lead the denominational work.

For example, the leadership of the denomination generally agreed that postwar America required a revitalized city missions program, a transplanting of churches, and additional funds for un-churched communities. The executives of the societies favored a program called "Churches for New Fron-

37 Interview with the adviser of the Research Committee.
38 *Yearbook*, 1956, p. 64. In a personal interview it was reported that on one occasion the executives of the missionary societies met with the Budget Research Committee to recommend an increase in the funds of the Council on Christian Social Progress for a special project. Several people pointed to this incident with pride, but it is primarily remembered because it was unique.

tiers" under the care of the Home Mission Society, but there was a general feeling that a new financial drive for this agency might detract from the promotional work of the other societies. In a group session the executives stated that they would be glad to permit the Home Mission Society to attempt to gain support for the program, but they would not lend direct assistance. One executive who was present at the meeting remarked that the Home Mission's secretary "has never been in such a meat-chopper in all his life."[39]

An executive who was caught in this kind of "meat-chopper" had some general observations to make including specific comments on the then-current reorganizational movement: "The heart of our trouble is the abysmal relations which exist between the city, state, and national organizations. I don't fear this reorganization business at all. It can't do any harm and it might do a lot of good. I'll tell you the seat of our trouble—autonomy! Everybody is autonomous. We have little dictators all through the Convention. I guess before I came to New York we had some here too, but we don't have any right now. But every man thinks his work is more important than mine, but I suppose some conflict is natural."[40]

Every executive must feel that his work is the highest expression of the Baptist evangelical imperatives. The work of the other agencies is recognized as legitimate, but it should never be over-emphasized. The Home Mission staff will state, quite correctly, that there is no possibility of a vital foreign program if the local front is neglected. But from the point of view of the Home Mission Society the local situations can never be dynamic enough to warrant a reduction in their budgetary allowance, no matter how critical the situation may be in Japan or Burma.

The executives of the societies are not unaware of the inefficiency involved in the constant competition for support from the constituency. One executive commented on this condition in relation to the competitive publications of the societies: "Every one of the societies has its own house organ

39 Interview with an associate secretary.
40 Interview with an executive secretary.

which is designed solely to publicize its work and attract funds. Now I know it would be better to have one first-class magazine which would do a better job for all of us. I've pushed the idea at executive meetings, but as things exist right now I'm not really serious. I'm afraid our work might be caught in the rush, or we might get an editor who would be unsympathetic to our work. So we go on publishing our expensive little propaganda pamphlets."[41]

Writing on this same problem, Archibald noted the unusually competitive relations of the societies. He suggested that nothing could be done under the present organizational system: "It must be noted that time, effort and money is spent by each of the national agencies in promoting its own specific program and interests, over and above what is done by the CMC. This is unavoidable inasmuch as each of our national agencies are set up as independent organizations, perpetuating their own ends within the fellowship of the ABC. . . . So long as they are independently organized societies with their own boards and interests, all our societies will feel the need for expending additional sums. . . . Until we have a general board of the denomination, with subdivisions of home and foreign missions, education, publication, etc., and the autonomous state of each of the present societies is thus merged into one board, I do not see how this internal kind of promotion can be eliminated."[42]

Competition and tension between the agencies of the Convention need not be totally dysfunctional. A diversity of interests, and the strains which arise from them, can be a source of new creative activities if the diversities are limited by common devotion to higher goals. But the executives often fail to seek for a redefinition of their private interests, and they seldom search for a synthesis of claims which will emerge into a new reality. They are unwilling to sacrifice their present gains in order to achieve a higher goal. Therefore, the problems of one society are not viewed as difficulties which all must face. The success of an agency, rather than a signal

[41] Interview with an associate secretary.
[42] Archibald, *Background Material*, *op.cit.*, pp. 20, 21.

for common rejoicing, acts as a threat to the position and prestige of the others. One executive described an inter-agency executive session in which an executive secretary pro-posed a new financial drive for his society:

"No one liked the idea, not because it would infringe upon our activities, but because we believed it would fail. But there was no real opposition, even though another agency had re-cently experienced a comparative failure in a similar drive.

"We should either kill these ideas or support them. If the bell tolls for one society it tolls for all of us. But it's hard to accept this idea. There is more cooperation than in the past, but we still operate as though the old autonomy still exists."

Even the common effort to reorganize the Convention and strengthen the General Council seems to be largely motivated by a fear of the growing power of the Council on Missionary Cooperation, as well as by a fear of the considerable influence of the state secretaries who are on the policy-making board of the CMC. This phenomenon is well-known in the relations between other organizational types. Speaking of the tensions between nations, Michels says, "the national oligarchies are willing to recognize the authority of international resolutions only when by an appeal to the authority of the International they can quell a troublesome faction in their own party."[43]

The societies fulfill a recognized and legitimate task in the denomination, but at the same time the executives are seriously limited with respect to their formal authority in the Conven-tion. This means that the executives must seek for sufficient power to achieve their goals within the informal system of power relations. The effects of this problem tend to be mu-tually contradictory. On the one hand, an executive may gain influence out of all proportion to his official status and author-ity; on the other hand, inter-agency and interpersonal com-petition tends to detract from the prestige, authority, and power of all the professional executives.

No matter how perfectly rationalized an organization may be, constant shifts in the balance of power will alter the actual

[43] Michels, op.cit., p. 196.

128

character of the organization. A powerful charismatic personality can appear in a business or military organization, or in the Roman Catholic hierarchy. But within the highly rationalized organization the presence of hallowed traditions, the authority of the organization's system of law, and the rational-legal authority of other members of the hierarchy will act as countervailing forces which will restrain the charismatic personality.

In the American Baptist Convention, where there is an influential hierarchy that is not legally legitimated there is a general lack of rules and ancient traditions to govern the executive relations. The organization is sustained by means of expediential adjustment to goal achievement and through the efforts of the executives to preserve their status and the programs of their agencies. The net effect is that the Baptist denomination, so proud of its heritage of social freedom and concern, is no less conservative and cautious than the highly rationalized ecclesiastical organizations.

ORGANIZATIONAL CONSERVATISM

The Situation of the Leaders

THE character of leadership is determined by social conditions, existing ideologies, and the nature of organizational forms no less than by the personal propensities and qualities of the leaders themselves. In fact, the constitution and purpose of an organization may have a greater effect upon the kind of leader who is recruited than the leader himself has upon the organization.[1]

Barnard lists the personal qualities of leadership in order of importance, placing vitality and endurance first, followed by decisiveness, persuasiveness, responsibility, and intellectual capacity.[2] But the Baptists—believing as they do that direction for denominational affairs should come from the grass roots, and aware that this direction is not forthcoming— are impelled to recruit their leaders from among the persuasive personalities of the "leadership pool." Men of this type are not readily available and many of them would rather preach than make policy and administer large organizations. In addition, the individual who appears persuasive in the pulpit often proves to be a displaced person in the administrative office.

Persuasiveness is difficult to define. The best that Barnard can do is to note that it includes all the other qualities of leadership and often involves talents "such as that of effective public speaking or of exposition or special physical skills or even extraordinary physique; and many others."[3] In any case the quality of persuasiveness probably approximates the "charismatic type" more closely than any of the other categories of leadership suggested by Barnard. Weber says, "the

---

[1] Chester I. Barnard, *The Nature of Leadership* (Cambridge: Harvard University Press, 1940), pp. 10f.
[2] *Ibid.*, pp. 11ff.   [3] *Ibid.*, p. 12.

natural [charismatic] leaders in distress have been holders of specific gifts of the body and spirit. . . ."[4] The charismatic personality "demands obedience and a following by virtue of his mission." If his followers recognize him as such, he is their leader "so long as he knows how to maintain recognition through 'proving' himself."[5]

The point is that a premium is placed upon extra-legal authority in the case of the persuasive or charismatic personality. Because the Baptist executive is not supported by rational-legal authority he must seek the support of the constituency through the exercise of his personality. Therefore the Baptist leader must conduct himself where few rules have been made, few traditions established, and where a serious mistake may result in the loss of his constituency. More important, this loss may involve something other than the displacement of himself as an officer; it may result in the elimination of the office itself. For example, the office of General Secretary of the Convention, which was established in 1952 and is as yet inadequately defined and limited in function, could be eradicated if the current incumbent made a precipitous effort to increase his power. Many Baptists who constantly seek for deviant action on the part of ecclesiastical officials would immediately malign the office as well as the office-holder.

Baptist executives are necessarily motivated by a desire to assure the survival and well-being of their own agencies. Herbert Simon has found this to be a customary motivation in all social groups because personal success is often closely allied with the success of the group to which one belongs and because the spirit of competition between groups engenders a reaction of self-preservation. Another reason is that an individual can consider only a limited number of issues at a given time, i.e., a Convention-wide orientation is difficult to maintain since the organization consists of so many agencies, goals, and loyalties that it is easier to attend to the needs of one group. In brief, Simon says, "it is a prevalent character-

[4] Max Weber, *From Max Weber: Essays in Sociology*, transl. and ed., H. H. Gerth and C. Wright Mills (New York: Oxford University Press, 1946), p. 245.
[5] *Ibid.*, p. 246.

istic of human behavior that members of an organized group tend to identify with that group."[6] A fourth reason for organizational loyalty can be added to Simon's, namely, that the structural pattern of the Baptist organization is such that it reinforces a limited loyalty configuration on the part of an agency's leaders.

An associate executive of one of the societies explained how the denominational structure forced him to conform to the needs of his own agency at the expense of others: "It's dog eat dog. If I'm not loyal to this society, no one else is going to be. There are times when what we do seems unnecessarily competitive with respect to the other societies, but when competition is the common practice the weakest competitor has to follow the rest of the procession."[7]

To return to Simon's first principle, in which he states that personal success cannot be disassociated from the well-being of one's group, it is important to record an additional observation of the same associate secretary. "Every staff member identifies himself with his own society. An attack on this society is an attack on my work."[8]

This rather obvious phenomenon does not need to be labored. Suffice it to say that the role-expectations of the executive leaders impel them to express a deep concern for the welfare of their own group and its policies. The labor of the executives and their staffs has been directed toward the successful fulfillment of the agency's goals and policies. An attack upon the agency, from the point of view of its members, assumes the form of a personal assault upon its personnel.

One of the principal dysfunctional aspects of intensified organizational loyalty is that it prevents the "organizational men" from making decisions which will accrue to the advantage of the whole Convention. In the decision-making process the needs and goals of one's own agency must be weighed against the needs of the other agencies. The disheartening

6 Simon, *op.cit.*, pp. 20-21.
7 Interview with an associate secretary.
8 *Ibid.*

thing to most executives is that all "the other executives fail to recognize the existence of wider needs and concerns."[9]

Another functional aspect of group loyalty proceeds beyond the tendency to protect one's own activities and programs. There is an anxious effort to gain legitimate jurisdiction and operational control over new activities. Thus a partial list of the work of the Home Mission Society includes operations which invade areas of endeavor which the casual observer would assume belonged to some other agency:

Alaska: Indian work and schools in the U.S.

Christian Friendliness: race and cultural relations within Baptist churches; refugee work.

Ministry to Servicemen

Church Extension

City Work: delinquency, ethnic groups, etc. (This work is distinct from the activities of the City Mission Societies which are "autonomous.")

Edifice Funds and Building Counsel

Evangelism

Homes and Hospitals

Latin America

Publications and Communications

Town and Country[10]

One executive alluded to this phenomenon of organizational acquisition when he referred to the increasing activity of another agency: "They are happy to add to their operations. Then their work becomes more essential to the churches. They become indispensable to the Convention. The more their activities increase the greater the number of contacts with the people out in the field and the more support they get. Also, they need a bigger staff and a larger budget and this increases their power."[11]

Writing in a secular context concerning this phenomenon, Michels observed that "the instinct of self-preservation leads

[9] This opinion was expressed in four personal interviews.
[10] *Yearbook*, 1956, pp. 292-308.
[11] Interview with an assistant secretary.

the modern state to assemble and to attach to itself the greatest possible number of interests."[12] The political party, like the state, also attempts to establish a wide base, "and to attach to itself in financial bonds the largest possible number of individuals."[13]

This tendency can be observed among the Baptists in a description of the personnel who are associated with the promotional agency of the Convention: "On the Council on Missionary Cooperation there are 115 elected and appointed members. On the various State and City Departments there is a total of 325 elected persons besides about 255 appointed by the National Societies. In addition to those who hold office, there is in every area a large number, totaling hundreds, who serve in special phases of the promotional work, serve freely and on call of the Director or Department."[14]

All executives would probably agree that a valid part of their task is to assure the well-being of their organizations, but they would not interpret this to mean that their own agencies are rightfully to be considered as ends-in-themselves. The leaders seem to believe no less firmly than the constituency that the agencies of the Convention were formed on a pragmatic basis and are not ecclesiastical organizations on the same level with the local church. Logically, this implies that any agency should be dissolved if it is no longer meeting a need as defined by the local churches. Actually, the tendency of agencies to duplicate operations already cared for by other groups presents an adequate basis for arguing that self-perpetuation is no less important as a guiding criterion than is the fulfillment of needs. The tensions which arise within the Convention as a result of this tendency are reflected in a discussion of the difficulties of allotting program time at the annual conventions: "We appreciate the urgency back of the national secretarial request for two-hour blocks of time for their organizations. We rejoice over the impassioned concern for their own areas of responsibility. We would not want secretaries who do not go all out for the promotion of the

---

[12] Michels, *op.cit.*, p. 185. [13] *Ibid.*, p. 187.
[14] "A Manual for the Department of Missionary Cooperation," *op.cit.*, p. 5.

Kingdom of God through their own societies. . . . [But] not without disastrous consequences can we try to make annual conventions a sounding board for every denominational agency."[15]

Seldom, however, is the existence of a denominational agency significantly threatened. But there is the limiting case of recently organized groups which have not grown in size, influence, or prestige. In such cases the problem is more acute than the mere maintenance of the budget and sustaining of the size of the staff at existing levels. The Council for Christian Social Progress faces this threat from time to time. Budget and staff maintenance is a minor problem for this agency compared to the intermittent pressure for a total reorientation of its basic goals.

There is no corresponding threat to the agencies which are well established and enjoy extensive support from the constituency. For the members of these groups the terms "self-preservation" and "agency survival" do not signify a fragmentary effort to ensure the existence of the agencies; rather, the terms point to the extension of an agency's activities until the well-being of the entire denomination is dependent upon the vitality of the agency.

It is often observed that the rationalized organizations of the bureaucratic type engender a conservative outlook among its members. Michels carries this further and says "bureaucracy is the sworn enemy of individual liberty, and of all bold initiative in matters of internal policy."[16] In this context "conservatism" is indicative of self-preservation—of an attitude among personnel which is characterized by organizational loyalty and group centeredness. The pure bureaucratic organizational type to which the American Baptist Convention bears only limited resemblance emphasizes "legalist punctilio, predictable promotion, seniority claims, merit rating, tenure, security, routine, and precedent."[17] Many of these categories

15 W. H. Porter, "We Consider Our Programs," *Background Material*, *op.cit.*, pp. 14-15.
16 Michels, *op.cit.*, p. 189.
17 Karl Mannheim, *Freedom, Power, and Democratic Planning* (New York: Oxford University Press, 1950), p. 147.

are not operative within the official activities of the Convention, but are included in the informal system of power relations. For example, tenure is not a factor among the professional executives because—according to the official bylaws—the executives are annually nominated and elected by the boards of managers. But as a matter of fact, the initial election of a top executive is often tantamount to permanent tenure since the executive is in a position to determine the choice of board personnel. Thus within the agencies of the Convention—at least at the informal level—there are many elements of bureaucratic organization. When Michels shifts his attention to a description of bureaucratic characteristics, his interpretation is less formal and more readily applicable to the American Baptist situation. He describes the machinery of rationalized organization in terms of "the harmonious co-operation of individual members, hierarchical relationships, discretion, [and] propriety of conduct."[18]

The fundamental reason for the conservative character of bureaucratic organization is the premium which is placed upon the established methods of achieving the goals for which the group was founded. Nothing is permitted which will detract from the apparent achievement of the original goals. Real achievement is not important so long as objective and impressive results are continually presented to the constituency. Thus the legitimacy of the organization will not be questioned and no effort made to eliminate it or alter its structure. The turnover of personnel, the advent of a new administration, and all other disruptive forces must be stabilized and controlled in terms which will ensure the efficient operation of the group. The effort, however, to stabilize the process of organizational coordination results in the displacement of the original goals by the methods of bureaucratic procedure. "Thus, from a means, the organization becomes an end."[19] The results are paradoxical since the goals which the organization was created to achieve tend to be displaced by the goal of organizational self-perpetuation. Philip Selznick speaks of this process

---

[18] Michels, *op.cit.*, p. 373.   [19] *Ibid.*, p. 373.

in terms of "organizational imperatives." The organization creates needs of its own which must be met before the group can attend to the goals for which it was established: "We can say that once having taken the organizational road we are committed to action which will fulfill the requirements of order, discipline, unity, defense, and consent. These imperatives may demand measures of adaptation unforeseen by the initiators of the action, and may, indeed, result in a deflection of their original goals."[20]

When Baptist leaders think of the work of missions, education, publications, or ministerial benefits, they must think in terms of the agencies which carry on these activities and of the organizational procedures which have been established. There is no possible way of organizing to achieve a goal and at the same time avoid the demands of organizational imperatives. The Baptists in local churches, when they consider the missionary enterprise, must necessarily accept the interpretation given them by the professional workers. It is not a false interpretation but neither is it derived from first-hand experience. The executives tend to interpret the mission work in terms of impressive budgets, numbers of missionaries, quantitative analysis of annual conversions, the world situation as viewed by a secretary in New York, public relations and personnel problems, and organizational difficulties.[21] In this context a public relations executive explained his technique for communicating the work of the agencies to the churches: "It is our job to interpret the work of the missionary societies in terms of what they need. We're trying to raise money to support programs, and the best way to do that is to talk about 'your Baptist missionaries and your Baptist organization' and what they are doing. It does not help to talk about pathetic situations in foreign lands. People hear about that all the time—they're hardened."[22]

On the one hand, the executives are dismayed because laymen do not have an accurate and up-to-date knowledge of the

20 Selznick, *op.cit.*, p. 256.
21 *Yearbook*, 1956, pp. 242ff., 523ff., 214, 211, 233f., 239, *passim.*
22 Interview with an assistant secretary.

missionary work and the postwar alterations in mission philosophy; on the other hand the executives are convinced that in order to fulfill organizational imperatives it is necessary to adjust the information on missionary work to conform to the latest fund-raising techniques.

In any organizational environment, shifts in commitments occur as an agency advances in complexity and influence. The security or status of an organization never fully satisfies the personnel; therefore the survival of the organization becomes the primary goal. The original purposes for which it was organized may maintain their relevance in the minds of the executive leaders, but these purposes tend to become a means for supporting and assuring the continued existence of the agency. This means that all activities which do not assure the continued life and growth of the agency are to be avoided. Under these conditions reassessment of activity-goals is accomplished within a context of organizational well-being rather than an evaluation of social conditions in the mission fields.

It has been indicated above that one of the original purposes for which the Convention was created was a renewal of the support of the ministry to the immigrants and the urban slum dwellers. In 1952 the Home Mission Society launched a publicity campaign for the support of a "church extension program." Attention was given to the sub-standard communities, that is, to areas where no material benefit was likely to accrue to the advantage of the agency.[23] But equal, if not greater, attention was given to those areas "where Baptists are not served by a Baptist church," and where there are people "who in the past have paid no attention to the church, but . . . have a new readiness to listen to its appeal."[24] On this subject one editorial said that the extension program is necessary not only "to meet the needs of hundreds of new communities that have been established by the constantly shifting population," but also, "enlightened self-interest makes such a Church Exten-

[23] G. Pitt Beers, "The Past Challenges the Future," *Missions*, 150 (April 1953), p. 20.
[24] *Ibid.*

sion Campaign an inescapable obligation for the future of the American Baptist Convention."[25]

This tendency to move from an almost total concern for the indigent to an anxiety involving "enlightened self-interest" is commonly attributed to the movement of all former sect groups toward a position of greater social prestige. In addition to the quest for communal status, it appears that organizational imperatives play an important role in the hastening of this process. The deflection from original goals mentioned by Selznick occurs at every level of the Convention, as can be seen from the following incident.

Younger men in the lower echelons of the Home Mission and City Societies indicate a dissatisfaction with the work of the agencies. They are stimulated by a belief that the societies are distorting the original imperatives. Fear of disciplinary sanctions, however, prevents an active protest. A sub-executive in one of the city missions referred to an instance when the executive secretary proposed a site for a children's day camp which could be conveniently located near a public housing zone. The board of managers disagreed and an executive from New York was called in to mediate. He supported the board and told the sub-executive: "We must not raise too much fuss on the small issues because these men support our work in the whole area. If we don't have a day-camp for their children we may not get financial support for anything."[26]

Not all people who are associated with the work of the agencies obey the requirements of order, discipline, and consent. But consistent refusal to bow before these commitments often results in a complete severance of one's relation to the Convention. In reference to such an individual, one young executive said, "it's people like R----- who always seem to leave the Convention." The man in question was interviewed later and his comments were heated: "The church extension program has been horrible. The Convention leaders are scared stiff. Many of the new churches on Long Island have been extremely conservative, even insisting on immersion for full

25 W. B. Lipphard, *Missions*, 150 (March 1952), p. 170.
26 Personal interview.

membership. But the executives are afraid to oppose them. They don't want to lose their support."[27]

Many Baptist leaders deplore the steady loss of trained ministers to other denominations, but no one has studied the nature of the motivation of the departing individuals. Certainly, with some it has been the theological controversies and the quandary of the Convention officials as to the most propitious method for handling the situation. With at least a few others, their departure has been precipitated by the conservative nature of a national organization more devoted to organizational imperatives than to social needs.

It is not clear that the loss of these "dissident" individuals is deplored by the national leadership. Speaking again of Mr. R one sub-executive said that "everybody in these offices agreed that it was extremely unfortunate that he left the Baptists. But in the year prior to his leaving, there was a job available which he would have been willing to take. . . . When I asked why it was offered to another man he was described as being 'more aware of Baptist distinctives and loyal to them.' " It can be understood why Mr. R was permitted to leave the denominational work if he voiced his concerns to the executives as he did during a personal interview: "Programming at the national level has been mediocre in design and intent. The aim is to satisfy the most conservative churches. We even have to keep the Southern Baptists happy to prevent them from finding ammunition to use in the explosive situation in southern California. But the New York office doesn't worry about the strong liberal churches. The assumption is that they will not leave the Convention and will make out adequately on their own. This hasn't been the case. They remain where they were ten or twenty years ago because they've had no intelligent guidance from the Convention."

This kind of situation, of course, is not confined to the Baptists. It occurs within all of the American denominations as they continue to rationalize their organizational structure: "Thus one unavowed and usually disavowed purpose of the

27 Interview with a former Baptist minister.

denominational church is to hold intact, at times seemingly at any cost, the organization itself. This interest is consistent with, in fact partly the unanticipated consequence of, the presence of a self-perpetuating bureaucracy."[28]

Some of the professional staff members deviate considerably from the generalized portrait which has been presented. There appears to be a direct relationship between the status of an agency in the Convention and the security and prestige of its personnel. If an agency is favorably regarded by the constituency, the executives enjoy greater freedom of action, their opinions are widely respected, and they may have an informal influence which far exceeds their official privilege. On the other hand, if the status of an agency is insecure, undefined, in flux, and generally unacceptable to the constituency, the corresponding status of its personnel will be placed in jeopardy. They will view their role as one which demands caution and a greater willingness to compromise, and the status and influence of the agency will undergo further diminution.

A board member of one of the missionary societies offered the Ministers and Missionaries Benefit Board as an example of the secure agency. This is the retirement board of the Convention, and, on an emergency basis, it offers a wide range of personal services to ministers and missionaries regardless of their theological perspective or educational status. Apparently the function of this board is so materialistic that its activities transcend theology; in any event, fundamentalists and liberals are impartially indebted to the work of this board and appreciative of its existence.

One executive member of this board indicated that he would not have "joined the hierarchy" in any other capacity. "I'm not at all interested in joining in the Convention wars." From this instance it is not possible to draw a generalization that the less secure agencies attract the more adventuresome personalities, while the "status agencies" recruit the conservative type. In fact, this is not true. There are men who shift from high- to low-status agencies because they believe a job needs to be done. But it has been observed by leaders of the Conven-

28 Page, op.cit., p. 146.

tion that the strain of political machinations places a tremendous pressure upon the executives. Men who have been designated as "progressive and imaginative" by their peers have been condemned as "turncoats and double-dealers" after a few years in the bureaucracy. Older Baptist leaders recall their high hopes for the revitalization of one of the societies when one of their contemporaries became the executive secretary: "He was just a few years out of seminary. He was the most persuasive preacher I'd ever heard. He was theologically progressive; he could handle people; he was brilliant in every way. All of us said, 'now, that society is going to change at last.' That was years ago and no essential change has occurred in the society. The organizational manipulations that he engineered would have been better left undone. But he changed. He was no less effective but he buried every radical notion he'd ever held."[29]

This judgment was made by a minister, well-known within the denomination for his social concern and liberal orientation. His disappointment with the executive secretary was rooted in a simple reliance upon the intellectual integrity of the powerful and dedicated leader. In a complex social situation the power relations and ubiquitous contests between constituent groups require something more for the transformation of the situation than that which is supplied by the personal virtues of a highly consecrated individual. The orientation of intellectuals who enter a bureaucracy undergoes a change derived from the "pressures for action." They tend to become "less theoretical and more practical." The executive of whom this minister was speaking was close to the actual locus of decision-making, a circumstance which demanded that he translate ideal policies into programs for action. The pressures emanating from actual situations over an extended period of time tend to reshape "the general perspectives of the bureaucratic intellectual; he comes increasingly to think in technical and instrumental terms of ways of implementing policies within a given situation."[30]

[29] Personal interview with a minister.
[30] Merton, *Social Theory* (1949), *op.cit.*, pp. 172f.

Although it has not been widely commented upon in the literature on bureaucracy, the process of organizational determination effectively operates in more than one way. Usually it is noted that group loyalty, the tendency to self-preservation, the normative goals of efficiency and maintenance of the traditional techniques of the agency, all tend to oppress the adventuresome and to restrain the progressive personalities. But an organizational environment appears to have quite the opposite effect upon the few people from the ranks of Baptist fundamentalism who have been able to ascend the barriers and enter into executive roles at the level of the state or national conventions. During interviews it was noted several times that organizational membership at the executive level places new responsibilities upon the recipient of the office. The process is the same with the fundamentalist and the liberal, although the former would probably register greater surprise at the end result. The fundamentalist might oppose the existence of the denominational organization but covet a position of power in order to engage in a project of organizational transformation. When such a person attains an executive position—usually at the level of state executive—he must evince a measure of organizational responsibility in order to maintain his position. When this has occurred, the pressures of the organizational environment converge upon him to alter his reactionary perspective. Furthermore, a greater intimacy of association with the executive hierarchy of the Convention often includes the double effect of conveying a new status upon the fundamentalist leader.

Leadership Types

In the preceding section it was argued that the nature and activity of leadership is largely determined by organizational forms, current ideologies, and the formal and informal goals of the social system. But since a perfectly rationalized social system does not exist, bureaucracies do not operate faultlessly or automatically. There still remains "a large area of indeterminate social action for a bureaucratically organized society. Bureaucrats are human beings, not automatons."[31] The desire to assure the continued existence of an agency is only one of a complex series of factors and goals which determine the actions of the executive personnel of the Convention. The ideational background of any bureaucrat plays a determining role in the decision-making process; and the social and religious heritage of the Baptist bureaucrat may be radically different from that of the bishop in the Episcopalian hierarchy or from that of the civil servant in a state bureaucracy. As Lipset points out: "a deterministic theory of bureaucratic behavior, such as that advanced by Robert Michels or James Burnham, neglects the implications of an alternative pattern of bureaucratic response."[32]

To interpret the Convention only in terms of political history—in terms of the power struggles between interest groups —may cause an observer to overlook the fact that individuals are determining agents in history as well as creatures conditioned by their environment. Furthermore, a theory of bureaucratic determinism also tends to ignore the fact that theological doctrines play an active role in the molding of historical events. Religious ideas are not only products of the secular social process; they have an independent development of their own, so that they become causal factors in the course of action and history.[33]

Having recognized that the personnel of an organization does not constitute an unchanging and neutral factor within the social matrix, the investigator finds himself faced with a problem far more complex than that subsumed in a theory of bureaucratic determinism. Since the American Baptist Convention is not a laboratory where tools and materials can be manipulated in accord with the purpose of the analyst, it is possible only to make some empirical generalizations which

---

[31] Seymour M. Lipset, *Agrarian Socialism* (Berkeley, California: University of California Press, 1950), p. 271.

[32] *Ibid.*, p. 271.

[33] Weber, *Essays in Sociology, op.cit.*, pp. 269f. Cf. also, Troeltsch, *op.cit.*, p. 1002.

will contribute to a sharper, but never a total, understanding of the organization.

For example, the method of typological generalization has been used for some years among the personnel of the Convention. They found it useful to distinguish between the fundamentalists, the liberals, and the "organization group." An acute statement concerning the third type was written in 1922, some years before sociologists became intensely interested in the theory of bureaucratic organization: "This group gives more attention to the practical situation and to questions of policy and expediency than to questions of doctrine; and, I say it in all kindness, when an issue arises between the other two groups the votes of many in the organization group are controlled by their conceptions of the probable effect upon the organization."[34]

No doubt, the organization men have their predilections and prejudices. But a more recent observation in this area by an associate secretary of one of the societies reveals that each of the groups has a special predisposition. "At a recent minister's retreat at Green Lake there were three emphases. The first was evangelism—the conservatives attended. The second was ecumenicity—the liberals attended. The third was the organization of the Convention—no one attended."[35]

Actually, within the denomination there are many more than three types of people and several ways of developing these. The groups can be distinguished according to ministerial or lay personnel, wealthy or poor, large church and small church, businessmen and laborers, those with a formal education and those who are naturally endowed, etc. But with respect to the Convention leaders, both lay and ministerial, it is most helpful to distinguish on the basis of four types: the pragmatist, the liberal idealist, the realist, and the Baptist dogmatist. This is arbitrary nomenclature and only roughly approximates the perspective of any single member within a type. Also, no individual is accurately and perfectly de-

---

[34] Charles R. Brock, "Confessions of Faith at Indianapolis," *Watchman Examiner*, 10 (May 6, 1922), p. 842.
[35] Interview with an executive secretary.

scribed by the typological generalizations. Finally, no exhaustive attempt will be made to delineate a type because of the admitted lack of investigation in the area.

RELIGIOUS BELIEFS

Liberal idealist: It makes little difference what a person believes so long as he is tolerant. Cooperation with the Convention is important but secondary since the goals of the kingdom of God are ultimate and the ABC is only an instrument to achieve these.

Pragmatist: It makes little difference what one believes so long as he cooperates with the Convention. The ABC may only be a means for achieving goals but it is the only one we have, so it must be preserved.

Realist: It makes a great deal of difference what one believes because his beliefs may determine his actions.

Dogmatist: It makes a profound difference what one believes and it must be true to Baptist traditions.

THE BAPTIST DILEMMA

Liberal idealist: The Baptist situation is chaotic because a small minority of conservative leaders is unwilling to accept the will and judgment of the majority as to the proper goals of the Convention. We must educate them to be more amenable to points of view which are different from their own.

Pragmatist: The Baptist situation is no more chaotic than any other organization in the modern world. There is always a dissatisfied minority which demands recognition and satisfaction. Give them some recognition and they will contribute to the work.

Realist: The Baptists do not know what they believe, so how can there be anything but chaos? We should investigate tradition, history, etc., and educate ourselves. We must discover the essential truths of the Christian faith and adjust our polity and government of the church to these insights.

Dogmatist (A sect orientation): Baptist theology must be kept pure. Good Baptists know what they believe, proclaim it and are true to it.

THEOLOGICAL CONSERVATISM

Liberal idealist: Dogmatic beliefs constitute an undesirable threat to the work of the Convention as we seek to obey the commands of the Gospel.

146

Pragmatist: We have a job to do and responsibilities to meet. Dogmatic attitudes are deplorable if they thwart the goals of the Convention. Whatever we do, we should avoid controversial arguments—especially theological discussion—this hurts the efforts of the ABC.

Realist: Doctrines are desirable but their limitations must be recognized. Without a perspective, man cannot operate in society. Baptists should be loyal to their distinctives without becoming separated from other Christians.

Dogmatist: Baptist distinctives must be sustained and the ABC should be disbanded or its leadership changed if we are not true to these. Some kind of creedal test should be instituted to judge the performance of the hired professionals of the Convention.

The Baptist dogmatist has played a limited role at the national level of the Convention, but his activities have had a profound effect upon the leadership. The pragmatic type has been dominant among the leaders of the Convention. Some of the pragmatists have liberal tendencies, a small minority have been fundamentalist in theological persuasion, and in recent times a realistic note can be detected among the executives and the board members. All who actively work for the Convention place loyalty to the organization at least on a par with loyalty to one's beliefs. No special effort was made to discover *what* the policy-makers believed, but considerable attention was given to their *attitude toward* religious beliefs.

Among the younger sub-executives there is a new interest in theological thought which is in accord with the current trend in the seminaries and pulpits. Most executives of the earlier generation registered a disinterest in and sometimes a voluble distrust of theological ideas. The executives themselves were not unaware of this situation and some attempted to explain it. Most often, they mentioned the reaction to the fundamentalist controversy. It is firmly believed that the twenty-year conflict was detrimental to the efforts of the professional leaders; in any case, it left them with a morbid fear of all theological argument. A description of that period of tension portrays the effect upon the policy-making process and the efforts to achieve the goals of the Convention:

"Within thirteen years a storm broke; and at the Buffalo Convention [1920] chaos was king. . . . In the 1930's the annual conventions became increasingly a series of tedious days filled with addresses, presentations of denominational agencies and programs; while the real interest of the constituency centered in the exciting discussions that were carried on at night after the sessions were over, in the rival sociopolitical 'fellowships'—the Roger Williams Fellowship, the Fundamentalist Fellowship, the Conservative Baptist Fellowship. It was these informal, unauthorized groups, with leadership constantly changing, which sharpened the controversial issues and became the major instruments for the formation of denominational strategy for over a decade. . . .

"What this controversy has cost would be impossible to discover. Men who were once among our denominational leaders, men whose voices were once familiar at conventions and church gatherings, gave up in despair and in this dark period threw in their lot with denominations where there was less bickering and more harmony."[36]

During these hectic years the executives exercised considerably less control over the policy-making process than they believed was desirable for the smooth operation of Convention affairs. Theology became for them a symbol of denominational conflict although they were never unaware of the non-theological factors of the fundamentalist controversy, such as class and educational rivalries and the competition for control of the boards and agencies.[37] But theology was the focal point of the tension and at the present time the pragmatically oriented leaders of the Convention do not believe it is wise to discuss publicly Baptist problems in a theological context.

For the most part, the older executives received their seminary training at the height of the liberal Social Gospel movement. During personal interviews three executives expressed the hope that this study would not be written from a "neo-orthodox" point of view. Each of these leaders, of course, has a personal religious faith, but as denominational officials they

[36] Eugene M. Austin, "A Preliminary Statement," *Basic Papers, op.cit.*, pp. 3f. [37] *Ibid.*, p. 6.

must maintain a theological neutrality. Officially, they are not ecclesiastical leaders but administrators of church-related agencies. An administrator is not a theologian, and religious belief must remain an adjunct to the attainment of the goals which he has been directed to achieve. In short, there exists among the organizational men a "zone of indifference"[38] with respect to theological beliefs. They are not interested, in the first instance, in an individual's religious attitudes, but rather in his stance in relation to the work of the Convention and its agencies.

It will be seen that the factors which have been mentioned in this and succeeding sections combine in such a way that the executive professionals of the Convention bear a striking resemblance to the marginal man of sociological theory. In most cases the executive is an ordained minister who does not have the usual opportunities to express his beliefs or fully utilize his training. His priestly opportunities are limited; his prophetic expressions must be carefully guarded; and his preaching—when he enjoys the opportunity—should be expressed in such a way that everyone in the denomination will continue to contribute funds to his agency. Therefore, the executive professional is a minister and yet not a minister, and the ambiguity of his role invades almost every phase of his life. He is an urban worker whose Christian concern engenders a compassion for the people who live and work near his office; but he has no time to analyze and relieve the miseries within the city where he works. He is a commuter who cannot be an active member of his community because he is a travelling executive who may spend as much as eighty percent of his time away from his home. He is a local churchman who has little time to become involved in its affairs, and yet he is the advisor to local churches throughout the nation. Finally, the organization toward which he is loyally devoted and for which he has sacrificed a significant part of his life may not be recognized as "a proper Baptist agency" by many people with whom he is closely associated.

[38] Chester Barnard uses this phrase in another connection. (Cf. *The Function of the Executive, op.cit.*, p. 168.)

A marginal man has been described as one who lives in a "cultural no-man's land," who has emigrated from the society of his origin into a culture where the values and goals are radically different from those of his earlier life. This, in many ways, expresses the situation of the Baptist executive.

Organizational Survival

One of the first requirements of any dynamic religious group is the need for free and critical theological discussion. In the Free churches this is a fundamental requisite of the belief system. Baptists believed that the institutional means for achieving religious freedom was through the autonomy of the local church. But the movement which culminated in the sovereignty—as distinct from authority—of the local church tended to curtail denominational efforts to achieve more ambitious goals. Within the local congregation the individual member could still speak freely, but he was seldom heard beyond the walls of his own church. The freedom to speak without the opportunity of being heard by one's denominational brethren is a dubious power.

The principle of democracy espoused by the Free churches was based on the affirmation that the humblest individual must have an opportunity to express what the Holy Spirit has spoken to him. Freedom is often curtailed in local churches, but the problems are much less complex than when an entire denomination attempts to maintain the freedom of the individual, both to hear and be heard. The most obvious political means for sustaining this freedom at the national level was the formation of pressure or interest groups. During the fundamentalist controversy many Baptists proudly avoided and condemned this compromise with "pure democracy" and refused to join such groups as the Roger Williams Fellowship or the Conservative Fellowship. In more recent times the old alignments are breaking down. Members of the Conservative Fellowship have either left the denomination or quietly cooperate with the Convention's leadership after engaging in a symbolic protest at the annual meetings. With respect to the most significant issue of recent years—the debate on location of Convention headquarters—the Roger Williams Fellowship was sorely divided, which is probably the primary reason why this issue could not be resolved at the annual convention of 1957, and was finally resolved on a compromise basis in 1958. Among the younger denominational leaders there is great hesitancy as to what strategies to follow. It is apparent to them that they need some kind of group through which to express their opinions; but it remains an open question whether it is best to revitalize the Roger Williams Fellowship or form another group of their own.

James H. Nichols observes that democracy means more than "counting noses, or establishing the strongest pressure group. . . ." But he also points out that "democracy means entering into discussion, the submission of diverse views to mutual criticism, with the intention of discovering something new."[39] In this the Baptists are failing. The organizational men in the Convention are not interested in stimulating discussion because, as one board member pointed out: "Conditions are such at the present time that we cannot risk it."[40] Another leader, as associate executive of one of the societies, has the same fears: "Other denominations have the fundamentalist problem, especially in the rural areas, but not like the Baptists have it. Whatever the reason for this we have to live with it. If we started an open discussion of theological issues we'd blow the lid off a boiling pot. I know—we fear this more than anything else and it conditions everything we do and say."[41]

The sensitivity of the leaders to the theological conservatism of the constituency results in an organizational and policy-making conservatism of their own. Some of the younger sub-executives—perhaps because of a different theological perspective—deplore this situation. One sub-executive spoke of the impossibility of reaching the constituency through the denominational journals. He characterized as representative

[39] Nichols, *op.cit.*, p. 34.
[40] Interview with a member of the General Council.
[41] Personal interview.

the attitude of an editor of one of the largest denominational publications: "He thinks he's very courageous. It's just wishful thinking. He'll write articles on controversial subjects. He was quite proud of the fact a few months ago when he let a brief piece go through on 'The Value of the United Nations.' But the first letter he receives from a militant reactionary sends the whole editorial office into turmoil. We're not allowed to stand up on any given issue long enough to find out how powerful the right-wing really is. They may not have any support at all anymore."[42]

Some of the younger executives are encouraged by the regional theological conferences sponsored by the General Council and the Board of Higher Education. The participants for these conferences are drawn primarily from the ranks of the Baptist seminary professors, ministerial circles, and a few sub-executives of the Convention. In conversation with a subordinate, one of the most influential executive secretaries in the Convention expressed his opinion: "Don't pay too much attention to that thing. It's just a bunch of seminary crackpots with nothing better to do."[43]

On many occasions the executives have the power to stifle theological discussion. One instance involved a sub-executive who was requested to study a five-page report suggesting a theme for a youth conference. The theme might have had controversial implications. When asked at a later committee meeting if he would approve the report, he said, "I don't think so. I haven't had time to read past the first page, but it doesn't seem to make sense to me. I think we should go on as previously planned."[44]

The fear of the leadership regarding theological controversy is not entirely lacking in foundation. The American Institute of Management observed that the American Baptist Convention is the most diversified of the twenty-four Baptist groups in this country: "Bilingual churches have been common; in fact, the Convention has more bilingual work than

[42] Personal interview.
[43] Interview with a sub-executive.
[44] Interview with an assistant secretary.

any other religious group. The importance of this to the organization and life of the Convention should not be overlooked when considering some of its problems of unity. Throughout the Convention there are widespread differences between social and economic groups. Naturally, rural and urban memberships differ as well as the cultural background of memberships on a national scale."[45]

Temporarily, at least, the fundamentalists have been restrained as an active and powerful group in the denomination; this was accomplished more through political machinations than by means of open discussion of religious differences. Sidney Mead observed this process in most of the denominations of America: " 'Fundamentalism' in America, among other things, was a movement that tried to recall these denominations to theological and confessional self-consciousness. But it was defeated in every major denomination, not so much by theological discussion and debate as by effective political manipulations directed by denominational leaders to the sterilizing of this 'divisive' element."[46]

In addition to methods noted in previous sections, there are a variety of ways in which the leaders of the American Baptist Convention were able to neutralize the power of the fundamentalists. One of the principal sources of power for the fundamentalists was their ability to "pack" the annual meetings with "instructed" delegates. Fundamentalist churches which were unsympathetic to Convention policies and which were offering a major portion of their benevolence funds outside the Convention were at the same time sending a full quota of delegates to the annual meetings. These delegates were "informed" by the conservative leadership before voting on any major issue. But at the annual meeting of 1946 in Grand Rapids the liberal leaders amended the bylaws so that the number of delegates any church could send was made contingent upon the percentage of the benevolent funds that the church contributed to the Convention. It was denied

45 *Management Audit, op.cit.*, p. 5.
46 Sidney Mead, "Denominationalism: The Shape of Protestantism in America," Church History, XXIII, 4 (December 1954), p. 300.

that the amendment was a test between groups. "It is an ethical principle, and we must not delay action," was the sentiment expressed by the executive official who spearheaded the motion.[47] The amendment was eminently just in everything but intention, which was clearly to weaken the forces of the fundamentalists without joining in serious theological debate. Again, disruptive potentials were circumvented and relative harmony prevailed in the denomination.

Another event demonstrates the power of judicious compromise, a procedure which is followed whenever there is reasonable assurance that an unfavorable policy can be advantageously administered. When the Church Extension movement was discussed at the annual convention of 1953, a conservative group "wanted assurance that the churches would be, unquestionably, American Baptist churches, that they would serve their constituencies in accordance with traditional Baptist faith and practice. . . ."[48] An amendment was drawn up to this effect and was passed "almost unanimously." In describing this issue one executive deplored the general lack of candor among his colleagues: "We were unwilling to say we needed various kinds of Baptist churches. There are new things going on in the religious world today and I don't think it pays to define our programs too narrowly. But some people wanted churches that followed the traditional practices of immersion, closed communion, etc. This faction was fairly strong. At least they were strong-voiced. At any rate, the New York people were afraid to spell out their own policies in specific terms. We'd lose the support of some conservative churches. I don't know if that is the most important thing or not."[49]

This type of amendment does not hamper the activity of the executives and is not effective in accomplishing what the delegates intended. Although the delegates initiated this particular policy at the annual meeting, it is the executives who implement the policy and who can interpret as they see fit

[47] *Watchman Examiner*, 34 (June 13, 1946), p. 616.
[48] *Missions*, 151 (June 1953), p. 24.
[49] Interview with an associate secretary.

the meaning of the phrase: "traditional Baptist faith and practice." It is not to the interest of the executives to establish churches which are not loyal to the Convention, and since immersion and closed communion are often associated with non-cooperation, those who administer the Church Extension movement have not insisted upon a narrow interpretation of these two principles.

It is the desire of the policy-makers to minimize theological cleavage and to placate churches which will contribute to the financial health of the denomination. This is especially true in view of the recent history of the Convention. Statistics from recent years are not encouraging:

"Each day, since 1950, American Baptists have been losing 1.2 members per hour.

"On each successive Sunday, during the past six years, there have been almost 201 fewer people in our membership. American Baptists have been losing 10,473 members each year. . . .

"If the trend of the past six years continues, within a decade over 100,000 members and 500 churches will be lost."[50]

The losses have been due to proselytizing by other Baptist groups, church mergers, defections to fundamentalist movements, and cessation of operations on the part of some churches. The yearly budget of the Convention continues to increase but this is attributed to the financial health of the nation more than to any other factor. In this situation the executives are not going to argue with the conservatives who want churches established in accord with "traditional" Baptist principles, nor, on the other hand, are they going to quibble with the group of Baptists who want to establish a church and who have little concern for methods of baptism and explicitly desire open communion. One executive stated the situation in pragmatic terms: "We want to build new churches. We want them to be loyal to the Convention and make a contribution in all kinds of ways. Beyond that we don't have any

---

[50] James A. Scott and Edward D. Rapp, *American Baptists Today* (New York: American Baptist Home Mission Societies, 1957), p. 32.

rules. So far as I'm concerned if we tried to discover a definition of the true Baptist church we'd be able to get as many definitions as there are people in the Convention. When you have to operate in that kind of situation you act according to the dictates of your conscience."[51]

[51] Interview with an executive secretary.

BAPTIST DEMOCRACY

A Democratic Polity

THE BAPTISTS are unanimous concerning their faith in democracy. Everyone seems to agree that the "Baptists are the recognized democrats of the Protestant world."[1] Baptists declare that the polity of their denomination is "the most extensive experiment in pure democracy in all history."[2] These judgments are not confined to Baptist observers. In a recent project designed to discover more efficient operational procedures for the Convention, the American Institute of Management declared that "a study of the American Baptist Convention is of particular interest because both the weakness and strengths of the organization arise from a common cause—a democratic mode of operation."[3] According to this study the only major problem which faces the denomination is the need to reduce tensions which exist between democratic procedures and the methods of "managerial efficiency." The report continued: "The main problem then, in the adequate fulfillment of its social function, is for those charged with the responsibility of managing the Convention to bring about maximum efficiency and economy of operation and at the same time protect the genius of the denomination—its 'grass roots' design of operation."[4]

This assessment of the Convention has been of little help to its leaders, primarily because of the dubious assumption that the "grass roots design of operation" is still operating. A more critical analysis reveals that Baptist worship before the altar of democracy is little more than pious obedience to an honorific symbol. For years the Baptists have been looking at anarchy and seeing democracy. However, the use of the

---

[1] Mrs. W. A. Montgomery, "President's Address," *Yearbook*, 1922, p. 38.
[2] McNutt, *op.cit.*, p. 5.
[3] Management Audit, *op.cit.*, p. 1.
[4] *Ibid.*, p. 2.

term has a functional significance because it assists in the mobilization of opinion and the neutralization of dissident forces. This is an inevitable necessity in a social system in which so many members insist that freedom and autonomy are the fundamental principles of their faith. "Baptist churches decide for themselves. In the Baptist system—if system it can be called—the voluntary principle is paramount."[5]

The polity of the Christian Church cannot be evaluated solely by the principles of a political theory. P. T. Forsyth noted the tendency of the Free Church, guided as it is by the principles of liberty and democracy, to attack clericalism and ecclesiasticism, rather than to engage in a development of its own ministry and its own theology of the church: "It is in danger of overdoing its protest against a false Church, of spending more on that protest than on realizing a true Church, of denouncing a priestly Church till it lose its own sense of essential priestliness of the Church. The ministers of the Churches it opposes are, on the whole at least, as spiritual as they. They are as sure they have the truth, and as loyal to Christ as the truth."[6]

The tendency of the church which is oriented according to the principles of freedom, autonomy, and democracy is to own no other truth than itself. Its determinations therefore are as likely to be derived from culture as from Christ. Forsyth proclaimed that "the Church is the only society with a fulcrum outside the world; and therefore the only one that can move the world as a whole."[7] However, the church which claims autonomy and separation as the ultimate goal of its polity, so that it is exclusively dependent upon the Holy Spirit, is most likely to become involved in Christian aberrations.[8]

Viewed from the theological perspective the chief problem of the Christian church is manifested in the fact that the sources of its determination are both historical and divine.

---

[5] *Watchman Examiner*, 38 (March 23, 1950), p. 281.

[6] P. T. Forsyth, *The Church and the Sacraments* (London: Independent Press, Ltd., 1953), p. 8.

[7] *Ibid.*, p. 7.

[8] Horton Davies, *Christian Deviations* (London: SCM Press, Ltd., 1957), p. 12.

While in any final sense the polity of a church must not be guided by the principles of politics, it is inevitable that the Free churches will share the proceeds of the democratic political doctrine it helped to create. The theological thought of the Free churches is socially expressed through its polity. However, following Forsyth, some Baptists have observed that the church cannot be democratically ordered, but must be organized according to the principles of an absolute monarchy because Christ is king of the church.[9] But again, the absolute monarchy of Christ is a theological idea which requires translation into social forms and concrete polity structures. According to the intent of the earliest Baptist sectarians, the criterion by which all polity should be judged is the degree to which it successfully assures the freedom of God and the revelation of His sovereignty through the church.

Baptists believe that a democratic polity is the most certain means of assuring God's freedom, but this must be "pure democracy," undefiled by the compromises which secular democracy has found it necessary to make. If Baptist democracy is to be more than a shibboleth for the mobilization of opinion and the reduction of dissent, it is necessary to discover the new environmental forces which tend to alter the democratic process.[10]

Democracy as developed within the Free churches was a method for discovering the will of God. It was founded on the principle that the Holy Spirit may be active in the heart of the lowliest member of the community. Since anyone may receive the word of God, and because the members of the community must distinguish between God's word and the subjective imaginings of the individual, free discussion is the cornerstone of the democratic process.[11]

However, free discussion presupposes equality of access to the important sources of information, and in a large-scale society characterized by bureaucratic monopolization of technical information, manipulation of the masses by means of

9 Forsyth, *op.cit.*, pp. 12f.   10 Selznick, *op.cit.*, p. 264.
11 A. D. Lindsay, *The Essentials of Democracy* (Philadelphia: The University of Pennsylvania Press, 1929), p. 18.

propaganda, and the general separation of the leaders from the common man, the democratic process of free discussion tends to break down. The free expression of opinion is meaningless if the opinion is unsupported by knowledge. This problem faces every large organization, secular or religious, but, despite all the difficulties presented by modern environmental conditions, Baptists nonetheless, boast of their "pure spiritual democracy." Analysis of the procedures of the American Baptist Convention, however, reveals that they are not in accord with any of the criteria used to measure the viability of modern democracy.

Other essential principles of democracy are as follows: first, government by the leaders must rest upon the consent of the governed. This implies that the governed have responsibilities and duties as well as freedoms; but in order to meet these responsibilities they must enjoy the freedoms of speech, press, and assembly.[12] Second, no qualified person is to be excluded by any arbitrary measures from the opportunity to govern. This indicates that democracy, as is true of any other political process, requires leadership, but the leaders are chosen according to universal and not particular criteria.[13] Third, "Because of the size and complexity of modern society, pure democracy is an impossibility. . . . Modern democratic government is representative government."[14] Fourth, John Hallowell believes that the political party is "an essential democratic institution, and no democracy is conceivable without it."[15]

One may agree that within a political state party politics is the best method for the preservation of the democratic ideal. But it is not necessarily true that ecclesiastical parties are essential for the preservation of a democratic polity. Undoubtedly, there are differences of opinion among the churchmen in every denomination concerning the best policies to follow in order to realize the goals of the church. There are also disagreements as to which men are best equipped to as-

---

[12] John H. Hallowell, *The Moral Foundation of Democracy* (Chicago: The University of Chicago Press, 1954), pp. 48ff.
[13] *Ibid.*, pp. 51f.   [14] *Ibid.*, p. 57.   [15] *Ibid.*, p. 53.

sume the highest ecclesiastical positions. But these differences need not be formalized as developed in the party system of a modern democratic state. There is a sense, however, in which some form or prototype of political parties must exist in a pluralistic social system as large and geographically dispersed as the American Baptist Convention.

The preceding analysis has indicated that the Convention operates, at least in part, according to the principles of pressure politics. Interest groups were most necessary and most evident during the time of the fundamentalist controversy. At the apex of the controversy during the second decade of this century the area of common agreement between the two contending groups was very small. Their disagreement extended not only to theological differences but also to the method for achieving the denominational goals, the nature of the goals themselves, and the particular personalities who should lead the denomination. It was during this period in the history of the Convention that a system of party politics almost reached a point of formal development. At the Convention of 1922 the fundamentalists placed several men on the nominating committee and "tried to ram through a conservative ticket."[16] But it was also at this time that the existence of the Convention, as it was then known, was most seriously threatened. The areas of agreement were so narrow that it seemed for a time that the conservative and liberal groups could not possibly operate in the same denomination. Many men from both ends of the spectrum departed from the Convention.

There will always be politics in the church, but it is doubtful that a system of formalized political parties can operate effectively within a single denomination. In a religious group where convictions are so passionately held, the "zone of agreement" must be significantly greater than in secular political government. The "zone of difference"—that is, the area in which the group shall agree to disagree—must be more limited. Pressure or interest groups are necessary and desirable in the large ecclesiastical social orders, especially if the religious group is devoted to a democratic polity. In this way

16 Furniss, *op.cit.*, p. 112.

the Spirit can be free to transform existing methods and orders, and to pronounce judgment upon the corruptions which appear within the churches.

There remain three principles of democratic procedure to which Free Church polity must give serious thought: the principle of free discussion; the principle that no member be excluded from ecclesiastical office unless he lacks natural ability or formal training; and the principle that legislation and policy-making be executed in accord with methods of representative government.

In practice, these are mutually interdependent factors, and in analyzing the procedures of the Convention no effort will be made to separate them. For example, in discussing methods of representation it will be discovered that recruitment of leadership does not always operate by means of objectively established and universal criteria. Most of the non-executive leadership appears to be drawn from the larger and wealthier churches. In many cases, this is probably where the men of ability and training are to be found, but these are always relative qualifications, and in a denomination which boasts 53 percent rural churches, half of these having a membership of 140 or less,[17] it appears that leadership from small rural churches would probably be highly competent interpreters of this important aspect of the denominational work.

Methods of Representation

Most Baptists are not apologetic about the inequality of representation in the denominational organizations. They believe the individual must be absolutely free and that no one can effectively represent him. They also affirm that no individual can express the mind of a local church at an associational meeting, so it is not according to Baptist principle to permit delegates to such meetings to have "legislative" power. Curiously, they affirm at the same time, that "pure democracy" is a possible form of government even in a large religious denomination. The Baptists maintain a contradictory amalgam

[17] Milton C. Froyd, "We Consider Our Ministry," *Background Material, op.cit.*, p. 2.

of beliefs, namely, that representational democracy is not "pure democracy"; that, therefore, a delegate from a local church cannot possess "delegational authority"; that "pure democracy" exists so long as the churches are directly represented by their delegates.

A former president of the Convention says that Baptists believe the individual is an end in himself.[18] It is on this basis that representation is an anathema to Baptists. Another American Baptist, the late Edwin Aubrey, more accurately observed that "respect for the individual . . . is the core of individualism but not of democracy, for democracy is a collective life, and its central conviction must be a conception of community."[19]

Most Baptists could agree with this but would argue that the only true community of the Holy Spirit is the local church. The result is that Baptist leaders whose experience in the denomination is exceeded only by their hopeful idealism believe that because there should be no wider ecclesiastical power, there is none: "Baptists have no hierarchy, no centralized control of religious activities, no headquarters' 'oversight' of churches or liturgies, practices or regulations. The local parish church is a law unto itself. Its relations with other churches, its acceptance of any resolutions formulated at conventions—all these are entirely voluntary, without the slightest degree of compulsion."[20]

The Baptists are not opposed to direct representation. Ideally, everyone in the denomination should be able to attend the annual meetings. This is clearly impractical, but the Baptists, nonetheless, insist that a mode of direct representation exists because delegates are sent from the churches, not from local associations of churches. A committee of the Convention reported that through all organizational changes: ". . . we have retained the New Testament concept of the local church

18 Pruden, *Interpreters Needed, op.cit.,* p. 57.
19 Edwin C. Aubrey, "Building a Better Democracy," *Religion and the Present Crisis,* ed. John Knox (Chicago: University of Chicago Press, 1942), p. 17.
20 W. B. Lipphard, "What Is a Baptist?" *A Guide to the Religions of America* (New York: Simon and Schuster, 1955), p. 3.

163

as the basic unit. The whole Baptist idea of representation is directly from the local congregation to the Northern Baptist Convention. This must not be forgotten. No missionary agency . . . can stand between the local church and the convention. All the agencies of promotion and collection are subject to the will of the churches as expressed by democratically chosen delegates from the churches to the convention."[21]

The same committee answers those people who complain of "plans and pressures handed down to them" from the Convention. "The plans are rather *handed up* to the churches from the servants they employ. . . . And 'pressure' is but the urgency of getting the work done."[22] This casuistic statement indicates that Baptists leaders want to believe that the voice of the churches is heard, and that a method of free expression is adequately safeguarded by means of the Convention's bylaws and traditions.

Under the system of "direct" representation established by the constitution each cooperating church of the Convention is permitted to send two delegates to the annual meetings "and one additional delegate for every one hundred members above the first hundred. . . ."[23]

It was noted above that if all churches were fully represented there would be a minimum of 12,744 voting delegates at the annual meetings. Actually, between three and four thousand delegates attend the conventions, indicating that considerably more than half of the churches are not represented since many churches, especially those which are nearest the annual meeting place send their full quota of six to ten delegates. Obviously, three thousand delegates cannot intelligently participate in the policy-making process. This method of representation has been criticized since the inception of the Convention. Theodore Soares wrote that "the basis of representation

---

[21] *Yearbook*, 1950, p. 155.   [22] *Ibid.*

[23] *Yearbook*, 1956, p. 13. No church can send more than ten delegates, and if a percentage of its benevolent contributions is not assigned to the united budget of the Convention, the number of delegates is reduced in direct proportion to that percentage. The first two delegates are not affected by the rule.

is clearly unsatisfactory, and is only workable because so large a number of the churches do not send delegates."[24]

Even a meeting of three thousand delegates cannot be defined as "workable," and the method which the Baptists have evolved to create a reasonably efficient policy-making process seems to vary in no significant way from the procedures followed by secular democracies. A small elite makes policy, and the delegates strive to vote as intelligently as possible under conditions which do not favor an intelligent response to issues. Nonetheless, Baptists insist that the policies of the Convention "are subject to the will of the churches as expressed by democratically chosen delegates from the churches to the convention."

The process of choosing delegates from the congregations has been described by several ministers of local churches. The procedure does not seem to vary from one church to another. Actually, delegates are seldom "chosen" by the church membership. Since almost all lay delegates finance their own passage to the annual meetings, only the more affluent members of the churches are able to afford an active part in the life of the denomination. Those local church people who are willing and able to attend the annual meetings inform the church meeting of their inclination. Many times this is not done until a week or two prior to the annual convention, so churches generally empower the minister or board of deacons to appoint the delegates. Churches seldom inform the delegates concerning issues which will arise at the convention, or how they should conduct themselves with respect to the questions of the meeting. In the minds of many Baptists it would constitute a violation of the principle of the "soul competency" of the individual if the delegate were instructed to act in accord with the will of the local church. But at a more practical level, it is not likely that delegates who are paying their own bills to the conventions will agree to follow the guidance of their church.

[24] Theodore G. Soares, *A Baptist Manual* (Philadelphia: The American Baptist Publication Society, 1911), p. 90.

Even if the churches wanted to inform their delegates, it is doubtful that they possess an adequate method for accomplishing the task. There is nothing new about this within the Convention. The committee which surveyed the denominational situation in 1925 discussed this problem:

"The increasing number of organizations, the absence of adequate machinery for providing representation for local Baptist churches on program matters, the increase in the number of employed personnel, and the increase in the size of all programs of various denominational organizations, have all combined to bring about a situation under which the policies of the denominational organizations are determined more by those executing the programs than by those who sponsor and finance them. There is practically no means of providing the local Baptist churches with sufficient opportunity to inform themselves and to express their preferences regarding the programs of denominational organizations.

"Not only are policies determined by those who subsequently carry them into effect, but the results are appraised and approved by these same groups and individuals.

"There is not only a high degree of centralization of legislative functions, but executive functions are centralized in organizations which are virtually self-perpetuating."[25]

The Distribution of Power

It had often been stated during some of the interviews that representation on the boards and committees of the Con-

---

[25] *Report of a Survey of Fifty-eight Organizations*, *op.cit.*, pp. 38-39. Two changes have occurred in representational procedure since the Convention was founded. The original bylaws provided for representation from local associations on the basis of two delegates from each association and one additional delegate for every ten churches above the first ten. Each state association enjoyed the same representational privilege. When this practice was discontinued those churches which could not afford to send delegates to the conventions lost their only possible means of representation, indirect though it may have been. (*Annual*, 1907, pp. 4ff.) Another early bylaw provided that any individual or local association could appoint one annual delegate for every fifty dollars contributed to the work of the national societies. Any individual could be personally appointed by contributing ten dollars. Presumably, if an individual desired to control an annual meeting he was limited only by a shortage of fifty dollar bills. (*Annual*, 1910, p. 211.)

vention is generally derived from the larger and more affluent churches of the denomination. To investigate this claim more systematically, a spot check was made of representatives from five states. The following procedure was used: (1) Yearbooks from five states were obtained: Massachusetts, 1943; Connecticut, 1954; Iowa, 1955; Kansas, 1955; and Maine, 1955. (2) A check was made of the alphabetical list of persons named on the boards of the American Baptist Convention. The *Yearbooks of the American Baptist Convention*, 1943, 1954, 1955 were used. (3) The names of the people from the various states mentioned above, whose names were also recorded in the yearbooks of the national Convention, were checked against the church directories to be found in the state yearbooks. Only ministers could be systematically located, so the study was confined to ministerial representation. (4) The statistical data found in Tables 1-5 is derived from the five state yearbooks.

For example, in Massachusetts in 1943 there were four ministers who were represented on the boards and agencies of the Convention. The average membership of their churches was 1,250, and the average contribution of these churches to the Unified Budget of the Convention was $5,439. On the other hand, the average membership of all the churches in the state was only 307 persons, and the average contribution of all the churches in the state to the Unified Budget was only $686.

It is evident, at least in the case of ministerial leadership, that one of the primary criteria for choosing Convention representatives is the budget contribution of the minister's church and the quantitative membership of the church. But it is probably not astounding to discover some kind of spoils system operating among the outstanding democrats of the Protestant world. The succeeding tables offer more detailed information on the five states.

Only six persons were represented from Iowa in 1955 on the national boards: four lay people, the state secretary, and one minister. The minister served one of the largest churches in the state.

167

TABLE 1
Ministerial Representatives to ABC from
Massachusetts in 1943

Minister and Church	Membership	Contribution to ABC	Total Budget of Church
G. Bigelow			
Beverely First	1,174	$2,956	$21,194
C. Brownville			
Tremont Temple	2,558	11,572	83,742
L. Jackson			
Winter Hill	363	1,091	8,218
C. Arbuckle			
Newton Ctr.	907	6,136	27,950
Total (4 churches)	5,002	$21,755	$141,104
Total (337 churches of the state)	103,611	$241,563	$1,994,694
Average (4 churches)	1,250	$5,439	$35,278
Average (337 churches of the state)	307	$716	$5,918

TABLE 2
Ministerial Representatives to ABC from
Connecticut in 1954

Minister and Church	Membership	Contribution to ABC	Total Budget of Church
W. B. Molnar			
Sillman Memorial	135	$440	$7,598
K. Maxwell			
Hartford Central	1,738	33,483	98,992
P. M. Humphreys			
Waterbury First	764	3,613	27,387
Mrs. M. H. Mason (wife of minister)			
New London First	822	4,420	23,993
M. L. Johnson			
Hartford Memorial	426	2,891	20,345
Total (5 churches)	3,885	$44,847	$178,315
Total (108 churches of the state)	25,323	$163,488	$985,045
Average (5 churches)	777	$8,969	$35,665
Average (108 churches of the state)	234	$1,514	$9,121

TABLE 3
Ministerial Representatives to ABC from
Iowa in 1955

Minister and Church	Membership	Contribution to ABC	Total Budget of Church
H. Bjornson			
Waterloo	817	$8,621	$39,400
Total (175 churches of			
the state)	28,440	$201,027	$1,289,412
Average (175 churches of			
the state)	162	$1,149	$7,350

TABLE 4
Ministerial Representatives to ABC from
Kansas in 1955

Minister and Church	Membership	Contribution to ABC	Total Budget of Church
R. Fredrikson			
Ottawa First	987	$9,819	$31,843
M. Morgan			
Topeka First	1,239	13,652	56,026
R. Paslay			
McPherson First	621	9,633	23,429
F. B. Thorne			
Wichita First	3,578	35,597	103,443
Total (4 churches)	6,425	$68,702	$214,741
Total (298 churches of			
the state)	58,006	$401,956	$1,973,526
Average (4 churches)	1,606	$17,175	$53,685
Average (298 churches of			
the state)	195	$1,348	$6,622

It is evident that few ministers from small churches have an opportunity to work at the national level of the American Baptist Convention. In a denomination organized on a basis of synods or presbyteries, this would probably be less noteworthy. Such denominations do not emphasize the autonomy of the churches or other "democratic" principles of ecclesiastical organization, nor do they believe that these principles should be the ultimate criteria of church order. Perhaps more significant, in these denominations, is the fact that every local

169

TABLE 5

Ministerial Representatives to ABC from
Maine in 1955

Minister and Church	Membership	Contribution to ABC	Total Budget of Church
A. W. Geary			
Bangor-Columbia St.	739	$7,273	$34,869
E. J. Holt			
Auburn, Court St.	521	4,689	24,719
Wm. Powell			
Caribou	956	5,207	29,515
O. Stairs			
Presque Isle			
Bethany	170	2,110	39,925
Total (4 churches)	2,389	$19,274	$129,028
Total (290 churches of the state)	26,970	$123,097	$1,312,507
Average (4 churches)	597	$4,818	$32,257
Average (290 churches of the state)	93	$424	$4,525

congregation is indirectly represented by elders or deacons from a presbytery or diocese.

It has often been observed that no form of government or church polity is more susceptible to anarchy than is democracy. Hallowell says, "in no government does the choice between order and anarchy depend so largely upon the thoughts, actions, and decisions of individuals. If democracy fails . . . the fault lies clearly with the people themselves."[26] This is true, but it is difficult to see how the chaotic system of representation in the American Baptist Convention is to be altered when the power to change the system must be obtained by those people who at present have the least opportunity to gain power. Many difficulties in the Convention clearly arise from lack of interest and intelligent action on the part of the constituency, but it would be unjust to condemn any particular group—whether it be the leaders or the constituency—and burden them with all the denomination's problems. In the present situation it appears that no group possesses the power, authority, security, or will to affect significant transformations of church order.

[26] Hallowell, *op.cit.*, pp. 48f.

During interviews with various informants another claim was often made. It was generally worded somewhat as follows: only a few people can be called the active leaders of the Convention; they are the individuals who are active on the boards and agencies at the national level; probably the top executives are more active than anyone else on these boards and agencies.

The Yearbooks of the Convention can again provide some kind of objective test for these statements. Four yearbooks were used which spanned a ten-year period: 1946, 1949, 1952, and 1955. The purpose of the study was to discover how many people were on the boards of the Convention during the ten-year period, how many boards each of them was on, and what kind of people were on the various boards. It was found that there were 1,487 people on the boards during the four representative years. These people shared 4,246 places on the boards, an average of 2.8 positions for each person. There were 904 lay people who held 1,972 positions, an average of 2.3 positions per individual. In contrast to these figures, there were 18 top-ranking national executives who held 274 positions, an average of 15.2 positions per person.

In Tables 6 and 7 the first and last columns of figures offer the important data. The intervening columns constitute a breakdown of the last column. In Table 6 absolute numbers are given. Table 7 offers the same data translated into averages.

The tables are complex because they are describing a complex operation. But if studied carefully they yield interesting results. In comparing the tables we discovered that there are 18 national executives on 274 boards, an average of 15 positions for each executive. The executives are best represented on the Convention Committees, possessing an average of eight committee memberships per person (column 3). The rest of the data can be calculated in a similar manner.

Several generalizations can be derived from these tables:

1. The closest "competitors" of the national executives are the state and city secretaries, who average 6.9 boards and committees per person. This relatively high average is due to membership on state boards and automatic membership on

TABLE 6
Number of Persons on Convention Boards

| PERSONNEL CATEGORIES | NUMBER OF PERSONS ON BOARDS (1) | BREAKDOWN ACCORDING TO BOARDS THEY ARE ON | | | | | | | TOTAL NUMBER OF BOARDS THEY ARE ON (9) |
| | | American Baptist Convention | | | Cooperating Organizations | Associated Organizations (6) | State Conventions and City Societies (7) | Trustees (Baptist Schools) (8) | |
		General Council (2)	Convention Committees (3)	Subsidiary Councils (4)	Mission Societies (5)				
Lay People	904	53	263	147	702	406	309	92	1972
Women	*320*	*13*	*107*	*53*	*439*	*96*	*27*	*26*	*761*
Men	*584*	*40*	*156*	*94*	*263*	*310*	*282*	*66*	*1211*
Ministers	385	67	262	166	288	57	113	82	1035
Educators	53	5	55	15	84	3	11	12	185
Ntl. Execs.	18	7	144	58	45	12	2	6	274
Sub. Execs.	51	8	74	35	103	31	...	1	252
State-City Executives	76	2	73	174	17	5	179	78	528
Totals	1487	142	871	595	1239	514	614	271	4246

TABLE 7
Average Number of Persons on Convention Boards

| PERSONNEL CATEGORIES | NUMBER OF PERSONS ON BOARDS (1) | BREAKDOWN ACCORDING TO BOARDS THEY ARE ON | | | | | | | AVERAGE NUMBER OF BOARDS THEY ARE ON (9) |
| | | American Baptist Convention | | | Cooperating Organizations | Associated Organizations (6) | State Conventions and City Societies (7) | Trustees (Baptist Schools) (8) | |
		General Council (2)	Convention Committees (3)	Subsidiary Councils (4)	Mission Societies (5)				
Lay People	904	.05	.29	.16	.77	.45	.34	1.02	2.18
Women	*320*	*.04*	*.33*	*.16*	*1.37*	*.30*	*.08*	*.08*	*2.37*
Men	*584*	*.07*	*.27*	*.16*	*.45*	*.53*	*.48*	*.11*	*2.07*
Ministers	385	.17	.68	.43	.75	.15	.29	.21	2.69
Educators	53	.09	1.04	.28	1.58	.05	.21	.22	3.49
Ntl. Execs.	18	.39	8.00	3.22	2.50	.67	.11	.33	15.22
Sub. Execs.	51	.16	1.45	.68	2.02	.61	...	.02	4.94
State-City Executives	76	.03	.96	2.29	.22	.06	2.36	1.02	6.95

the Council on Missionary Cooperation. The CMC is a "Subsidiary Council" of the Convention (column 4) and the state and city executives obtain a high average in that column. Their influence in the denomination is primarily at the state level.

2. All the executives, state and national, are poorly represented on the General Council since, with the exception of the General Secretary of the Convention, they cannot be represented on the council. However, since the tables include a ten-year span some executives are recorded as members of the council during years they did not hold executive posts.

3. One cannot judge an individual's power simply by discovering the number of boards and committees he represents. For example, the General Secretary of the Convention was represented on 27 boards and agencies—more than any other individual. But he is not considered by the denominational leadership to be the most powerful person in the Convention.[27] But these tables do supply corroboration of the other data concerning executive influence. In addition, it is probably one of the best indicators of the power of a non-professional leader. For example, one laywoman was on 17 committees, another was on 15, and a minister who held no professional post was on 12 committees during the ten-year period. If a list of the 100 most influential people in the Convention were to be formulated, these people would undoubtedly deserve consideration.

4. The state executives are far better represented on the boards of trustees of Baptist schools and colleges than are the national executives.[28] Lay people, however, are as well represented on the boards of schools and colleges as the state executives (Table 7, column 8). Before this study was initiated it was hypothesized that the national executives would be very active on these boards. In actual fact, they occupy

---

[27] This opinion was derived from interviews with several informants. The individual mentioned most often as "the man to talk to" was the executive secretary of one of the largest agencies; but he held only 12 positions on boards and committees, three less than the average for other executives.

[28] Annual catalogues from thirty-two Baptist-related seminaries, colleges, and training schools were procured in order to obtain the data for column 8.

comparatively few positions on the school boards. Generally speaking, the schools draw their board membership from their particular geographic area. The smaller Baptist schools which have maintained closer denominational ties—such as Sioux Falls, Shurtleff, and Rio Grande—usually included the state secretary on their boards, in addition to laymen and ministers from the surrounding territory. Better known schools, such as Denison and Franklin, had a few national leaders on their boards. Schools like Chicago were not represented by Baptist leaders.

5. Many people call the Convention "a minister's organization." But the lay people are almost as well represented on the boards and agencies as the ministers, although both fall considerably behind the executives. The ministers are represented on an average of 2.7 boards per individual, while the laymen are on an average of 2.2 boards. The difference is probably not significant. Of course, due to the fact that there are fewer ministers in the denomination than lay people, the former are proportionately far better represented than the latter.

6. Many of the people recorded in the tables were on less than four committees during the ten-year period. If only those individuals are counted who were on four committees or more during that period, there are only 333 people who can be considered "very active" in the affairs of the Convention. They can be categorized as follows:

TABLE 8

Number of Persons on More than Four Boards
During the Ten-Year Period

Personnel Categories	Number on Boards
Laymen	65
Laywomen	68
Ministers	66
Educators	17
National Executives	18
National Sub-executives	36
State & City Secretaries	63
Total	333

During the interviews various hints were dropped concerning the number of people who "actually run" the Convention. These suggestions, of course, were highly speculative in nature, but the estimates ran anywhere from 400 to 700 persons. Upon closer examination even 333 seems too high. Included in that figure are approximately thirty people who are represented only on state boards but are not active at the national level. In addition, there are about twenty laymen among the 333 leaders who are active only on the "National Council of American Baptist Men." It is impossible to determine how many people can be called the foremost leaders of the Convention. Any estimate would be no more useful than the validity of the criteria used in establishing the estimate. But it is certain that the number is low. Even among the Baptists not everyone can be a king.

Of greater importance is the fact that under the present system of church-order a significant number of people in the local churches cannot possibly be represented by the leadership. A few years ago a committee reported that "less than one-half of our churches are represented at any one annual meeting."[29] But adjustments on a basis of indirect representation are widely condemned as "republican or presbyterian—not democratic and not Baptist."[30]

It is important to note at this juncture that one of the most significant threats to the power of the national leadership is the influence of the state secretaries. Within their own "bailiwicks" they seldom have a peer. The reasons for this are generally no different from the explanations offered for the power of the national executives. They exercise considerable control over the means to technical information; they are full-time workers with a staff; they usually control the membership of their own boards; and they possess some degree of rational-pragmatic authority. In addition, they have greater opportunity than the national executive for personal contact with their constituencies, which proves to be an invaluable aid in

[29] *Yearbook*, 1950, p. 162.
[30] These words were used by a board member during a personal interview.

gaining support. They are usually responsible for the fund-raising programs for both the national and state work, and they may exercise considerable control over those funds.[31] Finally, the state secretary assists in the recruitment of ministers in many churches which cooperate with the denomination.

Representation by state or local associations has long been opposed by the many influential leaders of the Baptist movement. Ostensibly they fear violation of the autonomy of the local church. Several decades prior to the formation of the Convention, Francis Wayland defended direct representation: "The power to enforce the laws of Christ rests with each church itself. . . . It is truly a violation of the independence of churches, and the right of private judgment, when several hundred brethren meet in some public convention, and manufacture public opinion, and adopt courses which their brethren are called upon to follow, on pain of the displeasure of the majority, as when they establish a formal representation, to whose decisions all the constituency must submit."[32]

Winthrop Hudson writes that Wayland was an early advocate of associational representation, but after gaining power "it must have occurred to him . . . that to have men sent as delegates by State Conventions . . . would provide a balanced body in which the influence and power of those who had been most active in denominational life would be sharply reduced."[33]

Since Wayland's time, the occasional proposals in favor of a more equitable representation have been extinguished in order to uphold "autonomy and freedom," or simply because "no change is deemed necessary."[34]

The denominational leaders alone cannot be castigated for the failure of the Baptists to create a more balanced system of church-order. There has never been a dearth of people, influential in their own local congregations, who recognize that a system of greater justice would detract from their own

31 *Yearbook*, 1951, pp. 64, 65.
32 Francis Wayland, quoted in an editorial, *Watchman Examiner*, 38 (March 23, 1950), p. 281.
33 Hudson, "Stumbling into Disorder," *op.cit.*, pp. 14-15.
34 *Yearbook*, 1950, p. 171.

parochial powers. The majority of people in the local churches in all probability honestly believe that to invest particular individuals with authority will necessarily mean that they must divest themselves of their right to self-government. But is it not more likely, as Maritain asks, that people, "when they invest certain men with authority, *keep* their right to self-government and their authority to rule themselves?"[35]

In the case of the Baptists this seems to be true. They have appointed leaders without conferring authority upon them. They have not been able effectively to minimize the power of their leaders. The leaders, in order to meet their responsibilities, were forced to seek and gain that which was not rightfully theirs. The people have little right to take away from the leaders that which they did not give them in the first place. The only adequate way in which the people can gain their right to self-government is to invest their leaders with an authority which can be rightfully removed if violated.

[35] Jacques Maritain, *Man and the State* (Chicago: University of Chicago Press, 1956), p. 129.

THE ORGANIZATION MEN

Promotional Work

SIDNEY MEAD associates the voluntary principle of American Christianity with the significant emphasis upon promotional activism which characterizes the contemporary religious life of America: "In relation to the voluntary principle Christianity itself tends to be conceived primarily as an activity, a movement, which the group is engaged in promoting. If the group *has* a confessional, its attitude toward it is likely to become promotional and propagandistic, as for example, witness Missouri Synod Lutheranism."[1]

It is true that the voluntary principle and the disappearance of state-supported religious institutions does result in a greater need for promotional activity. But this need occur only when there is a large religious organization to support. By itself, voluntarism is not necessarily related to huge promotional endeavors. The left-wing sects of the seventeenth and eighteenth centuries are not noted for the advertising campaigns for which they had neither the resources, the desire, nor the need. The twentieth century, however, is not unique in its projects of mass persuasion and promotion. It has been shown that the inclusive Christian church of the sixteenth century engaged in one of history's most fervent and systematic promotional campaigns, a circumstance which was important in leading Luther to his search for reform.[2] Large sums of money were essential for the support of the tremendous organizational program of the church and for the comfort of an affluent hierarchy.

Promotional activity is a requisite of any large-scale organizational activity, whether it is voluntary or inclusive, religious

[1] Mead, *op.cit.*, p. 299.
[2] Roland H. Bainton, *Here I Stand: A Life of Martin Luther* (New York: Abingdon-Cokesbury Press, 1950), Chapter 4.

or secular. American Protestantism's general acceptance of the methods of mass communication is in the first instance motivated by the need to support an ambitious organizational and missionary program. The institutionalized work of all the large religious groups in America is characterized by rationalized social structures with special staffs of executives, sub-executives, office secretaries, file clerks, business managers, editors, bookkeepers, file workers, missionaries, etc. Among all these workers the promotional men enjoy a unique position. They can make the claim that they husband all the activities and provide the essential income for the work of the organizations. In many cases their position is supreme, for nothing must stand in the way of promotion. The Baptist situation in this respect is perfectly described by a paragraph from Mead's article: "Anything that seems to stand in the way of or to hinder the effectiveness of such promotion is likely to be considered divisive and a threat to the internal unity and general effectiveness of the group. For example, insofar as theology is an attempt to define and clarify intellectual positions it is apt to lead to discussion, differences of opinion, even to controversy, and hence to be divisive. And this has had a strong tendency to dampen serious discussion of theological issues in most groups, and hence to strengthen the general anti-intellectual bias inherent in much of revivalistic Pietism."[3]

Many people within the denomination from both ends of the theological spectrum find the emphasis upon organizational security and the sanctity of promotional programs a difficult burden to bear. Eugene Austin points out that the new theological peace which has descended over the denomination is due only to the departure of "men of strong left- and right-wing theological opinion. . . ."[4] He goes on to observe how the immediate and pragmatic needs of the organization displaced theological concern: "Middle-ground men were in the central positions of leadership; and the people rallied to their support because of the pressing practical problems which confronted the Christian community in the post-war period.

3 Mead, op.cit., pp. 299-300.
4 Austin, Basic Papers, op.cit., p. 1.

179

. . . Controversy—that tense, exciting process by which new ideas are placed on trial and old ideas are re-examined and reshaped—was regarded with increasing distaste."[5]

The promotional function of the annual meetings of the American Baptist Convention deserves some attention since it is at these gatherings that the Baptists claim to formulate their policies for the succeeding year. At these meetings Baptist democracy is put to the test. Most leaders, at least in their public statements, appear to believe firmly that the delegates to the conventions have every opportunity to participate in a meaningful and democratic experience. It is only in the semi-public documents or in private statements that the liberal leaders and the executive professionals raise critical questions about the political process of the annual conventions.

An editorial in the *Crusader* prior to the convention of 1956 summed up the problems of the delegate but concluded that these are not insurmountable: "Only the delegate can know the excitement of grappling with convention problems on the spot, of first-hand participation in the shaping of denominational life. . . . His is the responsibility of seeing the issues clearly and voting with unbiased intelligence—no small task in the fast-moving round of reports and presentations that will engulf him if he is not alert. This very difficult task will be a welcome challenge to the delegate who takes seriously the principle that rule by the people is the cornerstone of Baptist polity."[6]

The conventions have often been criticized because the inexperienced delegate does not know how to operate in the caucuses, when to speak in the open meetings, how to gain entry to the crucial "backroom" discussions, or how to unravel the tangle of technical reports which perplex him. Lengthy discussion of issues and an opportunity to cast a vote cannot compensate the delegate who requires longer hours of preparation to comprehend the proceedings. But this is the balm which is offered the wounded spirit of the inexperienced dele-

[5] *Ibid.*, pp. 1-2.
[6] *Crusader*, XI (February 1956), p. 2.

gate: "Since 1930, I have attended every Northern Baptist Convention but one. The charge that ample and full time is not given for discussion of any and everything any delegate might have on his mind is not according to the facts. . . . At Grand Rapids . . . full discussion eventuated, and long votes were taken to decide democratically the issues involved."[7]

Actually, delegates to the conventions have little voice in the affairs and the policy procedures of the societies and the Convention proper. In part, this is the fault of the delegates themselves. They possess the requisite authority but seldom exercise the time and effort to familiarize themselves with the issues. However, the doctrine of soul competency which assures individual freedom also implies a separation from the other delegates and the annual meetings. The primary weakness of the delegates arises from their isolation from one another and their resulting inability to acquire the technical knowledge necessary for the understanding and formulation of policy. As observed above, the recruitment of delegates in the churches is generally a very casual affair. Many delegates look upon the conventions as opportunities to renew old friendships, to gain "spiritual uplift," and to discover what the national agencies can contribute to the work of their churches. Interest in the business sessions and policy-making of the conventions is admittedly secondary. As a result the delegates seldom affect the basic policies of the Convention and when they do it is considered a singular event.

For example, in 1949 the need for overseas relief and a strengthened mission program was foremost in the consciousness of American Christians. The delegates to the Northern Baptist Convention requested the Finance Committee to grant substantial increases in the percentage of funds to the four foreign societies. The description of this incident indicates the rarity of such action on the part of delegates: "The resolution came as a surprise. It was proposed that it be referred to the Budget and Research Committee. A motion to refer is not debatable. It was promptly voted down. Thereupon . . . the

[7] Hillyer H. Straton, "Northern Baptists," *Watchman Examiner*, 38 (May 4, 1950) p. 437.

resolution was adopted. Seldom in Baptist history has a motion offered from the floor expressed so realistically the mind of the denomination."[8]

The issues are seldom so clear-cut as in 1949 and "the mind of the denomination" is rarely so unified. More often, the budget of the Convention is passed with little attention from the delegates, primarily because they are unable to decipher its complexities. A conservative journal of the denomination makes periodic complaints concerning this problem. An editorial writer pointed out that funds and assets of the Convention total more than $75,000,000, that the budget is so complex that no ordinary delegate can comprehend it, and that their inadequate efforts to do so constitutes a threat to "our spontaneity and democracy."[9] One year later the same publication reported as follows: "A. J. Hudson, chairman of the Finance Committee, offered the report of that body. He presented the budget for the coming year. The budget requires a total of $7,360,296. . . . There are many technical elements in this report, and it will require a policy specialist and an accountant to understand it. . . . This large budget was passed by the Convention at a time when there were less than five hundred people in the hall. One wonders what is happening to our Baptist people in this Convention, that they have such little interest in their own affairs."[10]

The dilemma of the Baptists is not unique. They face the problems encountered by every large democratic organization. But the Baptists have attempted to solve the problem in two ways: by direct representation to the annual conventions, and by minimizing the authority of the executive professionals. It has been indicated that neither of these efforts is realistic. The Baptists are peculiar, however, in their insistence that these practices represent the democratic process at its best. Such an ideational stance results only in a failure to become aware of the inequities which do occur. While the denominational leaders continue to protest that democracy is alive on the

8 *Missions*, 147 (June 1949), pp. 334-335.
9 *Watchman Examiner*, 38 (April 13, 1950), p. 356.
10 *Watchman Examiner*, 39 (June 28, 1951), pp. 647, 648.

floor of the conventions, it is readily apparent that the actual function of the annual meeting is to generate enthusiasm for the work of the societies and other agencies, and that policies are often established by the leaders of these groups several weeks before the conventions meet.

A. D. Lindsay observed that large public meetings are gatherings for purposes of propaganda where only the most formal business is presented and voted upon. "A public meeting," he said, "cannot do anything."[11] Undoubtedly, this is an extreme statement, but a Baptist historian noted the same sort of situation in relation to the work of the national societies prior to the founding of the Northern Baptist Convention: "The denominational societies, nominally the creatures and servants of the churches, have become in fact great independent corporations that control the churches, so far as their united efforts in missionary and educational enterprises are concerned. The annual meetings of the societies are in theory composed of delegates from the supporting churches; in fact they are mass meetings composed of any who care to attend. The officials seldom have any trouble in directing such a meeting into any channel agreeable to them."[12]

Although the Convention was created to unify the benevolent work of the denomination and reduce the power of a small coterie of leaders by improvement of representational procedures, there has been no material change in the situation described by Vedder. The original purpose of the annual conventions was to transact business, establish policies, and form an organization to carry on until the next convention. These sober goals were soon overshadowed by four unanticipated functions: oratory, fellowship, entertainment, and promotion.

In the present stage of their development, the annual conventions bear a singular resemblance to county fairs. Almost a hundred booths advertising the work of every agency and sub-agency are located in the basement of the convention hall and thousands of delegates and visitors wander through the

[11] Lindsay, *op.cit.*, p. 29.
[12] Henry C. Vedder, "Fifty Years of Baptist History," *The Chronicle*, IX (October 1946), pp. 163-170. (Written in 1900 and republished.)

displays renewing old friendships, planning spontaneous re-
unions, purchasing material from the booths, and window-
shopping at others. As business progresses on the main floor
of the convention the population surrounding the booths undergoes shifts in character. The individual delegate soon
learns where to look for his friends, depending on their mutual interests and the nature of the program on the floor of
the convention.

The sheer size of the annual conventions and the introduction of mass media such as the denominational magazines tend
to displace the convention floor as a forum for the discussion
and exchange of ideas. All relevant and irrelevant ideas are
exhaustively explored during executive sessions months before the convention convenes and selectively transmitted over
thousands of miles to the future delegates of the convention.
This means that the "democratic" mechanics of meetings designed to exchange ideas and experiences become routine, ob-
solete, and boring. Speeches are no longer a spontaneous response to a given issue but are prepared hours or weeks in
advance by specially chosen leaders. The "parliamentary procedures" are relegated to the hotel rooms and the local restau-
rants, and the president of the convention entertains key mo-
tions so much by prearrangement that he often must jog the
movers into moving.[13] When something does occur sponta-
neously it is recorded as a unique event in the procedures of
the convention.

Generally speaking, the programs are divided into three
parts. The morning is devoted to business; the afternoon to
reports from committees, boards, and agencies; and the evening to worship, music, and speeches. In the early years of
the conventions—until the year 1928, when a change was instituted—considerably more time was allotted to business and

13 This was especially notable at the Seattle meeting in 1956 when the
problem of reorganization was discussed. The writer was on the stage
behind the speaker's rostrum during some of the most heated sessions.
During these periods the chairman of the meeting would move from one
back-stage group to another to make sure that the various groups had
their next speaker in immediate readiness.

reports than is now the case.[14] Since the founding of the Convention the programs have been controlled principally by the Executive Committee of the General Council. The guiding principles of this group are stated as follows: "The Committee has pursued the policy of encouraging open sessions, and of promoting the business aspects of a deliberative assembly composed of representatives from the churches. It has been deemed wise to provide for evening sessions that should be inspirational rather than deliberative."[15]

Apparently, it was soon discovered that business sessions were cutting into the time the society executives believed they needed to cultivate their own endeavors. As early as 1912 promotional work started to displace the "deliberative role" of the conventions: "Sufficient time should be given to the various societies to enable them to present their work effectively without curtailment from the other business of the Convention. To this end no Convention business has been placed in the afternoon sessions, except on the last day of the Convention. As far as practicable the mornings have been left free for the consideration of the work of the Convention and its various Committees, Boards, and Commissions."[16]

In a social system the size of the American Baptist Convention where there is only a limited opportunity to gather delegates to formulate policies it is unrealistic to suppose that the Baptists, as distinct from any other group, are better able to sustain the democratic process through the instrumentality of the annual convention. It has been estimated that through the years 1907-1951 the Convention met in annual session for a total period of 2,628 hours. Slightly more than one-fifth of these hours (550) were devoted to deliberation and business.[17] The promotional presentations of the three largest societies—Home Missions, Foreign Missions, and Education-Publication—consumed 602 hours; 285 hours were devoted to worship and prayer; 138 hours to

14 Porter, *Background Material, op.cit.*, pp. 1, 13.
15 *Annual*, 1910, p. 71.
16 *Annual*, 1912, p. 59.
17 Porter, *Background Material, op.cit.*, p. 7.

Christian social action; and the remaining 1,053 hours were divided between fourteen other types of activity.[18]

Among all these facts there is little which would stimulate the interest of the social analyst if it were more candidly admitted by the Baptists that the primary functions of the conventions were inspirational and promotional. But the significant criticisms of the parliamentary procedures of the annual meetings are to be found only in semi-public documents which are mimeographed and not widely distributed among the constituency. For example, one of these problems is outlined in a report to the General Council: "Should action on the budget be placed in an inspirational setting? Or should it be held to a colorless, business-type meeting? For the first approach, a great address on the spiritual nature of the budget is considered necessary. That is the approach usually followed by the Program Committee. On the other hand, such a setting tends to shut off genuine democratic discussion and debate of the issues at hand. Whether due to that cause or some other cause, the budget usually brings little discussion or debate. Probably many delegates hesitate to ask critical questions for fear it would make it harder to raise money if any criticism were voiced. Few would presume to tangle on a technical matter with the Financial Committee experts. . . . And so, with only a modicum of understanding and no other choice before them, the delegates usually approve the budget on which the Budget Research Committee and Financial Committee have labored long and earnestly."[19]

In the conservative press, criticism of convention procedures is more direct. As noted in the previous tables the rural-conservative ministry receives less attention from denominational leaders than do their brethren from more affluent churches. The delegates from outlying districts who are able to attend the conventions find it difficult to determine their own role amid the ostentatious display of missionary and evangelistic promotional wares. A journalistic spokesman for these

[18] *Ibid.*, p. 7.
[19] Carl W. Tiller, "A Study of Budget Preparation," *Background Material*, p. 14.

delegates is more caustic than his liberal counterparts: "The American Convention is less of a genuine democracy of voluntarily assisted churches than ever. . . . Less and less of the real business of the Convention comes before its sessions. These meetings are largely the display-window of the wide system of activities carried on by the agencies of the churches. The real business is not brought to the Convention in board meetings, commissions, committees and group assemblies. . . . But if these were dealt with by the Convention, the showcase aspect, with the dramatic presentation, would have to be abandoned. Even then, the time of the Convention would have to be expanded."[20]

On the average, the annual conventions list forty to fifty speeches extolling the work of the various agencies and calling the delegates to new heights of dedication and stewardship. One outspoken liberal commenting on this phenomenon called it a "panorama of Baptist ecclesiasticism whereby we smugly assume that every Baptist cause has had an adequate hearing so long as a handful of people sit and listen."[21]

Concluding his article on the programs of the annual meetings, the Assistant General Secretary of the Convention suggested that the most immediate need is to improve the quality of the programs: "Concentrate on great preaching, inspiring speakers, impressive pageants, rich music, wholesome fellowship, and important business to the end that our programs may be *qualitative* rather than *quantitative*."[22]

This emphasis upon emotion and promotion is not only stimulated by the organizational imperatives of the Convention's missionary agencies. The delegates themselves—if attendance at meetings is any criterion—indicate a greater interest in the inspiring speakers and impressive pageants than in the business of the denomination. Nonetheless, the needs of the national agencies are the primary motivation for the expenditures on the promotional work of the denomination. The decision to engage in new campaigns involving millions

20 Editorial, *Watchman Examiner*, 39 (June 28, 1951), p. 658.
21 W. B. Lipphard, quoted by Porter, *Background Material, op.cit.*, p. 16.
22 Porter, *Background Material, op.cit.*, p. 16.

of dollars and a major output of time and emphasis rests ultimately with the professional executives and the promotional
men. If their surveys signify that funds can be raised the new
policy is given favorable support. But if the surveys indicate
that support for the venture will be difficult to acquire, the
new proposal may be put aside no matter how great the need.
It now appears that "the adventurous Baptist missionary
spirit" can be accurately measured, but if the prognostication
appears negative it is not likely that a program will gain the
enthusiastic support of denominational leaders.[23]

As mentioned above, one of the most important functions
of the annual conventions is to appoint personnel and establish an organization which will carry on the work of the denomination for the succeeding year. Every effort is made to
enable the delegates to participate in the process; or at least
every effort is made to impart to them the impression that they
are participating in a significant manner. From the official
point of view, the process is free and democratic and undefiled
by the "demonic wiles" of the executive professionals. As a
result, the elected personnel for the succeeding year are ostensibly elected by the whole convention through the familiar
mechanism of the nominating committee. In actual fact, the
process is chaotic and only the most experienced delegates
operate effectively within it. Therefore, a few representatives
who are favorably disposed to the requirements of the executives are able to control the system. As a result the elected
personnel for the succeeding year are actually chosen on the
basis of their merit and their desire to meet the needs of the
organization as conceived by the standing leadership. Thus
there is no assurance that the democratic processes as under-

[23] For example, an elaborate survey was conducted by Marts & Lundy,
Inc., for the Board of Education and Publication. A twelve-page printed
report was presented to the Convention at the annual meeting in 1957. On
the basis of this report—a complex of statistics and recommendations—the
delegates approved a new $7,500,000 venture in behalf of Baptist educa-
tion. The need is apparent, but even if it were not the delegates would
have had great difficulty in comprehending and refuting the impressive
work of these publicity experts. ("Report and Recommendations of the
National Survey Commission on Christian Higher Education," printed
for use by the American Baptist Convention by Marts & Lundy, Inc., 1957.)

stood and developed by the Baptists can work effectively within a convention of over 3,000 uninformed delegates.

Probably the only reason the organization continues to operate effectively is that the nominating procedures are largely controlled by the informed executive professionals. No one knows better the needs of the organization and its sub-groups, and no one is better equipped to discover the appropriate personnel for the boards and agencies. All of this presupposes, of course, that the organizational imperatives are the criterion by which the success or failure of denominational activity must be measured. On the other hand, if the denomination is to engage in more venturesome programs and a more prophetic witness, probably no group is less able to choose its colleagues than the leaders whose first duty is to sustain the existing modes of operation.

From the point of view of the leadership, there is a sense in which chaos itself has a significant function within the organizational process of the American Baptist Convention. Since the system of formal executive authority plays a subordinate role to the system of informal power, a process which could be called "institutionalized anomie" is necessary for the sustaining of the organizational imperatives. The prosperity of the informal system of power is dependent to a large extent upon obscurity and a lack of definition with respect to official responsibilities and roles.

The prevailing chaos can best be illustrated by a discussion of the nominating procedures of the Convention. Rather than present the bylaws and articles,[24] it will be more effective to consider a description of the system by a board member of one of the societies. "The nominating system of the Convention is insane. You know there are 34 people on the Nominating Committee of the Convention, as there are 34 members on the other three Convention committees [Order of Business, Place and Preacher, and Resolutions]. The 34 state associations meet in caucus to nominate one person to each of these committees. . . .

"In the state caucus somebody shouts out a name. It may be someone who knows something about Convention business,

[24] *Yearbook*, 1956, pp. 16, 23, 26.

and what kind of people should be nominated to the various boards, or it may not be. Oftentimes people will be placed on the Nominating Committee who have never attended a Convention before. But someone from their state thinks it would be nice if that person could get on the inside of the process. Or it might be quite the opposite: a well-informed and 'instructed' fundamentalist might be placed on these committees. Most often, though, the people are not informed and know nothing about the real workings of the societies: who is on the boards, whose term is running out, who should be appointed, the type of person who is needed, and so on.

"You may wonder how this works, but it is very simple. Each society and agency has its own nominating committee. We send a representative from that committee to the Nominating Committee of the Convention. In this way they receive competent direction as to what is desired by our board of managers."[25]

The Baptist Dilemma

The possibility that "undemocratic procedures" could appear in the denomination has been publicly discussed by some of the leaders. The Commission of Review warned that "we must be ever alert and vigilant, lest strong personalities and pressure groups betray our historic Baptist freedoms."[26]

[25] Interview with a board member. Interviews with other people lent support to the process depicted above. In addition, a description of the behavior of the Committee on Resolutions is also quite similar to the activity of the Nominating Committee. "Each year 34 people, one from each state, with no advance notice of appointment, and with little regard for fitness, are nominated in state caucuses and perfunctorily elected as members of the Committee on Resolutions. These 34 people then . . . toil long into midnight hours to draft a set of usually perfunctory, often poorly written, hastily formulated resolutions on sundry topics and various issues of current concern. . . . On the last day of the Convention, when the vast majority of delegates have gone home, the resolutions are presented and debated, sometimes mildly, sometimes vigorously. . . . Eventually the resolutions are adopted with whatever amendments their persuasive, argumentative, sponsoring zealots succeed in getting approved. They are buried in the Convention's yearbook. . . . And since the Convention cannot commit any local Baptist church to any expression of opinion, it is unethical to publish to the world a series of resolutions as the reasoned conviction and corporate opinion of one million American Baptists." (Lipphard, *Background Material, op.cit.*, pp. 8-9.)

[26] *Yearbook*, 1950, pp. 155ff.

They further affirmed that the goal of the Commission "is to detect any undemocratic trends in our structural development, with a view to making the whole denomination more flexible and responsive to the will of the churches."[27] But again the conservative Baptist press carries stronger denunciations against the leaders of the Convention than are to be found in the official statements of the *Yearbook*. The leaders of the Convention do not forget the bitter polemic carried against them during the height of the fundamentalist controversy and they make every effort to avoid a repetition of the following caustic remarks: "There has been an organized and determined endeavor to keep conservatives off the boards and out of the prominent committees, salaried secretaries being often the partisan leaders of such successful attempts. In order to do this every Convention has witnessed illegal voting, such, for instance, as an election by plurality instead of majority vote. . . ."[28]

W. B. Riley was equally incensed with respect to another incident. He believed that an election of board officials which favored the liberals was determined by two hundred men. "Who were these 200 men? There is not an intelligent member of the Northern Baptist Convention that doubts that they were salaried servants, many of them cogs in the machine."[29] Riley said of one of the elected officials: "Dr. Moore has long lived by ecclesiastical office. We are saying exactly what we mean. . . . The office was to him a promotion, not an opportunity; a living, not a life."[30]

The unfortunate spirit and language of these statements cannot, however, obscure the substantial truth upon which they rest. In all probability Dr. Moore was acting with integrity and according to the best of his capabilities. But no matter what nomenclature the Baptists may choose, Dr. Moore was working in an ecclesiastical office; his advancement did constitute a promotion as well as an opportunity, and

[27] *Ibid.*, p. 156.
[28] W. B. Riley, "Shall Northern Baptists Automatically Exclude Ultra-Conservatives?" *Watchman Examiner*, 10 (May 11, 1922), p. 589.
[29] Editorial, *The Baptist*, 9 (October 20, 1928), p. 1,282.
[30] *Ibid.*, p. 1,282.

the office was a living as well as a life. Neither the fundamentalists nor the liberals are able to recognize the realities of
executive ecclesiastical office. Like any other executive office
it requires power in order to realize opportunities. Sometimes
in private conversation the executives are willing to support
these observations. One official described the operation of the
annual meetings in realistic terms: "Each year the secretaries
abdicate for one week. We stand behind the curtains and the
delegates play at policy-making. This maintains the fiction
of the churches as the real policy-makers of the Convention."[31]

But the leaders are involved in a complex dilemma. In the
first place, they are forced to maintain a semblance of democratic polity. If they publicly admit that procedures are undemocratic it would be almost tantamount to an admission
by an Episcopalian or Presbyterian that their polity is un-
Christian. Since freedom, autonomy, and democracy stand as
the cornerstones of Baptist church-order any erosion of these
ideals can be interpreted as an ultimate failure of the current
leadership.

Second, through all their studies and reorganizational efforts the denominational leaders have been unable to discover a
viable alternative to the present mode of organization. So long
as the denomination is dedicated to an evangelistic program
which extends beyond the boundaries of the local churches,
there must be some kind of rationalized organization which
compromises the purity of a congregational polity. Since the
majority of Baptists hesitate to reevaluate their church-order
the informal system of executive power is an inevitable substitute for a formal system of authority.

Third, the experience of the executive leadership has convinced them that they are not the only power-seekers in the
denomination, and that those who most blatantly protest for
the support of traditional Baptist symbols are representatives
of power groups which are no less calculating in their efforts
to gain control of the Convention. The fact that some of these
groups are momentarily disfranchised does not impress the

[31] Interview with an associate secretary.

executives. Short of heaven itself, they are inclined to note, there will be ecclesiastical powers and rumors of power even among the Baptists. In addition, Baptist polity enables inadequately trained men to become ordained ministers and gain positions of influence within the dissident centers of power.[32] Thus the present leaders engage in an effort to prevent these groups from undermining the common goals of the denomination.

In the light of these conditions, the Baptist situation is acute. If the leaders strive for reformation of the Convention, the establishment of more representational procedures, and a consideration of the entire Baptist system of church-order, they will open the gate for the invasion of those who will wave the banner of discord and perhaps even risk the destruction of the present missionary effort. On the other hand, if they do not strive "to detect any undemocratic trends" and to make "the whole denomination more responsive to the will of the churches," they will be filled with anxieties, tensions, and guilt which arise from the failure to maintain their loyalty to a fundamental Baptist ideal.

Responsibility for these problems does not fall entirely upon the executives and other leaders of the national organization. The Baptist dilemma starts with the churches and with the failure of the local associations and state conventions to sustain the necessary discipline and authority which is rightfully theirs. But it will be seen in the succeeding chapter that state and local associations can make no claim to have approximated the Baptist ideal.

[32] According to Baptist polity every local church has complete power to examine and ordain any candidate for the ministry. Many churches, especially in outlying areas, are served by ministers with nothing more than a high-school education.

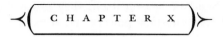

NOTES ON STATE CONVENTIONS AND
THE LOCAL CHURCH

State Conventions

REFERENCE has already been made to the relations between the American Baptist Convention and the state conventions. It has been observed that the problems of the authority and power of the state executives are no different from the issues faced by the national executives. Even though the state conventions have not been systematically analyzed to the extent attempted at the national level, it is desirable to draw some general observations in order to bring the denominational situation into perspective.

Throughout the nineteenth century, the state conventions had developed as mission agencies within specific geographic areas. These organizations were similar in function to the national missionary societies.[1] By the beginning of the twentieth century the state conventions had lost much of their prestige and importance due to a shift in operational emphasis from the state to the national level. This condition was criticized by Shailer Mathews while he was president of the Convention: "Our denomination has not given much importance to the State Convention. We have been so much afraid of Presbyterian presbyteries, and Methodist conferences, and Episcopalian dioceses, that we have looked a bit askance at Conventions of Baptists within the various states. . . . Unless my vision is hopelessly distorted, the development of our denomination for the next decade will be in the field of the State Convention."[2]

Mathews' vision was partially distorted. In one respect these organizations have become extremely important and powerful; in another respect they are weak and ineffective.

---

[1] Pruden, *Basic Papers*, *op.cit.*, p. 27.
[2] *Annual*, 1916, p. 23.

The state conventions have often been described as "miniature American Baptist Conventions." A sub-executive of one of the national societies elaborated this definition: "They don't differ in any important respect from the ABC. There are fewer executives to make policy and fewer important laymen and ministers to support the executives. The conflicts are just as radical and sometimes more bitter than at the national level. The participation of the laymen and the local churches is no more effective at the annual meetings than it is at the Convention. There is one big difference. The state secretary oftentimes controls the whole show. It's a much more limited operation, especially in the small states. There are always some unhappy churches and sometimes they gain control but not very often."[3]

From a policy-making point of view the local associations within the states are most notable for their impotence. They meet at various times of the year and have no professional leadership unless the state sends an executive to the meeting. Their primary function, beyond the opportunity to enjoy annual "fellowship," is to operate as centers of stimulation and organization for state and national promotional work. In some cases, however, the local associations bear a resemblance to feudal baronies. A minister of a liberal church within such an association described his experience when he first moved into the situation:

"The policies of the whole association were controlled by J----- T-----. He was originally a mildly conservative minister in the First Baptist Church in L----- [a city of about 80,000 in the center of a predominantly rural area]. He cooperated with the Convention until about 25 years ago when his son, who was a foreign missionary, was expelled by the Foreign Missionary Society on a morals charge. JT was not big enough to take that. He got his son a rural church and he gradually pulled the other churches away from the Convention. That wasn't hard to do because his church gave financial support to several smaller churches in the association. That's how he got control of the whole association.

[3] Interview with a sub-executive.

"It was odd the way we broke his power. It happened at the first association meeting that I attended. I only knew two other ministers in the area because they were active in the Roger Williams Fellowship at the Conventions. They explained how things were run. For example, the moderator of the association was from one of JT's churches. He really didn't know what was going on and everytime he got confused he'd look toward JT and get an affirmative or negative nod.

"Five of us ministers met after the first meeting. They were all graduates of CRDS and Crozer. They told me that the ordination councils were stacked and how more of the churches were being filled by high school and Bible school men from JT's group. . . .

"We didn't make any plans at all, but the next day was the nominating session and after the moderator had presented the committee's slate of officers, I stood up and nominated R---- from the floor. The moderator stood still for a full minute. I thought he was frozen. There wasn't anything he could do, so finally he asked for a rising vote—by golly R---- won the vote and the meeting was adjourned. JT came storming up to me and took me by the lapels. 'You've drawn a line here that'll never be erased. You're an unscrupulous tool of a dishonorable machine.' I told him I didn't know of any machine and then he left.

"He lost power from then on. It was simply because nobody knew it was going to happen and JT didn't have a chance to load the meeting with delegates from his churches. Once his power was challenged he was broken because he wasn't really very popular in any of the associations. I don't mean he disappeared, but at least he wasn't an absolute power any longer."[4]

Baptist experience with autocratic associations indicates that congregational polity does not automatically prevent an inordinate concentration of power even at the local level. This

---

[4] Interview with a local minister. During this extensive interview in which many aspects of the denominational organization were discussed the writer freely took notes. This procedure was not followed except in the case of one other interviewee, who also knew the writer well enough to be undisturbed by this procedure.

is especially true when the doctrines of the church sanction the ordination of untrained or poorly trained ministers. The problem of ministerial education has been fully discussed elsewhere.[5] The issue cannot be separated from the traditional role of the minister in the Baptist movement and the problem of ecclesiastical authority. If all that is required for ministerial ordination is for the applicant to experience a "spiritual call," there is little possibility of establishing standards which can be respected by all the churches. In such a situation whatever authority the minister obtains will be derived from qualities of personal leadership and the extent of his popularity. This method of conferring authority, not only at the local level but also in the Convention itself, often means that the individual who is the most passionately concerned and who has the largest following will exercise the greatest control over the policy-making process. The situation can arise even though a leader has little knowledge of the complexity of the issues with which he is dealing.

It was observed above that the national executives bear a close resemblance to the marginal man of sociological theory. The state secretary is also beset by tensions and conflicting values which are no less difficult to resolve. It is equally difficult for him to define rationally his role within the framework of denominational activity. His personal power within the state may be greater than that experienced by the national secretaries within their own spheres of action, but he must always walk as though on eggs. A success in one area may spell failure in another because he is more intimately involved in the liberal-fundamentalist controversy. If he publicly announces his loyalty to the national organizations he will be criticized by the conservative constituency; and the reverse is true if his concern for the state activities seems to distract his attention from the national work. The national officials can never be fully satisfied with the compromises the state executive is forced to make. Speaking of the relations be-

5 Hugh Hartshorne and Milton C. Froyd, *Theological Education in the Northern Baptist Convention; A Survey, 1944-1945* (Philadelphia: The Judson Press, 1945); Froyd, *Background Material, op.cit., passim.*

tween the Council on Missionary Cooperation and the state officials, one reporter observes: "There seems no adequate way for the General Director [of the CMC] to insure that men whose prior loyalty must be to their state or city society shall maintain a national point of view. When such men are hired, for example, in some areas the General Director is called in for advice. In other areas the choice of a secretary is made without any consultation with the General Director at all. . . . At present there is really no adequate plan for maintaining the national point of view in respect to their prior loyalty which many promotional men give to their state or city societies. This is one of the real problems of our Convention."[6]

Originally a missionary organization of the local churches, the present purpose of the state convention is not clearly defined. Today it functions primarily as a promotional outlet for the work of the local and national agencies: "Again, the dual function of the state and city promotional men leads to a confusion as to what is promotion. They give time and effort to raising the quotas for their areas; they collect the monies; they handle the literature and publicity; they arrange for missionary speakers, meetings, etc.; and they give a great many services to the churches in their respective areas. It is no wonder that many of them say, 'Everything I do is promotion!' They cannot, therefore, because of the highly individualistic methods of proceeding, give an account of the portion which their state or city society receives of the . . . funds marked for their use. . . ."[7]

The emphasis upon promotion and advertising has been present since the formation of the Convention. Bylaws on the relation between the states and the national Convention are almost exclusively devoted to the financial aspect of the work. In the *Yearbook* of 1910 it is resolved that any state convention may affiliate with the national organization if it will adopt the following: (1) promote the work and aims of the Convention; (2) consider the work of the Convention at all its annual

[6] Tiller, *Background Material, op.cit.*, p. 15.
[7] Archibald, *Background Material, op.cit.*, pp. 15-16.

meetings; (3) ". . . appoint a State Apportionment Committee, which shall receive annually from the NBC the budget assigned to its field, and shall apportion the same without change . . . to the churches of the State. . . ."[8]

The emphasis upon promotion and budget has an effect upon the attitudes of the lay constituency which cannot be considered salutary from the Baptist point of view. There exists no sense of participation on the part of the lay people in the work of the missionary societies even at the state level. With respect to national work this situation was noted early in the life of the Convention: "Each Society is corporately distinct, and legitimately feels that it has satisfied its trust when it has carefully and wisely expended the funds entrusted to it for the purpose designated. Each organization is zealous for its own work, and commendably so; but to the constituency of the NBC to whom all the organizations appeal for funds, the home mission work is one big business, and the various organizations only departments."[9]

The American Baptist Convention was originally formed to unify the work of the denomination. The achievement in this line has been relatively successful but only concerning the financial aspect of the denominational activity. Even in this area serious shortcomings have been noted in the past. In 1914 a report at the national level observed that the national societies expended $84,000 in one state, of which amount the state secretary was unaware of $22,000. Some radical suggestions were made to remedy the situation:

"The point is not that this official was ignorant of the work, but he seemed not to have known the cost. Similar conditions of incomplete or inaccurate knowledge . . . exist in practically all the states, and in some a duplication and profusion of workers, due to incomplete cooperation and imperfectly centralized supervision.

"[This] is the natural result of extended growth on the part of separate organizations. . . . Individualization should give

---

[8] *Annual*, 1910, pp. 138ff. The content of the bylaws has not changed since that time; *Yearbook*, 1957, p. 24.
[9] *Annual*, 1914, p. 77.

place more generally to socialization among our societies."[10]

On the whole, the states are no better organized today. The national leaders, who necessarily concentrate on the work and survival of their own agencies, assume little interest in the activities of the states beyond their concern for the promotional work. On the other hand, if a state executive refuses to co-operate to the desired degree, or if the state work is more than he can handle alone, the CMC will appoint a promotional director to the state.

In addition to his role as promotional director, "pastor's pastor," arbitrator of inter-church and inter-sectional disputes, one-man speaker's bureau, and numerous other tasks, the state executive is also the chief policy-maker within his area. One state secretary writes concerning his relations with his boards and committees: "The committees naturally depend upon the leadership of the state secretary and follow his suggestions at the point of program building and the features pointing up the ongoing work of the state. We have made it very clear at this point that the committees are not to take verbatim the things that we suggest . . . but they have been very coopera-tive in incorporating our suggestions and any adaptations or deletions that seem proper at the point of helping the commit-tees to do an effective job. . . . The setup is such in our state that it seems that all boards and committees look unduly in the direction of the state secretary for leadership. However, we are trying to elicit thinking on the part of our board and committee chairmen that they in turn may be able to propose and project programs after counseling with us that will be effective in our over-all program."[11]

The appearance of national organizations had a grievous effect upon the rational development of the state conventions. The denomination was nationalized before an adequate foun-dation was secured at the state and local levels, so that the local groups were forced to become the servants of the national missionary societies. Many of the problems of the denomina-tion which appear to originate at the level of the national or-

[10] *Ibid.*, p. 78.
[11] Personal correspondence to the writer.

ganization actually are located in an inadequate and partial development of the grass roots organizations.

The foundation of the American Baptist Convention is thin. Rather than lend effective support to the national activities, the state and local associations are faced with the same problems of legitimate existence and the same tensions between the formal system of authority and the informal system of power that exist at the national level. The inevitable result is competition between all the denominational agencies at every level of their work. This is in accord with Mannheim's observation that "most of the symptoms of maladjustment in modern society can be traced to the fact that a parochial world of small groups expanded into a Great Society in a comparatively short time."[12]

The social organization of the denomination demands a system of pluralistic loyalties which few individuals are capable of comprehending. Most people who are active in denominational affairs—both laymen and executive professionals— tend to be selective in their loyalties. If they work at the national level they are not likely to be active in state affairs. If they participate on the boards and committees at the state level they probably know little about the national work. Undoubtedly, part of this exclusiveness is due to necessary economies of time. But the tensions between the states and the Convention point to something deeper.

The Baptists do cooperate, but the unity which they feel is due less to their common name and to a common interpretation of the nature of their church than it is to the cohering force of the organized missionary and evangelistic movement. When the various groups within the denomination disagree concerning the purpose of the national organization the Baptist movement starts to fragmentize. This was one aspect of the fundamentalist-liberal controversy. Faced with differing interpretations of the goals of the missionary, educational, and evangelistic work the denomination itself was threatened. Since there was no Baptist theology of the church which could

[12] Karl Mannheim, *Freedom, Power, and Democratic Planning* (New York: Oxford University Press, 1950), p. 4.

serve to hold the disparate groups together, the educational, theological, class, and ethnic tensions were so intensified that the existence of the Convention itself was in doubt.

The Local Churches

At this point an effort will be made to analyze the actual autonomy of the local churches. Autonomy is a relational term. It is defined as "the degree to which a group functions independently of other groups and occupies an independent position in society."[13] This concept of autonomy implies economic self-sufficiency as well as political independence. Any social unit which engages in extensive social participation cannot maintain the degree of isolation and independence necessary to fulfill the requirements of a perfect autonomy. This is simply because autonomy and cooperation tend to be mutually contradictory relations. A high degree of independence can be maintained only if a social group remains economically and politically self-determining. No congregation which cooperates with the American Baptist Convention can claim political independence, and no church in the denomination can be called economically and theologically self-sufficient. Many of the statements by leading Baptists concerning the autonomy of the churches cannot bear even a superficial criticism. The following quotation from a recent president of the Convention is typical. "The self-government of a church in its own affairs has never been affected by the sending of delegates to Baptist conventions. The church calls its pastor, elects its own officers, disciplines its members, votes on its building program; in short, it makes its decisions and spends its money without intervention or control from the outside. But a true church is not concerned with local matters only. It has its part of the responsibility for the evangelization of the world."[14] The implication is clear: the autonomy of the churches is compromised only because they engage in world evangelization.

On the contrary, if the delegates to the conventions do not return with ideas and suggestions which affect the life of their

13 Hemphill and Westie, *op.cit.*, p. 323.
14 Pruden, *Basic Papers, op.cit.*, p. 18.

own churches this merely constitutes a reflection upon the sterility of the national conventions. But these meetings are never sterile. The delegate may not participate in the important political process of the denomination, but he would have to be utterly shallow-pated if he remained unaffected by the Convention experience. If, in turn, the church should remain undisturbed by their delegate's new perceptions, it would indicate that the individual was not a very active local churchman.

True, the church calls its own pastor. But he too attended conventions and has probably been trained in schools that are part of the denominational structure. The training of the pastor is the strongest single determinant in the affairs of the local church. Actually, it is impossible to think of any category of activity in which the local churches are engaged which is not significantly affected by the work and character of the denominational organizations.

Other factors diminish the autonomy of the local church in relation to the state and national organizations. A state executive in New England revealed that many fundamentalist churches which withdrew from the denomination two decades ago are now making overtures toward renewal of formal relations. Two reasons were given for this reversal of attitude. First, the ministers of the separated churches are now reaching an age when it becomes increasingly difficult for them to carry on the activities of their own churches, but it is impossible for some of them to find other churches without the assistance of the state convention. Second, some of the younger fundamentalist ministers, recognizing the difficulties faced by their older friends, are not adverse to cooperating with the Convention at least to the extent that they will receive the advantages of the Missionary and Ministers Benefit Board of the Convention.[15]

The independence of the local congregations is compromised by other services they receive from the Convention. A partial list includes: religious education materials; lay leadership training programs; missionary education projects; teacher

[15] Interview with a state executive.

training and church organizational materials; youth work, which includes a variety of activities with leadership supplied by the state and national conventions; state agencies for pastoral relations and supply; financial support for new and old churches; etc.

The problem of congregational autonomy cannot be confined to the relation between the churches and the ecclesiastical bodies of the denomination. The fundamentalist-separatists are right: organized Christianity does represent a compromise of the gospel. But those churches which avoid all ecclesiastical connections are no less liable to secular influence than the churches which find courage and strength in unity. "The ethical failure of the divided church" will not be overcome by a simple faith in improved forms of religious organization, or even by a more perfect unity of the Christian churches. Autonomy, separation, and disunity have generally proved to be an even greater burden, if for no other reason than the greater susceptibility of a divided church to the values of Caesar than to the teachings of Christ.

Even the fundamentalists recognize this danger and speak favorably of "spiritual cooperation" while deploring the efforts of the schismatics in their midst: "For the local Baptist churches to draw off by themselves under the mistaken conception that the independence permits this spiritual isolation . . . is to be guilty of schism and is certain to defeat the great objective of Christ in the church. Some churches cannot so learn from the New Testament."[16]

The Christian Church has been unable to avoid the dilemmas created by the desire for catholicity and the desire for holiness. Those within the Baptist movement who insist upon the absolute independence of the churches have not been able to escape ethical and spiritual compromise through their emphasis upon doctrinal purity and renunciation of ecclesiastical authority. With no fellowship beyond its own neighborhood the theology of these churches is characterized by an implicit championship of a parochial secular ideology, although it may be expressed in theological terminology.

[16] *Watchman Examiner*, 38 (May 4, 1950), p. 435.

Insistence upon pure autonomy has had another unanticipated effect upon the life of the churches. One of the original purposes of the Convention was to serve the churches and assist them in the achievement of their common goals. The compromise of local autonomy which occurred because of the formation of the Convention has not received general recognition in the official statements of the denominational leaders. Therefore the encroachment upon the freedom of the churches has been consistently counteracted by an official reaffirmation of the belief in congregational independence. Thus it can be seen that every group within the denomination experiences a real threat to its existence. It is not only the Convention and the leaders of the national agencies who suffer from the menace of diminution of their authority and power. The local churches also fear a sinister effort to reduce their legitimate authority. Their thoughts are not entirely unrealistic.

The local congregations originally constituted the sole stronghold of the Baptist movement. It was once believed that the freedom of God could be assured only through the medium of the local churches and that their autonomy was essential for the realization of this high goal. But the independence which they cherished has proved to be the source of their greatest weakness. The refusal to recognize the authority, however limited, of the local association of churches means that the congregations now stand separate and alone. Seldom can grass roots criticism be brought to the attention of the Convention leaders since the laymen have no adequate institutional means for expressing their inspirations. In the minds of the constituency the needs of the local churches are submerged beneath a frantic effort to sustain the program of the national organizations.

The national leadership is not unaware of this but do not know what remedial procedures to follow. The General Secretary of the Convention recently formed a list of ministerial complaints of the national agencies:

"We are tired of the Crusade idea and procedure.

"The yearly emphasis is not really a total denominational

program, but the strengthening and projection of certain established departments within the organizations.

"Such programs take too much of a pastor's time. He gets the feeling that he is engaged mostly as the promotional agent for a denomination.

"We need something new, total, local church and pastor centered."[17]

Thus the original function of the Convention—to serve the churches and help them achieve their common goals—has been drastically altered. The preservation of the Convention's organization and program has now become an ultimate purpose of the denomination. In a sense the role of the churches has been displaced by the role of the Convention. It is now the purpose of the congregations to increase and preserve the life of the national organization. The organizational imperatives of the Convention are now so stringent that the ministers are the local servants of the Convention and the executives are the national servants. One minister expressed the idea in cryptic form. "The Convention is bigger than any of us or any of our churches!"

[17] Reuben E. Nelson, "We Consider Our Planning," *Background Material*, *op.cit.*, p. 9.

WEBER'S CATEGORIES OF AUTHORITY AND NON-AUTHORITARIAN GROUPS

THE BAPTIST DILEMMA of authority and power is not peculiar to that denomination, nor is it a problem which is confined to religious organizations. Every voluntary and non-authoritarian association in America—trade unions, service clubs, patriotic and veteran's groups, quasi-religious groups, and business associations—become involved in the problem of the authority and power of their leadership. Internal conflicts between the national and local units is a constant source of tension in such groups as the American Legion, the DAR, and the Teamsters' Unions. The issue can be more specifically defined and analyzed as it exists in the Free churches because of the *explicit* allocation of authority to the local unit and their refusal to grant legal authority to their ministerial and administrative leaders. Of all the highly rationalized, voluntary associations in America probably the Baptists have been most radical in their insistence that the social system can operate effectively without recourse to well-defined lines of authority. But no group can function without leadership, and it has been argued that when leaders are divested of authority they will necessarily seek and gain power in order to meet their responsibilities; the power they acquire may exceed that which ordinarily accrues to leaders in non-totalitarian, hierarchical institutions.

Extension of the Categories of Authority

Carl Friedrich has observed that Max Weber's categories of authority are primarily applicable to authoritarian and hierarchical social organizations.[1] This has resulted in a lacuna

---

[1] Carl J. Friedrich, "Some Observations on Weber's Analysis of Bureaucracy," *Reader in Bureaucracy*, ed. by Robert K. Merton, et al. (Glencoe, Illinois: The Free Press, 1952), p. 31.

in the study of the problems of power and authority as applied to non-authoritarian social systems—those social groups which are explicitly or implicitly dedicated to a minimization of centralized control and supervision. Although non-authoritarian groups are present in every strata of our pluralistic society, in England and America this social type is represented in its classic form by the religious groups which emerged from left-wing Protestantism. By the turn of the current century voluntary organizations, both religious and secular, found it increasingly difficult to make an effective impact upon their social environment. Existing organizational trends in business, labor, and government forced the voluntary associations to develop large-scale bureaucratic hierarchies in order to witness effectively to their purposes.

Presumably, in an investigation of the power and authority structures of the Episcopal, Roman Catholic, or Lutheran churches, or of General Motors and Standard Oil of New Jersey, Weber's typology of authority is readily useful without serious alteration. In a study of social groups which place a high value upon the autonomy of the local unit and the freedom of the individual, new analytical tools are necessary in order to comprehend the power-authority relations of these groups.

It is perhaps advisable to restate Weber's basic theory. He taught that the key to understanding the authority relations of any social system was the basis of legitimacy for the persons in authority. The nature of this claim determines the type of authority as well as the mode of social organization. Since no social system can operate over an extensive period of time on a basis of power alone, the leaders of the group will seek to establish a legitimate right to exercise their power. Legitimacy, according to Weber, is rooted in tradition, law, or the charismatic qualities of the leader himself.

The value-orientation of the congregationally-ordered, democratic churches which emerged from the left-wing of the Calvinist movement indicates that their attitude toward authority was motivated primarily by a fear of ecclesiastical and civil power. In the case of voluntary secular organizations in America, suspicion of authority has been transferred to all forms of centralized power. Every effort to define authority, whether in the name of sacred tradition or merely by the established laws of the group, seems to be in radical opposition to a fundamental tenet of the American democratic ideology.

Nonetheless, voluntary associations in America have formed complex and impressive organizations which bear striking resemblance to the social structures more commonly associated with the highly centralized spheres of government and business. In addition, the national officials of these associations have obtained a significant degree of influence over the affairs of the local units. However, rational-legal authority—as the term was used by Weber—has not been conferred upon the national officials of these voluntary associations.[2] Actually the national leadership of these voluntary associations —as was explained in Chapter Four, in reference to the Baptists—does exercise a form of rational authority which is not explicitly defined by Weber. We called it *rational-pragmatic authority*.

Our observations of the American Baptist Convention may make it possible to develop further theoretical generalizations concerning the nature of rational-pragmatic authority and to compare it to rational-legal authority as delineated by Weber. He wrote that "the purest type of legal authority is that which employs a bureaucratic administrative staff" and functions according to specific criteria.[3] The fact that the voluntary, anti-authoritarian social groups of the modern world have found it necessary to organize in accord with bureaucratic principles without conferring upon their leaders a rational-legal authority has resulted in an important distinction with respect to their modes of social organization and activity. It is this phenomenon which makes it desirable to reassess Weber's categories.

Some of the criteria by which officials function in prag-

2 If it has been conferred, as apparently is the case in some closed-shop unions, they can no longer be strictly defined as voluntary and non-authoritarian associations.

3 Weber, *Theory*, *op.cit.*, pp. 333f.

matically sanctioned organizations are similar to those listed by Weber as functional characteristics of the legally sanctioned groups. First, there is "a continuous organization of official functions bound by rules."[4] Even though these rules are not conceived as legally grounded, they are based on practical experience and are no less binding upon the sub-administrative personnel. The incumbents of office are personally free and subject to higher authority only in their official capacity. That is, no sub-official can be *legitimately* requested by his superiors to devote his "whole self" to the point of sacrificial giving in the exercise of his tasks.

Obviously, in the voluntary, democratically-organized social group, as in the authoritarian system, it is also "a matter of principle that the members of the administrative staff should be completely separated from the ownership of the means of production or administration."[5] Also, the officials are remunerated by fixed salaries and the salary-scale is graded according to the status or rank of the official in the organization.

There is strict discipline and control in the conduct of office although in the pragmatically sanctioned organization these controls are more likely to be informally established by custom than enforced by a formalized legal code. Finally, "administrative decisions and rules are formulated and recorded in writing, even in cases where oral discussion is the rule or is even mandatory."[6]

The differences between legal and pragmatic authority arrangements, however, are discovered in the following categories: first, the organization of offices follows the principles of hierarchy only in a limited sense. Resemblance to hierarchical organization is usually an anathema to the members of the non-authoritarian social group. Offices are organized in terms of function or purpose rather than in terms of subordination and super-ordination as in the legally sanctioned social systems. Oftentimes, and quite paradoxically, even greater weight is placed upon technical knowledge *acquired* by the officials of the voluntary association than is the case

[4] *Ibid.*, p. 330.   [5] *Ibid.*, p. 331.   [6] *Ibid.*, p. 332.

in the legally established system. In the pragmatically sanctioned system the only rational ground for authority of office is knowledge and experience. The situation is ironic because, unlike the legally sanctioned system, officials are not *appointed* primarily on the basis of their technical qualifications. Since legality and hierarchy are deplored by the constituency of the non-authoritarian associations, formal provision for the training of future administrative personnel is kept to a minimum— e.g., the fear of the educated "pork chop" union leader. In the Baptist situation the highest executive of the board of missions or the board of education is more likely to be a former minister with an engaging personality than an educator or missionary with administrative training. These officials do not obtain the same degree of formal authority as that possessed by a bishop or the president of AT & T, but they are obeyed for other reasons of which there are three possibilities. First, they may be obeyed because they are recruited on a basis of personal charisma and upon entering office immediately attract a loyal constituency. Second, they may be obeyed because of the requirements of expediency and on a basis of pragmatic authority. Finally, what seems to occur most often is that they acquire charisma in office because of their success on the basis of their pragmatic authority. They are never obeyed simply because they hold office, as in the case of legally legitimated authority.

Within the non-authoritarian bureaucratic system, as in the legally sanctioned system, there are "specified spheres of competence" and officials do operate in accord with a systematic division of labor, but they generally lack "the necessary authority to carry out these functions."[7] It is characteristic of the non-authoritarian social group that the leaders are bound with responsibility to achieve the group's goals but are not given sufficient formal authority to fulfill their responsibilities. It follows that the informal system of power, which reflects the propensity of individuals and sub-groups to control the conditions of their existence, will be an absolute impera-

[7] *Ibid.*, p. 330.

tive for the continued operation of the non-authoritarian social group.

According to Weber's principles of rational-legal authority, "the necessary means of compulsion are clearly defined and their use is subject to definite conditions."[8] In the voluntary association there is no recognition of the existence of necessary compulsion. Nonetheless, mechanisms to compel normative behavior do exist whether or not they are recognized. They are not formalized, they are seldom defined, and they never operate on a basis of legalized procedures. Again, the informal system of power in which an official can bring pressures (economic, political, etc.) to bear upon other individuals and groups is vastly more important in this organizational system. At the root of their failure to rationalize the necessary instruments of compulsion is a utopian attitude on the part of the members of the non-authoritarian group. Thus they are compelled to operate according to the standard procedures of social organization without admitting or even recognizing that they are doing so.

Finally, in the non-authoritarian social system an office seldom constitutes a "career." More likely, the office will be viewed as a "calling." All efforts to make a formal career out of one's office, even if it assures more efficient and successful operation of one's agency, is viewed with contempt by the wider constituency. Activity in office will be most enthusiastically approved if it is treated as an inclusive calling, involving total devotion of all personal resources to the fulfillment of one's task. Of course this must be a voluntary act on the part of the official incumbent. It cannot be commanded by his superiors.

Charismatic and Traditional Authority

Another source for the validation of authority according to Weber is the charismatic power of an individual who "is set apart from ordinary men and treated as endowed with supernatural, superhuman, or at least specifically exceptional powers or qualities."[9] Necessarily, there is far greater dependence

[8] *Ibid.*   [9] *Ibid.*, p. 358.

upon the executive of the wonderful personality in an authority system legitimated on pragmatic grounds. This represents an interesting amalgam since charismatic authority is "outside the realm of everyday routine and the profane sphere. In this respect it is sharply opposed both to rational, and particularly bureaucratic, authority. . . ."[10]

As in the case of Weber's category of rational-legal authority another sub-type needs to be delineated. It will be called *quasi-charismatic*, since this contains no normative or pejorative connotations, as the term "pseudo-charismatic" might imply. The quasi-charismatic leader denotes a successor to the original charismatic founder.[11] He is obeyed by the constituency because they believe he is endowed with sufficient qualities of the original leader to warrant obedience. There is also an expediential motivation for this kind of authority. Weber noted that the process of routinization of charisma is motivated by the ideal and material interests of the followers and by the even stronger interests of the administrative staff.[12] The expediential aspect of quasi-charismatic leadership is intensified by the fact that the latter-day leader must "produce" in accord with the needs of the community and with the established norms and ideals laid down in general terms by the charismatic founder.

Quasi-charismatic authority has greater significance for the non-authoritarian bureaucracy than for the "pure type" of bureaucratic staff which is undergirded by legal authority, simply because rational-pragmatic authority is not legitimated as is its legal counterpart. Conditions are more favorable in the pragmatically sanctioned system for the development of charismatic movements because the institutional order has not advanced so far in the process of rationalization. In fact, it can be argued that the non-authoritarian groups make conscious efforts to curtail the process of rationalization and demystification. Deeply rooted sentiments against carrying specialization and division of labor to extremes of rationaliza-

[10] *Ibid.*, p. 358.
[11] In the case of the Baptists, this is Jesus.
[12] *Ibid.*, p. 364.

tion are fully operative in this type of social system. However, this fosters institutional instability in which established routines and traditional symbols may be broken under the attack of a new quasi-charismatic leader. The administrator who is supported only by pragmatic authority may believe it is essential to convince the constituency of his own charismatic gifts and of the need to revolutionize the existing order.

This study points toward the possibility of further development of Weber's conceptual scheme. Two sub-categories of authority have been suggested which may impart greater flexibility to Weber's typology without at the same time making the system so complex as to be useless as a tool for sociological generalization. Perhaps a third sub-type can be developed.

There seems to be empirical evidence that the affluent or politically powerful leaders of contemporary social systems rally support for traditional symbols and methods of action which no longer contain their former affective meaning. (The DAR, of course, is the outstanding example of the inversion of tradition.) In such a situation social activity gains support in the name of tradition without containing the usual validity of "long-standing" practice which extends beyond the memory of all the members of the social group.[13] This could be called *mimetic-traditional authority* and would be used to denote the effort of a society to seek support for the purely practical purpose of sustaining existing norms and procedures and preventing *anomie*. It indicates a spontaneous effort to mimic tradition in order to establish a legitimate basis of authority. But as Weber observed, "the choice of this rather than some other basis of classification can only be justified by its results."[14]

---

[13] "Long-standing" is placed in quotation because a tradition does not necessarily extend over a long number of years. In some cases, most notably in schools and colleges, it requires only three or four years for a new "generation" of students to appear and to establish traditions which extend beyond the memory of their immediate followers. It is not the passage of time so much as the attitude of the group toward an activity "without regard to changes in the functional implications of its operations," which determines the strength of a given tradition. Levy, *op.cit.*, p. 108.

[14] Weber, *Theory, op.cit.*, p. 325.

Contrary to Friedrich's view, it is possible that Weber was interested primarily in authoritarian and hierarchical social systems because he recognized the ultra-instability of the non-authoritarian social forms. While the latter may contain many values which are attractive to their adherents, such as the ability to sustain freedom for the individual and the autonomy of the sub-groups, grave dangers constantly threaten these values because of the unstable character of the system. Friedrich believes that Weber's writing "vibrates with something of the Prussian enthusiasm for the military type of organization."[15] But, as Parsons observes, Weber considered traditional organization to be more stable than the rational-legal type which frustrates the constituency by the segregation of roles and the "depersonalization of the individual."[16]

For whatever reasons Weber chose to develop his conceptual scheme on a tripartite basis, one fact stands out. Social systems which attempt to eliminate formal authority structures are subject to radically disruptive influences and must seek alternate methods for the allocation of power. For this reason the non-authoritarian system must balance itself on a precariously narrow fence. It must depend on quasi-charismatic leadership but at the same time avoid appropriation of the administrative machinery by a new and radically charismatic revolutionary. The leaders must foster loyalty to stabilize traditions without establishing tradition itself as the cohering element of the system. Obviously, these necessities are in contradiction with each other and a marked instability exists within the system.

Recognition of the potential anarchy of the non-authoritarian social system does not enable the observer to predict the future of these groups. But one event is inevitable: the leaders will seek to stabilize their sub-groups by establishing themselves as the legitimate holders of power. Whether this must necessarily result in establishment of charismatic, legal, or traditional forms is not clear, but the leaders will seek

[15] Friedrich, *op.cit.*, p. 31.
[16] Talcott Parsons, "The Institutionalization of Authority," in Weber, *Theory, op.cit.*, p. 68.

legitimacy in order to maximize stability and gain consistency of control.

All of this seems to signal the demise of the democratic intentions of the non-authoritarian group. Therefore it is of critical importance to recognize that the presence of power is not eliminated by noble purpose. Power in a social system is shared by those who are able and willing to mobilize the political, economic, psychological, and ideological resources of the community. In modern social experience this has been accomplished most effectively by the central administrative leaders. But over-centralization can become dysfunctional.

It appears that a balance can be established only if the local units can gather their own forces and create a viable rationale for their existence. The freedom of the individual and the autonomy of the local group cannot be sustained in absolute terms. It is only within a local community of individuals gathered for a common cause that the voice of the people will be spoken. But it is only within active associations of local groups, gathered to mobilize the opinion of all their company, that the voice of the people will be heard.

CHAPTER XII

POSTSCRIPT FOR BAPTISTS

THE PROBLEM of authority and power in the American Baptist Convention is grounded in discrepancies which exist between Baptist polity and the Baptist doctrine of the church. Efforts toward resolution of these discontinuities have been stimulated more often by pragmatic needs than by thoughtful consideration and application of principles derived from a consistent theology of the church.

Baptists have been seeking in vain for a valid and rational locus of ecclesiastical authority under God. Having rejected presbyterial and hierarchical connectional polities and modes of authority, the entire Free Church movement has been hard-pressed to discover a fundamental church-order which is generally acceptable to a majority of its members. Throughout their history Free churchmen have posited various entities as their primary locus of authority. Some Baptists declared the individual to be competent of soul and able to stand alone in his judgment of all matters of faith and practice. Others affirmed the congregation as the locus of authority and said that it must be absolutely autonomous and free to direct its own affairs. Other Baptists sought for an absolute authority in the Bible. But while even today the Bible enjoys a normative significance for all Christians, many have seen how the Scriptures can be used as a weapon to defend one's own presuppositions. Moreover, biblical criticism has made inroads into the authority of the Bible, thus demanding a more sophisticated understanding of biblical authority.

The ministers of the Baptist movement have never held the same authority of office as enjoyed by their counterparts in the hierarchical orders; but, ironically, it is the minister with the dramatic personality who often gains a higher prestige than that which is accorded the official priests of other religious movements. Like the authority of Scripture, the Lordship of Jesus Christ is duly acknowledged by all Baptists, but it has never been rationally defined in terms of a polity which permits "his crown rights" to be normatively expressed. In desperation some Baptists seek to eliminate all vestiges of authority and operate on an expediential basis in which controversy is minimized and response to situations is made on a pragmatic basis.

Few Baptists have seen that authority rests with none of these alone but with all together. According to the intention of the original founders, each has its function as a mode of revelation and each should contribute to the authority of the others. Free Church theology affirms that under God, and under the Lordship of Jesus Christ, there is no absolute authority. The Baptists must seek for new rational forms which will assure the sovereign freedom of God as he acts in history through the Baptist movement. In brief, this means that there must be a mutual expression of criticism and concern between the various units of the whole church.

The democratic ordering of the Free churches is based on several theological propositions. The primary doctrine is the absolute sovereignty of God and the Lordship of Jesus Christ within the universal church. In order to assure the freedom of God, the church must be unhampered by pressures from hierarchy, oligarchy, or state. No group may dictate to any of the others, whether it be a powerful fellowship of local churches or a professional leadership which possesses the technical mechanisms to control the policies of the denomination.

Second to the Lordship of Christ, the priesthood of all believers indicates that every man, no matter how humble his origin or attainment, has the power to seek and find the mind of Christ within the local church of which he is a member. No less important is the fact that if he hears the Word of God he must have an opportunity freely to proclaim what he has heard. This freedom to hear and proclaim includes every individual, whether he is a fundamentalist or an executive secretary.

Third, the doctrine of original sin points to the fallibility of all men, and indicates that there is wisdom in a multiplicity of counsellors. The revelation of God does not consistently appear with absolute clarity to any individual or group. The opposition, whether it be fundamentalist, liberal, or ministerial, has the right to act as a dike against the sin that comes from uncriticized authority and power. Dissent, as such, must not be restrained by any mechanism, formal or informal.[1]

Following upon the doctrine of the sovereignty of God, the earliest Baptists derived the principle that all ecclesiastical authority is penultimate and limited and has for its source the loving mercies of God. It is a tremendous temptation to seek for a final authority within history, and even though Free churchmen are dedicated to a frustration of all such efforts, in their actual church-activity they have been quite fervent in their attempts to establish an absolute locus of truth within the church. At no time, however, in their written letters and confessions of faith did the founders of the Free Church movement declare the local congregation to be an autonomous unit totally separated from the life of other churches. They were fully aware of the potentialities for corruption which existed within the congregations, so they never described the local church as a totally free and sovereign entity.

The Free Church tradition is opposed to every form of ecclesiastical caste system, whether it starts from the "bottom" with the churches or at the "top" with a General Council. In any hierarchical system the possibilities of a meaningful practice of mutual criticism are attenuated, and the doctrine of original sin is compromised in order to allow for the greater authority of the higher levels of the church-orders. According to the polity of the Free churches, the local church does stand in a position of primacy, not because of its essential purity and inviolate authority, but because within the gathered community of loving concern and disciplined criticism the Spirit may freely move with less hindrance from considerations of

---

[1] This, and many other sections in the book, are informed by James M. Gustafson, "A Study in the Problem of Authority in the Congregational Church Order" (mimeographed, 1954, Social Ethics Library, Yale Divinity School).

expedience, power, and organizational self-preservation than is found at the highest levels of an institutionalized hierarchy.

The principle of congregational autonomy is an unfortunate phrase which is descriptive of neither the theological intention of the Free churchmen nor of the real social relations of the churches and the associational groups. Established in comparatively recent years as an absolute principle within the Baptist movement, it violates the doctrine of the sovereignty of God and the freedom of the Holy Spirit. The founders of the Free Church movement recognized the potential corruptibility of the local church as well as the fact that not every church was equally gifted with respect to spiritual and material resources. Such churches should both desire and require the guidance and care of a parent church or an association of churches.

But, most important, freedom and authority are not antithetical but complementary terms. If local churches are to be free from domination by a secular power or from the authority of an ecclesiastical oligarchy, they must associate with one another, each recognizing the authority of the other, none claiming absolute autonomy or authority, and all recognizing the temporal but preëminent authority of the association of churches *so long as they wish to derive the advantages of associational membership.*

In this context authority signifies the right to demand obedience, but it does not follow that freedom and authority are inimical. According to Baptist tradition authority is grounded in the will of a people who are led by the grace of God to choose their leaders, and, if necessary, to depose them. This is in sharp contrast to the practices of dictatorial or oligarchical government. Dictatorship is based on naked power seldom supported by authority. For it is the fundamental character of totalitarian principles that the leaders are not concerned to hear the voice of the people and do not believe the people can be recipients of any revelation or special insight into the requirements of government. The only law to which the leader must be obedient is his subjective personal will—there is no other authority to which an appeal may be taken. But democratic government—whether ecclesiastical or secular—cannot dispense with authority, for there is no freedom without authority. In the absence of authority, freedom degenerates into an anarchy in which the most powerful group will rule. In great measure this is descriptive of the present Baptist situation.

Ecclesiastical authority is a derivative power. It is a gift freely bestowed by the grace of God. Just as authority is received by God's grace the ability to perceive valid authority is also a gift of God. Not all men perceived authority in the person of Jesus. In a similar way, the authority of some units of the church may not be recognized as legitimate by all its members.

Many of the difficulties faced by the Baptists arise from their failure to draw a meaningful distinction between power and authority. The assumption has long been prevalent that authority is merely a variant of coercive power, and that any group which is given authority will automatically attain power. The current situation among the Baptists belies this interpretation. According to their official doctrines, the churches have the authority to direct and criticize the denominational associations and conventions, but they lack the means or the power to utilize their authority effectively. On the other hand, the associational organizations possess no authority to legislate for or direct the churches; but, as previously demonstrated, they possess powers which often enable them to control the policies of the churches. In brief, few Baptists are aware that authority, although it can be misused, places limitations upon power by defining the extent, the functions, and the modes of power.

Without recognition of their authority, the leaders of an association of churches or the officials of the denomination are forced to operate behind the protective veil of the informal system of power. Denominational politics becomes the rule rather than an occasional support for the formal system of authority. Since the opportunities for power are often greater for the denominational official than normally enjoyed by any local church, or even by many local churches together, it is incumbent upon the Baptists to limit the power of their leaders through a more realistic and explicit definition of authority.

The purpose is not to weaken the executives; rather, it is to strengthen the local churches. In their constant effort to penalize each other, the various groups within the denomination attenuate the power and authority of the whole. In a democratic mode of government where all the units are linked together in a precarious balance of interdependence, the government can be no stronger than the weakest unit. If either the churches, the associations, the state conventions, or the national Convention is enervated, the total denomination must suffer.

While on the basis of the priesthood of all believers the Baptists hold that the individual has the "competence" to seek the Word within the covenantal community of the faithful, it is the congregation which covenants with God and not the isolated individual, no matter how competent his soul. The primacy of the local church is based on the principle that the church in its acts seeks to discern and be obedient to the mind of Christ within the situations in which it finds itself. The congregation is primary because in the local fellowship there is opportunity for a loving concern, mutual criticism, and a common discipline which can seldom be duplicated in an association of churches. The Free Church tradition teaches that the congregation is most responsive to the lively Word of God in history during the periods of worship, study, cooperative service, and monthly meeting. It is through the intimate and gathered community of common worship where individuals are expected to reprove one another in love that the Word of God becomes real and is truthfully proclaimed. When the same loaf and the same cup are shared by a community of neighbors the mind of Christ is most clearly discerned.

The intention of the Reformation was to proclaim that Christ is Lord of the whole church and not of any single unit standing in splendid isolation from the others. Christ may not be bound by the restrictions and functions of any institutional polity. Thus there is a basis for polity changes within new situations. This is particularly crucial for the contemporary Baptist movement, for the primary problems are at the level of the local congregation. This is where disciplined community needs most to be developed because the local church is primary and is most guilty of violating the ideals of a Free Church polity. If the churches cannot do it for themselves—and there is strong evidence that they find it difficult within the present social milieu—it is they which are most in need of critical discipline from some unit other than themselves. This is the Baptist dilemma. Every unit needs the support of all the others, and yet none of the units enjoys the respect of the others. The local congregations are undisciplined and weak; the associations are languishing; and while the state conventions are often vigorous, like the American Baptist Convention, they lack the authority and the means to strengthen the associations and the churches.

One of the problems never adequately faced by the Baptists is the adequate institutionalization or legitimation of dissident groups within the denominational structure. The fundamentalists are justifiably considered a threat to the stability of the denominational structure, but little is gained by pushing them aside and awaiting the day when they shall gain sufficient power to reverse the procedure. In the world of secular politics the rights of the opposition are preserved through such institutions as the party system, minority rights, and civil liberties. It is a strong indictment against the Baptists that they have not discovered any means to permit their own minorities to gain a voice in the Convention. In fact, by means of a representational system which fails to represent a shamefully large sector of the denomination the Baptists have made efforts to curtail all dissenting voices. In part, their excuse has been rooted in an experience of recent decades with a vocal minority which is bent on destroying the values of the denominational organization. But it has been shown that in all probability, even if the fundamentalists were to gain control of the national organization, they would find it necessary to be obedient to the organizational imperatives if they wished to remain in power.

It is a fundamental principle of democratic polity in the

Free Church that the local congregation and its membership remain free to hear the Word and proclaim it for others to hear. The contemporary practices of the denomination violate this principle by a separation of the churches from each other and by their consistent refusal to accept the authority of associational discipline. There is a greater emphasis upon independence than upon the interdependence which is essential for the maintenance of any significant degree of freedom. From the doctrine of the priesthood of all believers and the doctrine of original sin it follows that no single unit of the church can discern the mind of Christ in its fullness if separated from all other local units as well as from the associations and from the American Baptist Convention. In addition, it has been argued on the basis of sociological principles that the most effective way to bring a social system into almost total dependence upon the practices of power is to attempt to eliminate all forms of authority from the system.

The churches may enjoy the rights of formal authority without possessing the means for the effective utilization of this power. Perhaps their hope lies in new apprehensions of the faith and in the development of new and more adequate social forms. Until these are developed it appears that the Baptists must return to some kind of associational discipline. If the congregations were united in associations, the mind of Christ would be sought by the common gathering of the churches, and the association would legitimately proclaim the Word as discerned by the united churches. Perhaps if the leaders of the American Baptist Convention could hear the voices of the several associations, rather than the infinite clamor of a multiplicity of independent churches, they could act for the churches and be respected as a legitimate ecclesiastical power.

An association of churches is a covenanted fellowship, a communion of delegates gathered together under Christ to consider the work of all the represented churches. In this sense it is like a church; but, according to Free Church doctrine, it is unlike a local congregation in two important respects. It cannot possess the power of the keys to excommunicate an individual from the community of Christians. If this controversial authority is possessed by any unit of the church, it can be exercised only by the congregation. On the same grounds, only the local church can ordain a minister, but the association must reserve the right to examine the standards of ordination of the member churches and to expel any church which violates these measures. In every other way the association is a church. It seeks the mind of Christ for all the churches which maintain membership in the association; it can preach the Word and administer the sacrament of communion; and it can discipline any of the member churches which are unwilling to accept associational authority.

It is apparent that at the present time many Baptist churches would not agree with this formulation and that it would take many years to develop such a church-order within the denomination. It is difficult to discover in what other way the prophetic witness of the churches can be assured and the critical voice of the opposition be effectively heard throughout the denomination.

It is possible that this represents a futile effort to resurrect a system of Free Church doctrine which is dormant. But the Baptists have failed to create a "pure democracy," and therefore must seek alternatives to some form of associational polity which will provide a countervailing power to the apparently inevitable tendency toward centralization and rationalization of denominational power. In an age when organizational efficiency and concentration are accepted bywords to success it may be impossible to resuscitate the local associational units. But if the congregations can identify with and express themselves through nothing smaller than the state or national conventions it seems doubtful that they will overcome the problems incurred by impersonalization, distance, and a lack of technical knowledge. Indirect representation and occasional fellowship can never replace the advantages of intimate community, but it is probably better than no community at all.

The present system of representation to the associations is personal and direct, but grossly inequitable. On a basis of representation from local associations each church in the denomination would be indirectly represented. None would be totally ignored. It is true that the freedom to hear and proclaim the Word includes every individual, but this must mean more than the right to speak at an open convention—if one has the time and money to get there. Perhaps, in part, it means the right to be represented by a delegate with authority even if one cannot personally attend. Free Church doctrines do not signify an equal authority in all persons and units of the church. The principle of gifts, each man having "his own special gift from God, one of one kind and one of another,"[2] is sufficient justification for leadership and delegation of authority within the church. Although these may never be sovereign authorities, they are genuine leaders and genuine delegates who are chosen by God through the people to lead the churches and associations in the proper fulfillment of their tasks. They are not merely the people with a convenient supply of time and financial resources.

The delegates sent from churches to the associations and from associations to the conventions should have the authority to speak for the churches. Perhaps the associations and conventions would underwrite the expenses of the delegates from a common fund, thus assuring that no sector of the denomination would be unrepresented because it could not afford to send a delegate.[3] The delegates would not be "instructed" by their churches or associations, for no such delegate would be fully free to discern the mind of Christ within the associational meeting. The delegate would have an obligation to hear the Word as discerned by the association, for if the churches knew the Word before the associations met there would be no point in sending delegates.

Since the association consists of delegates elected by the churches, the associational meeting cannot transform itself into a self-perpetuating organization. If it attempted to accomplish this it would cease to be an association of churches. It

[2] I Cor. 7:7.
[3] On the basis of one delegate from each of the 372 associations of the denomination each state would have a voting power commensurate with the number of churches in the state. For example, New York would have 37 votes, Illinois 17, Rhode Island would have 3.

would have no enduring ecclesiastical status, for there can be no permanent council of executives or bishops within the Free Church order. However, the formal boards and agencies of the associations and conventions would probably continue to possess the same limited freedom which they now enjoy. The membership of these boards would be determined by the associational delegates, and in order to gain the values of efficiency and technical knowledge, such membership could be extended beyond that of a single term. The local associations, state conventions, and the American Baptist Convention would be authorized to speak and act for the churches in all matters of denominational concern.

Under such a polity some churches would probably withdraw from the Convention but that would not be a unique event. One might ask, on the other hand, if the dissident churches are more or less likely to depart from the denomination if they know for the first time that they are as fully represented as all other churches?

Free Church polity is predicated on the ground that every man has the ability to know the truth and the right to proclaim it. But it is also affirmed that those who possess the instruments of power will claim a monopoly on truth and will attempt to circumscribe the right of the minority to be heard. The polity of the Free churches reflects an effort to establish an equilibrium between these contending parties. The Baptists may have been wise when they removed the bishops from their places; but when they also eliminated the ecclesiastical authority of their own associations the bishops returned in business suits to direct affairs from behind the curtain of the center stage. Since their responsibilities are prodigious their presence is acknowledged. But paradoxically, their power is unrestricted because their authority is so limited. When Baptists recognize that authority is more than a grant to power and that it also defines and therefore limits the uses of power they may sustain the proximate harmony which they are seeking.

This is a selected bibliography. It does not represent all the books and articles which were used in research. Only those works are listed which were directly cited in this study.

BOOKS

Allison, William Henry. *Baptist Councils in America*. Chicago: Press of George K. Hazlitt & Co., 1906. (A dissertation submitted to the Faculty of the Graduate Divinity School of Chicago University for the Degree of Doctor of Philosophy.)

Bainton, Roland H. *Here I Stand, A Life of Martin Luther*. New York: Abingdon-Cokesbury Press, 1950.
Barnard, Chester I. *The Functions of the Executive*. Cambridge: Harvard University Press, 1938.
———. *The Nature of Leadership*. Cambridge: Harvard University Press, 1940.
Bingham, Walter V. D. and Bruce, V. Moore. *How to Interview*. New York: Harper & Brothers, 1941.
Buber, Martin. *Moses*. London: The East and West Library, 1946.

Crandall, Lantham A. *Henry Lyman Morehouse*. Philadelphia: The American Baptist Publication Society, 1919.

Davies, Horton. *The Worship of the English Puritans*. London: Dacre Press, 1948.
———. *Christian Deviations*. London: SCM Press Ltd., 1954.
Davies, Rupert E. *The Problem of Authority in the Continental Reformers*. London: The Epworth Press, 1946.

Flew, R. Newton (ed.). *The Nature of the Church*. New York: Harper & Brothers, 1952.
Forsyth, P. T. *The Church and the Sacraments*. London: Independent Press, Ltd., 1953.
Furniss, Norman F. *The Fundamentalist Controversy, 1919-1931*. New Haven: Yale University Press, 1954.

Hallowell, John H. *The Moral Foundation of Democracy*. Chicago: University of Chicago Press, 1954.
Heiman, Eduard. *Freedom and Order*. New York: Charles Scribner's Sons, 1947.
Hiscox, Edward T. *The New Directory for Baptist Churches*. Philadelphia: The Judson Press, 1894.
———. *The Standard Manual for Baptist Churches*. Philadelphia: The American Baptist Publication Society, 1890.
Horr, George E. *The Baptist Heritage*. Philadelphia: The Judson Press, 1923.

BIBLIOGRAPHY

Hudson, Winthrop S. *The Great Tradition of the American Churches*. New York: Harper & Brothers, 1953.

Jenkins, Daniel T. *Church Meeting and Democracy*. London: Independent Press, Ltd., 1944.

Knox, John (ed.). *Religion and the Present Crisis*. Chicago: University of Chicago Press, 1942.

Lasswell, Harold D. and Kaplan, Abraham. *Power and Society*. New Haven: Yale University Press, 1950.

Lazarsfeld, Paul S. and Rosenberg, Morris (eds.). *The Language of Social Research*. Glencoe, Illinois: The Free Press, 1955.

Levy, Marion J., Jr. *The Structure of Society*. Princeton: Princeton University Press, 1952.

Lindsay, A. D. *The Essentials of Democracy*. Philadelphia: The University of Pennsylvania Press, 1929.

Lipset, Seymour M. *Agrarian Socialism*. Berkeley: University of California Press, 1950.

Mannheim, Karl. *Freedom, Power, and Democratic Planning*. New York: Oxford University Press, 1950.

Maritain, Jacques. *Man and the State*. Chicago: University of Chicago Press, 1956.

Mathews, Shailer. *The Scientific Management of the Churches*. Chicago: University of Chicago Press, 1912.

Mayer, F. E. *The Religious Bodies of America*. St. Louis, Missouri: Concordia Publishing House, 1956.

McGlothlin, W. J. (ed.). *Baptist Confessions of Faith*. Philadelphia: The American Baptist Publication Society, 1911.

McNutt, William R. *Polity and Practice in Baptist Churches*. Philadelphia: The Judson Press, 1935.

Merton, Robert K., Fiske, Marjorie, and Kendall, Patricia L. *The Focused Interview*. Glencoe, Illinois: The Free Press, 1956.

Merton, Robert K. *Social Theory and Social Structure*. Glencoe, Illinois: The Free Press, 1949. (Also the revised and enlarged edition, 1957.)

Michels, Robert. *Political Parties*. Glencoe, Illinois: The Free Press, 1949.

Newbigin, Lesslie. *The Household of God*. New York: Friendship Press, 1954.

Newman, A. H. *A History of Baptist Churches in the United States*. New York: The Christian Literature Co., 1894.

Nichols, James H. *Democracy and the Churches*. Philadelphia: Westminster Press, 1951.

Niebuhr, H. Richard. *The Social Sources of Denominationalism*. Hamden, Connecticut: The Shoe String Press, 1954.

———. *The Purpose of the Church and Its Ministry*. New York: Harper & Brothers, 1956.

Parsons, Talcott. *Essays in Sociological Theory Pure and Applied*. Glencoe, Illinois: The Free Press, 1949.

———. *The Social System*. Glencoe, Illinois: The Free Press, 1951.
———. *The Structure of Social Action*. Glencoe, Illinois: The Free Press, 1937.
Pruden, Edward H. *Interpreters Needed*. Philadelphia: The Judson Press, 1951.

Rosten, Leo (ed.). *A Guide to the Religions of America*. New York: Simon and Schuster, 1955.

Scott, James A. and Rapp, Edward D. *American Baptists Today*. New York: American Baptist Home Mission Societies, 1957.
Schaff, Philip. *Creeds of Christendom*. Vol. III. New York: Harper & Brothers, 1877.
Selznick, Philip. *TVA and the Grass Roots*. Berkeley, California: University of California Press, 1953.
Soares, Theodore G. *A Baptist Manual*. Philadelphia: The American Baptist Publication Society, 1911.

Torbet, Robert G. *A History of the Baptists*. Philadelphia: The Judson Press, 1950.
Troeltsch, Ernst. *The Social Teaching of the Christian Churches*. Vol. II. New York: The Macmillan Co., 1931.

Underhill, Edward B. (ed.). *Confessions of Faith and Other Documents of the Baptist Churches of England in the 17th Century*. London: The Hanserd Knollys Society, 1854.
Underwood, A. C. *A History of the English Baptists*. London: Kingsgate Press, 1947.

Weber, Max. *From Max Weber: Essays in Sociology*. Translated, edited with introduction by H. H. Gerth and C. Wright Mills. New York: Oxford University Press, 1946.
———. *The Theory of Social and Economic Organization*. Translated by A. M. Henderson and Talcott Parsons. Edited with an introduction by Talcott Parsons. New York: Oxford University Press, 1947.
Williams, Robin M. *American Society: A Sociological Interpretation*. New York: Alfred M. Knopf, 1952.

ARTICLES AND EDITORIALS

Andrews, Charles R. "A Baptist Looks Backward and Forward," *Theology Today*, XIII, 4 (January 1957).

The Baptist, Vol. 6 (August 11, 1925); Vol. 9 (October 20, 1928).
Beers, G. Pitt. "The Past Challenges the Future," *Missions*, Vol. 151 (April 1953).
Bitting, W. C. "What Changes, if any, Are Desirable and Feasible in our Missionary Organizations and Methods?" *The Standard*, XLIX (December 28, 1901).

Crusader, Vol. XI (January 1956, April 1956, June 1956, Summer 1956).

BIBLIOGRAPHY

Encyclopaedia Britannica, 1953, Vol. 3. "Baptists."

Friedrich, Carl J. "Some Observations on Weber's Analysis of Bureaucracy," *Reader in Bureaucracy*, ed. by Robert K. Merton, et al. (Glencoe, Illinois: The Free Press, 1952), p. 31.

Hassrick, Romain C. "This Pays Dividends," *Missions*, Vol. 152 (January 1954).
Hudson, Winthrop S. "Are Baptists so Peculiar?" *The Christian Century*, LXX, 2 (November 18, 1953).
———. "The Associational Principle among Baptists," *Foundations*, I, 1 (January 1958).
———. "Stumbling into Disorder," *Foundations*, I, 2 (April 1958).

Mead, Sidney. "Denominationalism: The Shape of Protestantism in America," *Church History*, XXIII (1954).
Missions, Vol. 147 (June 1949), 150 (March 1952), 151 (June 1953).
Moehlman, Conrad H. "Baptists," *The Encyclopedia of Religion*, edited by Vergilius Ferm. New York: The Philosophical Library, 1945.

Page, Charles H. "Bureaucracy and the Liberal Church," *Review of Religion*, XIV (July 1951).

Riley, W. B. "Shall Northern Baptists Automatically Exclude Ultra-Conservatives?" *Watchman Examiner*, X (May 11, 1922).
Rylaarsdam, J. Coert. "The Doctrine of the Church and the Problem of Culture," *Christianity and Society*, XVIII (Autumn 1953).

Simon, Herbert A. "Decision-Making and Administrative Organization," *Public Administration Review*, IV (1944).
The Standard, Vol. 49 (June 1, 1901, October 26, 1901, November 16, 1901), Vol. 55 (March 30, 1907).
Straton, Hillyer H. "Northern Baptists," *Watchman Examiner*, XXXVIII (May 4, 1950).

Vedder, Henry C. "Fifty Years of Baptist History," *The Chronicle*, IX (October 1946).

Watchman Examiner, X (May 6, 1922), XXXIV (June 13, 1946), XXXVIII (March 23, 1950; April 13, 1950; May 4, 1950), XXXIX (June 28, 1951).

PUBLIC DOCUMENTS

Annual of the Northern Baptist Convention, 1907-1940. Philadelphia: The American Baptist Publication Society. (*Yearbook of the American Baptist Convention, 1941-1958*.)

The Board of Education and Publication of the American Baptist Convention, 44th Annual Report, 1955. Philadelphia: The Judson Press.

BIBLIOGRAPHY

Catalogues from thirty-two Baptist-related seminaries, colleges, and training schools. For a complete listing of these schools see the *Baptist Campus Directory*, Second Edition. Philadelphia: The Board of Education and Publication, 1950, pp. 15-49, 74, 76, 80, 100-114, 124-128.

The Connecticut Baptist Convention, 1954. Annual Report. Hartford, Connecticut.

Kansas Baptist Annual, 1955. Topeka, Kansas.

Massachusetts Baptist Yearbook, 1943. Boston, Massachusetts.

Minutes of the One-Hundred-Fourteenth Annual Meeting of the Iowa Baptist Convention, 1955. Des Moines, Iowa.

New Hampshire Baptist Yearbook, 1954. Concord, New Hampshire.

Proceedings, the Baptist Congress for the Discussion of Current Questions. Chicago: University of Chicago Press, 1895.

United Baptist Convention of Maine Yearbook, 1955. Augusta, Maine.

Yearbook of the American (Northern) Baptist Convention, 1941-1958. Philadelphia: The American Baptist Publication Society. (Cf., *Annual of the Northern Baptist Convention, 1907-1940.*)

Yearbook of the American Churches. Landis, Benson Y. (ed.). New York: National Council of Churches of Christ in the U.S.A., 1956.

UNPUBLISHED OR PRIVATELY CIRCULATED PAPERS

"Background Material for Special Meeting of the General Council." Mimeographed, 1952.

"Basic Papers Prepared for the American Baptist Theological Conference." Mimeographed, 1954.

"Basic Resource Papers for the East Central Regional Theological Conference." Mimeographed, 1956.

Fosdick, Raymond B., et al. "Report on a Survey of Fifty-eight Organizations of the Northern Baptist Denomination." Printed for private distribution, June 1925.

Harrelson, Walter J. "The Church and Its Baptism." Paper presented to the American Baptist Convention, Seattle, Washington, 1956.

"Management Audit: American Baptist Convention." Published by the American Institute of Management expressly for its members. New York: February 1955.

McClernon, Robert. "The Formation of the Northern Baptist Convention." Unpublished Bachelor of Divinity dissertation, Federated Theological Faculty, University of Chicago, 1956.

"A Manual for Department of Missionary Cooperation of a State or City Promotional Area." Mimeographed, no date, but issued by the Council on Missionary Cooperation within the last decade.

"Report and Recommendations of the National Survey Commission on Christian Higher Education." Printed for use by the American Baptist Convention by Marts and Lundy, Inc., 1957.

INTERVIEWS WITH PARTICIPANTS
IN THE AMERICAN BAPTIST CONVENTION

In order to maintain anonymity not all the interviewees are included in this list. Two omissions are important: a member of the General Council and a former board member of a national society. If their names were recorded each could be readily identified by reference to his remarks.

D. M. Albaugh. Director: Overseas Department, Foreign Missionary Society. February 17, 1956.

M. F. Ashbook. Executive Director: Ministers and Missionaries Benefit Board. February 15, 1956; June 20, 1956.

Miss B. Atkeson. Director: Baptist Student Movement. June 20, 1956.

H. R. Bowler. Budget Adviser: Budget Research Committee, American Baptist Convention. August 26, 1957.

M. P. Burroughs. Director: Department of University Pastor and Student Work, Board of Education and Publication. January 19, 1956.

T. M. Chastain. Executive Secretary: Home Mission Society. February 16, 1956.

D. B. Cloward.* Executive Secretary: Council on Christian Social Progress. February 15, 16, 1956.

Miss M. R. Corbett. Administrative Assistant: Council on Christian Progress. January 20, 1956; February 13, 1956.

W. F. Davison. Vice-Chairman: Council on Christian Social Progress. June 18, 1956.

R. B. Deer. Director: Ministerial Placement, Colgate Rochester Divinity School; formerly a state executive secretary. November 9, 1955.

F. L. Essex. Secretary: Radio-Television, Division of Communications, Council on Missionary Cooperation. February 17, 1956.

Mrs. C. D. Eulette. Vice President: Board of Education and Publication. January 19, 1956.

G. B. Ewell. Member: Budget Research Committee, American Baptist Convention. November 9, 1955.

M. C. Froyd. Director of Field Work: Colgate Rochester Divinity School; formerly an executive, Department of Higher Education, Board of Education and Publication. November 9, 1955.

R. D. Goodwin. Director: Division of Communications, Council on Missionary Cooperation. February 14, 1956.

R. C. Johnson. Member: General Council. January 20, 1956; September 3, 1956.

* Deceased.

BIBLIOGRAPHY

R. M. Johnson. General Director: Council on Missionary Cooperation. February 14, 1956.

K. S. Latourette. President: American Baptist Convention, 1952. October 5, 1955.

R. E. Nelson. General Secretary: American Baptist Convention. February 14, 1956; June 21, 1956; September 8, 1956.

W. H. Porter. Associate General Secretary: American Baptist Convention. June 17, 1957.

A. T. Rasmussen. Board Member: Council on Christian Social Progress. November 8, 1955.

W. E. Saunders. President: Colgate Rochester Divinity School; Chairman: Board of Education and Publication. November 9, 1956; January 19, 1956.

R. F. Smith. State Secretary: New Hampshire. May 9, 1956.

E. C. Starr. Corresponding Secretary: American Baptist Historical Society. November 7, 1955.

J. W. Thomas. Executive Secretary: Council on Christian Social Progress; formerly Associate Director: Ministers and Missionaries Benefit Board. February 16, 1956; June 18, 1956.

R. G. Torbet. Director: Department of Educational Services, Board of Education and Publication. February 17, 1956.

R. V. Wells. Associate Executive Secretary: Board of Education and Publication. June 30, 1957.

D. R. Wright. Associate Director: Ministers and Missionaries Benefit Board. February 16, 1956; May 8, 1956.

INDEX

Budget Research Committee, 73, 124f, 181, 186
bureaucracy, 120n, 136; American Baptist Convention and, xi, 70f, 135; Baptist ideology and, 86f; churches and, x-xi, 37; efficiency of, 36; definition of, xi; as end-in-itself, 136; as functional requisite, 71; goals and, 71; individuals and, 45n, 79, 86, 215, 225; intellectuals and, 142f; liberty and, 135; modern society and, x; policy-making and, 135; rationality of, xi; as self-perpetuating, 133; staff of, 70; technical knowledge and, 159; theory of, xi; voluntary associations and, 208. *See also* organizations, organizational men
bureaucratic determinism, 144
Burnham, James, 144
Burroughs, M. P., 235
business associations, 207
bylaws, 42, 95n, 153, 162ff

Caesar, J., 204
calling, 212
Calvinism, 3, 11, 23f, 27, 31, 33, 53, 208
career, 212
caste system, 219
caucus, 180f, 184, 189f. *See also* nominating committee
causal factors, 44
centralization, 40f, 43, 86f, 121, 167; function of, 86, 89, 216, 225. *See also* rationalization
charisma: anarchy and, 93, 214; defined, 14n, 75; leaders and, 14, 74, 76f, 85, 93f, 130, 211, 213; legal authority and, 76f; ministers and, 197, 217; of office, 211; policy-making and, 197; revolution and, 62n, 75, 215; state secretaries and, 76f; voluntary associations and, 211-14. *See also* authority, charismatic authority
charismatic authority, 4, 74-78; defined, 74f; executive professionals and, 78, 92; as functional requisite, 92ff; rational-legal authority and, 74; as supra-rational, 131. *See also* authority
charismatic founder, 213
charismatic leaders, 14, 74, 76f, 85, 93f, 130, 211, 213
charter, *see* confessions of faith

Chastain, T. M., 235
Chicago University, 174
children's camp, 139
church and state, 24, 28, 53, 178, 220
church councils, *see* associations
Church Extension Program, 72, 97, 116, 125f, 138ff, 154f
church-order, *see* polity
churches: absolutizing of, 102; affluency of, 167ff, 186; American Baptist Convention and, 15, 41, 100, 206; associations and, 13, 26, 29-34, 40, 49, 56-59, 66, 70, 102, 193, 220, 224; authority and power of, viii, 6, 13, 15, 27, 35, 55ff, 66, 102, 221; autonomy of, *see* congregational autonomy; corruption of, 5, 29, 30, 32, 54, 58, 162f, 220; debt of, 72; executive professionals and, 78, 149f, 176f; functional requisites of, 5; God and, 54, 58; isolation of, 204f; leaders in, 176f; loss of, 155, 227; mergers of, 155; mutual criticism in, 222; national societies and, 38, 40, 44f, 49, 57ff, 101, 183, 200; nature of, 4, 104; New Testament and, 52; number of, 3, 95n; policy-making and, 13, 77, 98, 100, 192; prestige of, viii; primacy of, 219, 223; purpose of, 4, 18, 40, 49, 104; rational-legal authority and, 6, 57, 66; rationalization of, 45f; representation of, 164, 167ff, 173ff; rural, 45n, 73, 162; schism and, 31n, 70, 204; secularization and, 6, 21, 44f, 58, 71, 102n, 204; social change and, 6, 128f, 214; as "synagogues of Satan," 30; urban, 73, 97; voluntarism and, 3, 24, 53. *See also* congregational autonomy, Free churches
Churches for New Frontiers, *see* Church Extension Program
City Mission Societies, 111, 124f, 139
civil liberty, 223
civil power, 208
civil servants, 144
class conflict, 148, 153, 201
Cloward, D. B., 235
coercion, 101, 221
Colgate Rochester Divinity School, 196
collective orientation, 8

239